PREPARING OUR SCHOOLS
FOR THE 21ST CENTURY

EDITED BY DAVID D. MARSH

ASSOCIATION FOR SUPERVISION AND CURRICULUM DEVELOPMENT
ALEXANDRIA, VIRGINIA USA

Association for Supervision and Curriculum Development
1703 N. Beauregard St. • Alexandria, VA 22311-1714 USA
Telephone: 1-800-933-2723 or 703-578-9600 • Fax: 703-575-5400
Web site: http://www.ascd.org • E-mail: member@ascd.org

Gene R. Carter, *Executive Director*
Michelle Terry, *Associate Executive Director, Program Development*
Nancy Modrak, *Director, Publishing*
John O'Neil, *Director of Acquisitions*
Mark Goldberg, *Development Editor*
Joyce McLeod, *Development Editor*
Julie Houtz, *Managing Editor of Books*
Margaret A. Oosterman, *Associate Editor*
Darcie Simpson, *Associate Editor*
Kathleen Larson Florio, *Copy Editor*
Charles D. Halverson, *Project Assistant*
Gary Bloom, *Director, Design and Production Services*
Karen Monaco, *Senior Designer*
Tracey A. Smith, *Production Manager*
Dina Murray, *Production Coordinator*
John Franklin, *Production Coordinator*
Valerie Sprague, *Desktop Publisher*

Copyright © 1999 by the Association for Supervision and Curriculum Development. All rights reserved. No part of this publication may be reproduced or transmitted in any form or by any means, electronic or mechanical, including photocopy, recording, or any information storage and retrieval system, without permission from ASCD. Readers who wish to duplicate material copyrighted by ASCD may do so for a small fee by contacting the Copyright Clearance Center (CCC), 222 Rosewood Dr., Danvers, MA 01923, USA (phone: 978-750-8400; fax: 978-750-4470). ASCD has authorized the CCC to collect such fees on its behalf. Requests to reprint rather than photocopy should be directed to ASCD's permissions office at 703-578-9600.

ASCD publications present a variety of viewpoints. The views expressed or implied in this book should not be interpreted as official positions of the Association.

Printed in the United States of America.

January 1999 member book (pc). ASCD Premium, Comprehensive, and Regular members periodically receive ASCD books as part of their membership benefits. No. FY99-4.

pc1/99

ASCD Stock No. 199000

ASCD member price: $16.95   nonmember price: $20.95

ISSN: 1042-9018

ISBN: 0-87120-335-9

04 03 02 01 00 99   10 9 8 7 6 5 4 3 2 1

1999 ASCD YEARBOOK:
PREPARING OUR SCHOOLS
FOR THE 21ST CENTURY

Introduction: An Opportunity That Comes Once
in a Millennium. 1
　　David D. Marsh

Section I.
New Directions for Our Schools—Trends and Issues

1. Getting to the Heart of the Matter: Education in the
　21st Century. 13
　　Delaine Eastin

2. Education and the Demands of Democracy in the
　Next Millennium. 25
　　Marc S. Tucker and Judy B. Codding

3. Education for the Public Good: Strategic Intentions for the
　21st Century. 45
　　Brian J. Caldwell

4. Rethinking Civic Education for the 21st Century 65
　　Todd Clark

5. Diversity and Education for the 21st Century 89
　　Belinda Williams

Section II.
Creating a New Era—Educational Reform for the 21st Century

6. The Role of Standards in Educational Reform for the
   21st Century 117
   Peter W. Hill and Carmel A. Crévola

7. Making Better Use of Resources for Educational Reform . . . 143
   Allan R. Odden

8. Leadership in the 21st Century: Using Feedback to
   Maintain Focus and Direction 165
   Sherry P. King

9. Life Inside a School: Implications for Reform in the
   21st Century 185
   Myranda S. Marsh

Section III.
The Year 2000 in Schools: Celebrating, Synthesizing, and Reflecting

10. Using the Year 2000 in Schools: Celebrating, Synthesizing,
    and Reflecting 205
    Patricia O. Pearson

About the Editor 219

About the Authors 219

About the 1999 Yearbook Committee 223

ASCD 1998–99 Board of Directors 224
    Executive Council 224
    Members at Large 224
    Affiliate Presidents 225

ASCD Review Council 227

ASCD Headquarters Staff 228

Introduction:
An Opportunity That
Comes Once in a
Millennium

David D. Marsh, Editor

T his is a very special time in history. We are on the eve of a new millennium, a transition that matters to everyone in every age group.
Although some cultures across the world use a unique calendar to
map their religious or cultural lives, nearly everyone uses the Gregorian calendar to define their public lives and the worldwide community. And by this collective calendar, we will soon enter a new reality
and a new perspective about ourselves and our world. We are about to
enter an era that quite literally comes only once in a thousand years.

This yearbook focuses on the educational opportunities this new
millennium signals—opportunities to help ourselves and our students
synthesize, celebrate, and offer perspective about our collective journey,
and opportunities to rethink the way our schools will work in the 21st
century. More than ever before, we as educators now have a special responsibility, for we are in the "business" of helping all our students prepare for the future. We do this by offering facts and skills, but more
importantly, perspective on and pathways to the future. We have a lot
of work to do.

Looking back a thousand years, Reston (1998) describes the eve of
the current millennium as follows:

> As the millennium approached, Europeans feared the world would
> end. The old order was crumbling, and terrifying and confusing
> new ideas were gaining hold in the populace. Random and horrific

violence seemed to sprout everywhere without warning, and without apparent remedy. (Jacket cover)

Fifty years later, the world had changed dramatically—Europe had literally been transformed. A new reality and a new perspective framed the Western world.

Now we are called to share in shaping the perspective for the next millennium, and the task will not be easy. Perspectives are controversial—the 500th anniversary of the "discovery" of North America by Columbus and his crew raised considerable controversy both about the facts of the "discovery" and about the value of the new era that the voyage led to. Perspectives are also bound by life experience—many of the senior citizens in our society use the Great Depression and World War II to mark the stages of their lives, whereas many of our youth find the Beatles, the civil rights struggles of the 1960s, and the Vietnam War to be ancient history. And perspectives are formed by societal factors well beyond the school—by television for example. Henry Giroux (1997) has described the many ways that television unfairly shapes the image of our young people, and the tremendous problems this image creates both for adults and for young people. Educators compete with powerful and terrifying images of ourselves and our society. The perspectives we seek to develop in our students will, of course, be nested in values and controversy, be connected to the life experiences of a new generation of students, and be framed by the forces of the broader society. This is a given.

Education itself can influence our students, and we, as educators, have three challenges. The first is concerned with the purposes of our schools. Whether a teacher, a school, or a district chooses to emphasize critical thinking, academic core subject matter, or vocational training, that choice is building toward three common purposes of schools: helping students participate in a democratic society, engage in a productive work life, and engage in lifelong learning. Our specific choices reflect our views about how those common purposes can best be achieved.

Consider, for example, educating students for participation in a democratic society. We face an interconnected world in which information increasingly comes as "sound bites," and we expect, for the first time in history, to educate all our youth to a high level. What should be the role of schools in this work? How will we help our students understand social problems in a world characterized by increasing specialization of knowledge and complexity of effects? And now, diversity is the common ground in our society. What will this mean for schools in building a democratic society? We must rethink what educating students for participation in a democratic society will mean.

Enabling students to participate in the new world of work will be equally challenging. If "thinking for a living" is the new reality in the world of work, will thinking for an education become the norm in our schools? The Third International Mathematics and Science Study (TIMSS) suggests we have a long way to go in this regard. And how do we build a viable perspective about work in a world characterized by increased international and dynamic competition? Many students in Southern California believe that they will work as computer programmers doing routine tasks for a high hourly wage. They and the schools they attend ignore the facts: Many U.S. corporations are already sending their routine computer programming tasks to other countries, via satellite, and most U.S. students currently lack the perspective, knowledge, and skills to compete in this international arena. Moreover, across the globe, the work of the future will often be done in small and rapidly shifting organizations characterized by tight deadlines, strong teamwork, new attention to quality and results indicators, and frequent partnerships with external groups. In this environment, students will also need skills in self-monitoring and teamwork to be successful in the 21st century.

In short, our first challenge is to rethink the three purposes of our schools in light of the new millennium. The good news is that for the first time in 200 years, the demands of a democratic society, the workplace, and lifelong learning converge around similar educational knowledge, skills, and perspectives. Complex problem solving based on strong understanding of core academic knowledge and core values is at the heart of the new citizen and the new worker.

Our second challenge is to rethink how schooling in the 21st century will work and how schools and districts can make this transition. The last two ASCD yearbooks have made wonderful contributions to these needed changes in schools by focusing on the role of the new technology as it is linked to learning and the change process. But related issues about schools for the 21st century need attention as well. Many schools and districts are developing standards and working to redesign their schools so that all students can meet these internationally benchmarked expectations for performance. Much work remains in picturing what these standards might be and how they can be framed, and how curriculum, assessment, instruction, and organizational conditions can be reshaped to support the standards.

As Brian Caldwell alludes to in Chapter 3 of this yearbook, hospitals have evolved so dramatically over the last 100 years that a physician from the turn of the century would be entirely lost among the equipment, drugs, and procedures of the modern hospital. The same confusion might not hold for a teacher from the turn of the century. Unfortunately, almost everything about our schools would be all too familiar to that teacher, which is not to blame our current teachers or school leaders. Our schools are in need of dramatic revision, and fortunately, almost everyone agrees on this need even if the prescriptions for change vary considerably. The standards-based reforms and the reframed purposes of schooling are the basis of a dramatic new approach to schooling for the start of the next millennium.

This yearbook offers a view of the key elements of schooling in the 21st century and the nature of the change process that will be needed to create such schools. These key elements are drawn from the experience of educational reform in several countries and reflect a growing consensus about which elements will help all schools achieve both excellence and equity in student performance. This yearbook also offers concrete pictures of how schools and districts can create standards-based education, and it discusses the real issues surrounding the role of teachers, the nature of the change process, and the reallocation of resources. We've included the voices of teachers and district leaders in talking about these changes and worked to make all the chapters connect with the realities of schooling and the aspirations of school leaders—whether they are formally designated leaders like superintendents and principals or equally important informal leaders who serve as teachers.

The third challenge addressed in this yearbook is the way that schools and districts can use the year 2000 effectively as a source of celebration, synthesis, and reflection in the education of students. People across the world are already viewing the year 2000 as an important milestone. Interestingly, the year 2000 has been more actively a focus for community improvement and discussion in Europe than in the United States. For example, signs along the highway as one approaches an English town describe the town's "England 2000" project, which typically includes historical restoration and community improvement. And at the national level, England is actively working on the idea of "rebranding" itself—replacing an image of elderly gentlemen in tweed coats with an image of a vibrant modern economy and style, set in a reframed tradition.

U.S. society and schools have found historical milestones similar to the year 2000 to be quite important. Near the turn of the 20th century, for example, the world's fair in Chicago set a sense of identity and momentum that shaped Chicago's development for the next 50 years. More recently, the United States Bicentennial celebration and the 500th anniversary of the voyage of Christopher Columbus were important events that shaped the American identity and the curriculum in U.S. schools.

Yet the year 2000 will be much more significant as a milestone for districts and schools than have been these recent major turning points. This focus is already evident. At a policy level, the Goals 2000 project framed desired educational results that the United States as a country is supposed to be striving to achieve by the year 2000. At many schools across America, early signs are already apparent, such as the banner that greeted the entering freshman class at a high school in Virginia near the ASCD office. The banner read: "Welcome to the class of the year 2000," but there was little consensus about what would be different for that class at that school. These are tentative beginnings that can grow to become part of an important worldwide effort, and an important educational purpose.

A safe prediction is that the excitement over the year 2000 will increase dramatically over the next year. Attention will expand beyond "Y2K"—the computer programming problem associated with the year 2000. Interest both within schools and across communities will be to "do something" about the transition to the new millennium—whether that transition is seen as happening on January 1, 2000, over the year 2000, or on January 1, 2001 (the official transition point).

The real issue for educators will not be whether to engage in the celebration of the new millennium, but what form the celebration will take. We'll all want to avoid the superficial celebration and party atmosphere that distracts from the core work of schools. Instead, we'll need to find ways to use the millennium as the impetus for meaningful celebration, synthesis, and planning both for our students and our schools. At best, a focus on the year 2000 can be a tremendous support for helping students meet standards. This yearbook offers some suggestions for curriculum and instruction in specific subject areas as well as for schools as a whole.

In short, the year 2000 will be a massive milestone that schools and districts everywhere must address. As educators, our choice is not whether the people of the world will be focused on the year 2000—they

5

will be in any case. Instead, our choice is whether we can make this milestone an educationally meaningful focus for our students and our schools.

ASCD has focused this yearbook on this milestone for several reasons. First, the year 2000 in itself will be a defining time for both students and schools, and it warrants a yearbook that reexamines purposes for schooling in the 21st century, provides an important impetus for strategic planning and school reform, and provides a framework for thinking about celebration and reflection for students, schools, and communities. Second, ASCD is using the focus on the year 2000 to continue its work in fundamental school reform that will make sense well into the 21st century. In this way, the focus isn't only about the year 2000, but also about the future of schooling. Finally, we as educators are in an important moment in time—approaching the year 2000—and we can either gather interesting and powerful ideas about our future or pay the price when others do this for us.

Picture two schools and a school district as they approach the year 2000 and consider how this yearbook can be of value to each of them:

> School A, a middle school in suburban Detroit, has undergone a dramatic shift in student demographics in the last few years. The community is feeling a rebirth of economic activity, but community and school people sense they are no longer "middle America" in a way that term has been understood in the last 20 years. School leaders are hungry for a sense of purpose for their school and how they should prepare for the 21st century.

> A school district in the state of Washington has students whose parents are employees at Microsoft and other major computer software companies. Both parents and school leaders know that information is reshaping our world and our sense of direction for education. They know that schools will be different in the 21st century and want to use the year 2000 as an impetus for their strategic planning.

> School B is a high school in Omaha, Nebraska, or in Calgary, Canada. The school has a strong academic focus and a strong urge to use the year 2000 as a source of celebration and excitement in the school community. School leaders and parents know what they don't want—another festival with music and food that is empty of deeper meaning and connection to the rest of the school. Instead, they are curious about how educators across America and the world are proposing to include the year 2000 as an event of celebration in the curriculum in many subject areas. For example, science teachers would like to use the year 2000 to trace the history of science concepts and help students understand the inquiry process

and the content of science in this way; social science teachers want to use the year 2000 to examine themes in world and American history and discuss social policy issues relevant to students in the 21st century; and foreign language teachers would like students to engage via e-mail with high school students in other parts of the world to write about student plans and experiences in the year 2000.

To respond to the needs of these schools, and schools like yours, the yearbook is organized into three sections. In the first, we look at new directions for our schools—trends and issues. The section provides a strong overview of the educational issues for schools in the 21st century. Delaine Eastin, the Chief State School Officer in California, begins with a view of work in the 21st century and how schools must respond to provide a standards-based education that will help all students prepare for that future. Marc Tucker and Judy Codding from the National Center on Education and the Economy expand on this view of work and of democracy in helping us think about enhancing participation in a democratic society and preparing for work in the 21st century.

We then turn to three more specific trends and issues that confront educators on the eve of the 21st century. All three trends are "big issues" that have tremendous implications for every school in every setting. Brian Caldwell from Australia has been looking at trends in public education both in the United States and other countries. He focuses our attention on "What should be public about public education?" and sets this discussion in the context of education for the public good and a "strategic intention" view of school reform.

Todd Clark then picks up the second issue: rethinking citizenship education for the 21st century. For him, citizenship education must focus more intently on the local community and be integrated with other socializing forces in the community and society. Our current efforts at citizenship education are weak. There is little consensus as to what should be included in the curriculum; the traditional U.S. government courses focus on the structure and function of the national government rather than on the local community, and the traditional curriculum provides little development of skills and strategies that are essential to democracy. Clark offers a new view of citizenship and describes some of the myriad of resources and current programs that have implemented portions of this view.

For our schools, diversity is the new common ground. Belinda Williams describes new dimensions of diversity and education in the 21st century and focuses on (1) the need to comprehend and accept the

7

paradigm shift in diversity as it is supported by new understandings of human development, (2) the need to centrally position new understandings of human development in reform proposals introduced to increase the learning success of a diverse student population, and (3) the need to integrate available models and strategies about diversity.

Section Two of the yearbook focuses on creating a new era of educational reform for the 21st century. Peter Hill and Carmel Crévola have done some of the best work in the world in early literacy efforts. They use their early literacy work to illustrate a discussion of the promise of standards-based education and the value of a design approach to improvement. Allan Odden then addresses the fiscal questions in these new reforms. He provides fresh and useful ideas about how much money is "enough" and how schools can use resources more effectively to support student success.

Sherry King, a school superintendent in suburban New York, recognizes that the work of schools for the 21st century will be to create systems that are characterized by continuous improvement. Using her district as a case example, she describes some strategies that are at the heart of good reform: examining achievement data, looking at student work, and engaging the public in the reform effort.

But in every classroom, the demands and promises of reform are layered among the demands of everyday work—work that has been poorly supported. Often the structure of the school day does not encourage the teacher to be reflective individually or with other professionals. Myranda Marsh, a teacher who has lived daily with these reform efforts, offers some sobering observations about the role of teachers to date, and proposes some key elements for the involvement of teachers in forthcoming reform efforts.

The final section of the yearbook focuses on the year 2000 in schools: celebrating, synthesizing, and reflecting. Patricia Pearson, a high school teacher in Northern Virginia, talks about the importance of celebration in schools and offers some celebration themes for the year 2000. She then gives some important examples of activities for celebration and study that focus both on student involvement and teacher professional development.

I hope you find the yearbook stimulating and useful to your work.

DAVID D. MARSH

REFERENCES

Giroux, H. A. (1997). *Channel surfing: Race talk and the* destruction *of today's youth*. New York: St. Martin's Press.

Reston, J. (1998). *The last apocalypse: Europe at the year 1000*. New York: Doubleday.

Section I.

New Directions for Our Schools — Trends and Issues

Getting to the Heart of the Matter: Education in the 21st Century

DELAINE EASTIN

I recently went to the Internet to browse for articles on employment trends for the 21st century. The search engine returned thousands of citations, but I was struck by an advertising banner across the top of the list that invited me to search 100,000 jobs online. The first Web site suggested by the search was titled "IBM Employment in Other Countries." On another employment site run by the Funeral Service Association, I found a message posted by a young man with five years of experience in the funeral business. He was looking for part-time work while attending college. When I was a girl, the conventional wisdom held that you had to personally know the head undertaker. Now he recruits on a Web site.

It is a different world today, in every way. Forty years ago, Levittown homes measuring 800 square feet sold for $8,000. They called it the American Dream, and they were not exaggerating. Families who moved into these homes had arrived. Today, new homes being built in California often have more than 3,000 square feet of living space, and the average price of a home in the San Francisco Bay area where I live approaches half a million dollars.

Most people who bought into Levittown had high school diplomas. Those diplomas, plus a willingness to work, were all it took to launch the good life. But that is not the case anymore. Anybody with just a high school diploma buying one of today's new homes must also have his face on a baseball card.

You have to wonder where all this money is coming from. Certainly it is not from rising real incomes. Twenty years ago the median wage in the United States was $33,000 a year. Today it is about $34,000 a year. I do not think that increase got us from Levittown to Hillview Estates.

What got us there, in large part, were women going to work in vast numbers. When I graduated from college in 1969, about 50 percent of women held paying jobs. Today more than 75 percent do. But even the two-paycheck strategy is not enough to explain the massive difference in consumption between the middle of the century and the present.

Another major factor is debt. Total consumer debt in 1969, adjusted for inflation, was $97 billion. Today it is more than $700 billion. In other words, this is a very highly leveraged society. And a high-leverage economy is a seriously challenged economy. Our typical two-career couple went to school longer and studied harder. The rewards for those who did are those big houses, the sport utility wagons, the foreign travel, and so forth.

As a society, however, we make a huge wager when we buy into such a high-cost living standard. We are betting on our ability to keep both production and productivity growing at very substantial rates—not just in our time, but indefinitely into the future. Few of us hold retirement nest eggs in sacks of cash. Rather, these investments are pieces of massive capital funds that remain solid only so long as the businesses they back continue to grow and prosper.

And businesses can do that only if they can continually find a fresh stream of new, skilled workers. Over the last 20 years, about 20 percent of U.S. wage earners have seen their incomes rise sharply, while 60 percent have had declines in real income. There is nothing arbitrary about who's who in this picture. Those individuals with the skills to generate major wealth-producing products and services do well. Those who do not languish.

This is a grim picture, but there is good news behind it. The parts of the economy that employ high-wage workers are looking for more people—many more people. Even now these businesses are running to stay in place. The U.S. society has a tiger by the tail. We cannot fail to supply great armies of well-educated young people ready to participate fully in what is now credibly forecast as a long, sustained period of worldwide growth with great democratizing and humanizing potential in it.

With its usual edgy attitude hanging out, *WIRED* magazine put it this way in the summer of 1997: "We're facing 25 years of prosperity, freedom, and a better environment for the whole world. You got a problem with that?" Author Peter Schwartz, chair of the Global Business Network, predicts world economic output doubling every 12 years for decades to come (Schwartz & Leyden, 1997). Stanford economist Paul Romer attributes the surge to a long-awaited kicking-in of computer networks, noting that it has historically taken about a generation for any revolutionary technology to reach full leverage. That is just now happening.

On top of information technology, or, more accurately, because of it, comes the biotechnology wave. The Human Genome Project, sometimes scorned as too great a stretch just five years ago, is now halfway complete, on schedule, under budget, and spinning off valuable discoveries already. It is now plausible to believe that cancer and AIDS will be conquered, not by compassion, but by the ambition of smart, well-educated workers in an entrepreneurial age. The cloning of sheep in Great Britain foreshadows a time in the next decade when animals will be used to develop organs that can be donated to humans. In addition, plant genetics will yield ultra-hardy, high-yielding grains to feed a still hungry planet.

But who will do these things? Not a thin subculture of elites. There simply are not enough of them. The world will share the great potential for wealth and opportunity with a large, highly productive majority, or these things will not come to pass at all.

This vision is not some possible, future boom. It is already in full vigor. In 1997, years into a surging expansion, the U.S. economy was forecast to grow by a little over 2 percent, a healthy number by post-Vietnam standards. It came in at more than 4 percent, and that was the seventh straight year with such rates of growth. As a direct consequence, the proverbial "best and brightest" companies already scour the globe in a frantic search for help. They need well-educated young people with a passion for creativity.

That is what the United States exports to the rest of the world in this Information Age—creativity—and it is not just the Ph.D's who produce it. Consider the case of Dana Corporation, a Toledo, Ohio, maker of auto parts (Pearlstein, 1998). It wins long-term contracts by guaranteeing that prices will not go up. (This kind of pledge is what has begun to convince the doubters that the long boom will not be drowned out in a flood of inflation.) But Dana's wages go up every year. So what is the trick?

The trick is this: Every Dana employee is expected to come up with two new ideas a month designed to improve productivity. Management is expected to implement 8 out of every 10 ideas. It is closing in on that goal. Last year some 70 percent of the ideas were used. Dana's profits went up 20 percent, with sales up 8 percent, wages up 4 percent, job security for everybody, and no price increases. That is real productivity. But it takes people who can think for themselves and work as team members. It takes a lot of them, not just the college-bound. The U.S. economy is adding 200,000 jobs a month, which is like recruiting an entire General Motors work force each and every quarter.

California is the epicenter of this whole expansion. The state added nearly half a million jobs last year, more than 100,000 over the forecast. Los Angeles, which suffered the worst of the defense cutbacks in the late 1980s, has recovered from the Cold War and is surging into the Information Age stronger than ever. While the U.S. economy is forecast to enjoy a 10 percent rate of job growth through 2005, the rate of job growth in Los Angeles is expected to be 17 percent.

Left by the military downsizing with more scientists and engineers than Massachusetts and Texas combined, Southern California was well positioned to become a giant in the fields of telecommunications equipment, genetic engineering, and a wide range of computer technologies. Los Angeles County lost 120,000 defense jobs between 1990 and 1994. In just two years, it has added more than 100,000 jobs in multimedia alone.

On top of that there is boomtown action in entertainment, international trade, and what author Joel Kotkin calls "artisanship." To take just one example among many, Southern California is fast becoming a world leader in furniture design and production, with innovative styles that push the edge of creativity.

But here again, the entrepreneurs who lead these growing businesses spend a disproportionate share of their time hunting for skilled help. People, not capital, are the bottleneck. These young firms need not just computer programmers, but "working-class youth to be designers, machinists, animators and skilled mold-makers," to cite Kotkin's report to the Milken Institute (1997). Without them, the whole powerful vision of a millennial future goes cloudy. With them, a marvelous path forward is crystal clear.

California is a place in the future, defined by racial diversity and cultural cross-pollination. Not perhaps one day. Now. One-third of all the immigrants in the United States live in California. Los Angeles is more than 40 percent Latino. The number of Latino-owned businesses doubled in the last five years to over 200,000.

Consider the case of Monica and Perry Lopez, a young couple who opened a little designer hot sauce shop in Pasadena two years ago (Torres, 1996). Hot Hot Hot is the name of the place. It offers a hundred varieties of hot sauces: Endorphin Rush, Satan's Revenge, Dave's Insanity Sauce. You get the idea. One morning, Perry Lopez arrived to open the shop, and he was met by a college student who wanted to design a Web page for the shop as part of a school project. Perry said, "Why not?" A few weeks later, it was all set: The little shop went up on the Internet. About 45 minutes later, in came the first order. It was from Tel Aviv. The second followed almost immediately—from London.

Young shop owners in their 20s are suddenly hot, hot, hot in the high-tech global marketplace. They are by no means alone. Young people, especially, understand what is going on, and some of their stories seem downright disorienting to those of us with traditional ideas about working one's way up a career ladder. The *Wall Street Journal* recently had a piece about a college student who was working on a paper. The subject was Internet search engines. Along came a man who had heard about the student's work, paid him $1.5 million for the *unfinished paper,* and made him a senior vice president of a billion-dollar company. Now that is what I call upward mobility.

A college student named Michael Dell tried to earn extra money by assembling computers for people. He bought the parts on the open market and put together just the machines his customers specified. In fact, he learned that you can even earn a living doing this. In 1997 Dell Computer sales were almost $8 billion.

Here is another story. A young man named Scott Adams was an aspiring cartoonist. A few years ago, he was a low-level worker at Pacific Bell. He published his comic strip in the company newspaper, and, through a syndicate, he also sold it to a few dozen suburban dailies, making just enough money to complicate his tax form. Then one day, Scott Adams put his Internet address under his name on the strip. Within a week he had thousands of e-mail messages from fans. He bundled the messages up and sent them in to the syndicate, which, in turn, showed them around to big-city newspaper editors. In a matter of months, his "Dilbert" strip was in virtually every paper in the country.

These stories are just the kind of thing the high-tech optimists see as the democratizing promise of the information revolution: little people, with the tools and the freedom to *go around the traditional gatekeepers* to make things happen for themselves, no longer held back by entrenched interests.

The big question remains, however: Do we prepare enough of our young people with the skills and entrepreneurial spirit to fill all the opportunities the great 21st century adventure will require? Right now, the answer is no. We leave far too many behind. That is an unacceptable human cost, but, in the cold, hard light of what is possible, it also amounts to leaving money on the table for the U.S. economy.

One human resources manager told the *Wall Street Journal* that if anyone could deliver a truckload of 500 computer programmers to his site, he could find them all jobs by noon. He is not the only one out beating the bushes. One morning a Silicon Valley firm announced a corporate restructuring. By 2:30 in the afternoon, there was a biplane circling its campus, dragging a banner: "For a good job, dial 1-800. . . ."

The hottest new specialty among human resources consulting firms is something called "retention experts." Meanwhile, 40 percent of firms in the industry have set up overseas recruiting operations. Last year the United States skimmed off the top 20 percent of India's computer science graduating class. It is a troubling notion that a rich country is systematically siphoning off the best and brightest from a developing country. But let us set that aside for the moment. There is a fairly solid national consensus that no country can go on borrowing money indefinitely. By the same logic, it seems unwise to count on borrowing talent forever. We need to grow our own.

I recently saw a list of 60 predictions for work force changes by 2008. Here are just a few examples:

- Jobs will become much more complex.
- People will still work 40-plus hours a week, but at times and places other than the office.
- Many more workers will need to be knowledgeable about other cultures, languages, and business practices.
- It will *not be possible* to survive in the workplace without computer skills.

What kind of people can do all these things, and the rest of the list? The answer is very well-educated people who are self-directed problem-solvers and team players, and who have a solid grounding in technology. These qualities will be necessary not just for management, but for everybody.

So it is no surprise to me that when I advocate for a more rigorous curriculum, the constituency that I have always been able to count on—without exception—has been the business leadership community. Because I have been in corporate management and politics and I have seen both sides and lived in both cultures, I am often asked, what is the difference between a business leader and a politician? The answer is easy: The business leader knows the difference between expense and investment.

A few months after being elected California Superintendent of Public Instruction, I proposed, among other things, in my first "business plan" that we reduce class sizes in kindergarten through 3rd grade to 20 students or fewer. Well, you would think I had set off the fire alarm. Politicians and others went running and hollering, saying this was going to cost too much money, and on and on. Here is what I found disappointing: Nobody even thought to ask about the results we believed this would yield. The only issue was expense.

But no sooner were we over the political hurdle when some said: "We're going to run into major, major implementation problems." Of course. Who could have imagined otherwise? California is a big state, and class-size reduction is a billion-dollar program. We were given two weeks to implement the program but not one cent to administer it. Naturally, there were problems. There were not enough teachers, not enough classroom space, and too little turnaround time.

Yet, after one year, 1st grade reading scores were up 18 percent in both San Francisco and Long Beach. This success is not hard to understand. It is easier to teach 19 children to read than it is to teach 35.

The goal of reducing class size is not simply tidiness. Instead, the goal is: *Make sure the right stuff gets mastered.* The *right stuff* implies a rigorous curriculum—in other words, high standards. *Mastered* implies some way to demonstrate the results, in some kind of intelligently comparable way. We need one statewide test, geared to the standards, but we also need multiple measures of achievement administered throughout the year, with clear communication to parents about how their child is doing. And *make sure* implies accountability. If something is not working, maybe we need to do something different, or maybe we have to give someone else a chance. Real systems of rewards and interventions must be crafted. When they are, real student achievement goes up, which is what has happened in Kentucky, North Carolina, and Texas. All of these states are on a steady curve of improvement after establishing clear, high standards, creating genuine assessment systems, and holding people accountable.

Who could possibly oppose bringing our reading and math standards into line with the challenging skill levels that are today the norm throughout most of the advanced economies of Europe and Asia? Well, the oddest of bedfellows—the left wing and the right wing. The philosopher Eric Hoffer once observed that we make a serious mistake when we assume that the far right and the far left are kind of like the numbers 1 and 12 on the face of a clock. "No government authority is going to tell my kids what to learn," say those on the right. On the left we have people who fear that any "raising of the bar" is a form of crypto-racism.

Excuse me? If I were a leader of an ethnic minority and someone came to me suggesting that our children should have lower academic standards that expose them to reduced life prospects, I would be enraged. In 10 years, there will be two kinds of people: the well educated and the hardly employable. It will be much, much better to be well educated. But there is still a lot of denial about that.

In every state that has established academic content standards, a furious battle has been waged. The lines have been drawn between two camps—those who want basics and those who want "basics plus." Clearly, children should learn spelling, punctuation, grammar, and arithmetic, but they need much more. Basic skills are important for us all, and they are the kinds of skills that were necessary—and sufficient—for the bygone agricultural and industrial ages. However, we must prepare children for the *future*, not for the past.

We now need to teach our children how to understand concepts, interpret and apply them, analyze information, and solve problems. That is what our top teachers, corporate leaders, and great university faculties all agree on. If students master only spelling, arithmetic, punctuation, grammar, and nothing else, what can they become? Secretaries? No. Secretaries today have spell-check. They make their money interpreting what they read. If they cannot read between the lines, they do not last. Nor are we creating a lot of jobs for people who are great at arithmetic. In fact, technology is eliminating such jobs, and it is creating jobs for people who understand the forces at work behind numbers, words, and ideas.

Even when we have to make compromises in the standards we adopt, having these standards is a big step forward. We can now build upon them—that is the way the system works.

On assessment, the task is to develop one major exam tied to standards, as well as multiple assessments administered throughout the year. If we do not reflect the standards in our assessments, we will not have a valid way to judge student achievement.

Finally, on accountability: Results are everything. An A for effort is a nice sentiment, but if performance is D or F, the effort is being misdirected somehow, and we need to redirect it. The school year is not over until the work is done. Any child who is not at grade level in May needs to go to summer school. Mandatory summer school will cost more money, but it is worth every dime. It is paying to get results. Maybe even more importantly it sends the right message to students. No slack is given—do not even ask. You can work until June or work until September. You choose. But you must make sure the right stuff gets mastered.

People ask, can our public education system really work? They wonder whether the system, for some reason we may not understand, is simply out of step with the way our society has evolved. If so, they ask, why should we fight to swim upstream like a salmon? Can we just give vouchers to parents and let everybody make their own arrangements?

The answer is no. Let me share a fundamental belief I have about public policy making: I do not believe in massive, uncontrolled experiments. We need to be careful. Few proponents of vouchers are. In *School's Out*, Lewis Perlman goes so far as to insist that vouchers should be disposed of in any way parents see fit (cited in Huitt, 1997). If parents decide to buy a computer for educational purposes, they can use the money for that. They can buy a curriculum package through the mail and let the child learn at home; they can hire a tutor or buy an encyclopedia. Perlman's point is, it is all up to the parent. At the heart of the idea is that how a child is educated is the parent's concern and nobody else's business. I reject that idea.

I also question the premise that our schools are performing so badly that there is a plausible prospect of improving the situation if we bail out into the open market. This assumption suggests that what we are aiming for—a quality education for every youngster—is a hopeless goal anyway, so we should save the students whose parents really care.

The premise is not only false, but demonstrably false. For example, after years of horror stories about public education's failures, there are 165,000 extremely high-achieving students enrolled in the University of California. Another quarter of a million are in the California State University system. An additional quarter of a million students attend good private colleges in California, and countless others are in

21

advanced technical training programs. Over one million students are enrolled in the state's community colleges. In contrast, a comparative handful are loafing on the street corner.

Where did most of those successful young people come from? Most are products of the public schools. Furthermore, they did not all come from elite magnet schools or well-to-do suburbs. The news media—and I impute no unworthy motives—have somehow cobbled together a mass belief that all schools, with the exception of those in very affluent suburban districts, produce nothing but lawless losers. That is simply not true.

I agree that we have some serious problems in our poor urban centers, and both justice and wisdom demand new and aggressive efforts there. However, the untold story is the real shocker—given the conventional wisdom. Take, for example, a 14,000-student district in the San Francisco Bay area suburb of Union City. Seventy-seven percent of its children are from minority families. Twenty years ago it was also a place with a large minority population. It was growing fast as a result of immigration. Its schools were not good.

Today, it is one of the better school systems in the state. Its technology infrastructure—a fiber-optic ring linking every classroom in the district—is said to be the most advanced example of education technology in the United States (McKenna, personal communication 1997). How did the district pay for that? The townspeople, a fair fraction of whom speak English as a second language, voted the bonds by a three-to-one margin. That is just one indication of local commitment. The high school is open from 7 a.m. to 8 p.m. It is *the* "place to be" for the teens of Union City. Moreover, achievement scores at all levels in the district keep going up—year, after year, after year. College placements are way over what the town's demographics would predict.

This district is by no means an oddball example. I visit a school a week on average. Although I have seen physical plants in dreadful need of attention, the stereotypical evening news "blackboard jungle" is not at all typical. This does not mean we do not have some very serious challenges in some districts, but we also have real success stories to balance that picture.

In Richmond, California, a private citizen named John Sculley has organized a program to support bright, very poor, mostly black youngsters by providing college students who tutor the children and take them to visit college campuses. These mentors paint a picture of something to aspire to. It works. At least half the participants in that program are going to four-year colleges; yet this is a group of children for whom cold statistical analysis would predict *almost none* could achieve that.

There is nothing wrong with these children! Yes, they often do lack family experience with the benefits of education, and that hurts. Yes, they often do lack parental support for their early intellectual victories, and that hurts. Yes—and this is the worst part—many do feel they have no business aspiring beyond their stations. That is Charles Dickens's philosophy. That is not ours. That is not the United States. That is not the 21st century in any country I want to live in.

John Katz (1998), *WIRED's* perceptive political writer, wrote a piece recently on a new study that found that whereas 73 percent of white students have access to a home computer, only 29 percent of black students do. He is chillingly on-target when he writes: "When the non-wired underclass figures out just how excluded they are from the good, clean jobs of the new global economy, it is difficult to imagine anything less than a political upheaval."

We are on the front porch of the 21st century, and public education in the United States is facing both enormous changes and tremendous challenges. Our world is evolving faster than at any time in our history, and we are literally rocketing out of the Industrial Age into the Information Age.

To prepare for this new age, we must ensure that all students receive the education and training they need to participate in the future—whether they pursue higher education, advanced training, employment, or community involvement. Clearly, if we ignore this responsibility and allow our education system to fall behind the tide of change in the larger world, we prepare our youngsters for bit parts at best. Let me repeat, the potential in the 21st century for our students will be fabulous, but only for those who are well educated—and only for those who have made sure the right stuff gets mastered.

To reach this potential, everyone must do their part. And everyone must reaffirm the values that launched this country and that are found in its charter: that all are created equal, that they are endowed by their Creator with certain inalienable rights, and that among these are life, liberty, and the pursuit of happiness.

But the pursuit of happiness takes *preparation*. Our schools are in the preparation business. We are all going into that 21st century together. We must *all* be in the preparation business. Let us never forget the words of H. G. Wells, who closed his thousand-page world history with these words: "Human history becomes more and more a race between education and catastrophe." (1920)

Education is the United States' first line of defense in the 21st century. In this sense, we should think of the country as being defended by its teachers, as well as its "top guns"; by its principals, as well as its Pentagon generals; by its moms and dads and mentors, as well as its missiles.

And the issue goes beyond preparing students for jobs; it means preparing them to be tolerant, good citizens who want to keep the values of democracy alive. The historian Theodore White once observed that the United States is the only multiracial, multiethnic, multireligious society on earth where people live in relative peace and harmony. This occurs even though people who live in the United States look more different from one another than, for instance, the people whose families are fighting in Bosnia.

Let us say it again: We must *all* be in the business of preparing our students for the 21st century. We must all make sure the right stuff gets mastered.

REFERENCES

Huitt, W. (1997). *Educational psychology: Success in the information age.* Paper presented at the Georgia Independent Schools Association, Atlanta, GA.

Katz, J. (1998, April). A restricted revolution. [21 paragraphs]. *Hotwired* [On-line serial]. Available http://www.wired.com/news/news/wiredview/story/11957.html

Kotkin, J. (1997, February 16). The LA economy: Back to basics. *Los Angeles Times.*

Pearlstein, S. (1998, May 2). An economy that just keeps growing. *Washington Post,* p. A1.

Schwartz, P., & Leyden, P. (1997, July). The long boom: A history of the future 1980–2020. *WIRED, 5,* 115–129; 168–173.

Torres, V. (1996, June 4). Hot hot hot. *LA Times.*

Wells, H. G. (1920). *The outline of history: Being a plain history of life and mankind.*

2

Education and the Demands of Democracy in the Next Millennium

Marc S. Tucker[1]
Judy B. Codding

A millennium ago, few were literate except the men of the church, who from time to time were borrowed by the crowned monarchs of the day to conduct their diplomacy, dispense their justice, and keep their books in Latin. Middle-class burghers with the money and time for books were a thing of the future. Field, farm, battle ax, and spear could be managed quite well without the written word. The extraordinary accomplishments in letters, drama, mathematics, architecture, and engineering of a millennium and more before were hidden away in the libraries of the clerics, not to be recovered for centuries to come.

---

[1]Marc S. Tucker is president of the National Center on Education and the Economy in Washington, D.C. This chapter is based on Tucker and Codding's (1998) *Standards for Our Schools: How to Set Them, Measure Them and Reach Them.* The book in turn is based on the work of the staff of the NCEE. This chapter describes the key features of NCEE's America's Choice™ School and District Designs (Commission, 1990).

How different it is now compared with a thousand years ago. To be illiterate is to be an outcast in this society, unable to cope in the most basic ways. And what it means to be literate is changing fast. For more than 60 years in this century, one could hold one's own economically with an 8th grade level of literacy. Not any more. For almost 25 years now, people with an 8th grade level of literacy—whether or not they have a high school diploma—have found that what they could purchase with their paycheck from a full-time job declined almost every year from the year before. It is now impossible to sustain a family above the poverty level with the wage they typically earn. Even the high school diploma—once a source of pride for its holder—now entitles family heads to a life of poverty in the United States.

That trend is, if anything, gathering force. It is now true that those with baccalaureate degrees are experiencing the same phenomenon—their paycheck buys less as the years go by. Now only a postgraduate degree seems to assure rising real incomes. There are millions of people all over the world who are willing and able to do work requiring only an 8th grade level of literacy for somewhere between 1/10th and 1/100th of what it can be done for in the United States at the minimum wage (Commission, 1990). Yet, year after year, more than a million youngsters graduate from U.S. high schools with only an 8th grade level of literacy—not nearly adequate to do college-level work.

All over the developed world, democratic governments are being pressed harder every year to provide openings in the higher education system for voters' sons and daughters. The perception is that, without a college or university degree, one's prospects are bleak.

Do we owe everyone a college education? We will not argue that point one way or the other here. What we will argue is that, as a matter of policy, we now owe every youngster an education in elementary and secondary school that will qualify them for a college education, without remediation, provided they are willing to work hard in school.

For as long as it has existed, this oldest of democracies has been absorbed in the question of what kind and quality of education government owes its citizens. In the opening decades of the present century, people resolved that question in an interesting way. Government, they believed, must make schooling mandatory through the age of 16. In that way, the state would assure a literate, informed electorate and make sure that its citizens were fit to earn a living.

At the time, the leading college presidents were proposing that everyone—whether they were going to college or not—should be prepared for a college education. That, said the opinion-makers, was an elitist idea unworthy of a democratic country. An elite education was fine for those who were going to assume leadership positions in the society and the economy. But surely, imposing the elite ideal on everyone was wrong, profoundly undemocratic. The democratic alternative was to provide different forms of education for different groups, so that those going off to other stations in life could have an education appropriate for them—less academic, more practical, and more hands-on.

The subtext here was that few educators believed that most students could do college-level work. They believed that an 8th grade level of literacy was all that could be expected of most students, not just that that was all they needed. In a democracy, one does not demand more of most students than they can actually do. This conception of the democratic ideal led to the something-for-everyone high school, to math courses without any math in them nestling side by side with AP math courses for the bright youngsters.

Well, here we are, 80 or so years later, and the widespread belief is that one is in real trouble without some kind of college degree. What does a democracy do now, on the eve of the next millennium? Do we still believe that only a few can really do college-level work? Do we still believe that, in a democracy, the state should expect no more than an 8th grade level of accomplishment from the mass of students even though that level of literacy will condemn millions of its citizens to a life of poverty?

It should be obvious that the answer to the last question is no. We believe that the minimum acceptable goal for elementary and secondary education at the close of the 20th century is to prepare all but the severely mentally handicapped to go to at least the local community college without remediation. We must, as quickly as possible, convert the high school diploma into a certificate set to that standard.

But remember that we conceived of the current system as democratic, in part because we thought it was undemocratic to impose an elite ideal on students who plainly could not do the work. Do we believe now what we did not believe then—that virtually all of our students, with the right preparation and enough hard work, can do college-level work in English, mathematics, and the sciences at their local community college?

Much depends on the answer. As it stands, community colleges are turning away young people who want two-year degrees in welding and auto mechanics because their English and math skills are not high enough for them to be able to do the work. If hundreds of thousands of young people are graduating from high school every year without the basic skills to enter college-level programs in auto mechanics and welding, what will they do?

Every year brings an increase in income disparity between the fifth of the population who earn the most and the fifth who earn the least. We are on our way to becoming a society that will inevitably be torn apart by the tensions between those who have a lot and those who have nothing left to lose (Commission, 1990). In such a society, democracy is not likely to survive because police action will be the only way those who have a lot will be able to protect themselves from those who have nothing. At the dawn of the next millennium, democracy demands that we embrace the very ideal rejected in the name of democracy at the beginning of the century—the goal of preparing everyone for college.

At the last turn of the century, being ready for college meant having a command of Latin, Greek, English rhetoric, some mathematics, and the sciences. For the purposes of defining a new standard for leaving high school, let's say that what we have in mind, at a minimum, is the ability to read and write well at the level expected of college freshmen who are really doing college-level work; to do mathematics through algebra, geometry, trigonometry, statistics, and probability; and to have a good basic knowledge of physics, chemistry, biology, and the earth sciences. Let's stipulate, too, that knowledge of these subjects isn't worth much unless the student can apply that knowledge to a significant range of complex, real-world problems. We would want our model high school graduate to have a working knowledge of the trajectory and meaning of human history, the evolution of democratic institutions, the basic elements of economics, and an appreciation of the finest human achievements in the fine and applied arts, including music. And we would want our schools to contribute what they can to the development of young people of good character, who are healthy and physically fit.

Suppose now that we take those goals and, wherever appropriate, convert them into standards that students will have to meet to graduate from high school—turn-of-the-millennium standards, if you will. We would want to be sure that these standards were as high as—though not necessarily the same as—the standards in those nations where the great majority of students perform at the highest level. And we would want to make sure that the standards made clear not only *what* the student should know and be able to do but also *how well* the student needs to know it and be able to do it.

So far, this chapter can be summarized in two propositions: (1) the goal of elementary and secondary education should be to get all but the severely mentally handicapped to the point that they are ready to begin a college-level education without remediation, and (2) the way to make that goal explicit and actionable is to actually specify the goal as a measurable standard.

It is important to recognize what a profound change this goal represents compared with what has gone before. Here we are saying that a high, clear standard must be set and the job of our schools is to make sure virtually everyone meets it. That is in sharp conflict with the implicit goal of most of the current century.

Currently, by contrast, the goal for the most part has been to sort students out by "ability" and to educate each student accordingly for his or her "station" in life. The probability that those assigned in kindergarten or 1st grade to a low-ability group would eventually escape that assignment has been very slight. Once placed in the track, a child stays in the track. Needless to say, the children of poor and minority parents typically have been placed in the lowest tracks and the children of the wealthy and white in the upper tracks. This is a profoundly antidemocratic system of institutionalized low expectations.

In this system, not only are the students in the lowest tracks not expected to perform at high levels, but their failure to perform at high levels is in no way reflected on their teachers. Failure is thought to be a function of the genetic inheritance of the students. To develop explicit, high, and measurable standards for all students is to institutionalize a system of high expectations, and is therefore to stand on its head the system that has been in place through most of this century. In the next sections of this chapter, we consider what it will take to institutionalize a system of high expectations, a system designed to get all but the severely mentally handicapped to high standards, a system for the next millennium.

One thing is certain: Simply putting the students who *have not* succeeded into the programs in place for those who *have* succeeded will not work; they will not be able to do the work. Simply telling students that they will not be promoted to the next grade when they have failed the last will not by itself work; they will not know how to do better in the future what they could not do in the past. Simply threatening educators in schools that are failing will not work; it will just demoralize them and persuade capable educators to avoid problem schools. It is crucial to remember that getting all students to a high standard is a task for which the current system was never designed. If that is the goal, then we will have to design a new system to reach it.

Actually, make that two systems. The first is an instructional system. The second is a policy, organizational, and management system. We'll discuss each in turn.

THE INSTRUCTIONAL SYSTEM

The instructional system begins with standards. The problem is not that we have had no standards. We have had standards; but they have been, for the most part, implicit rather than explicit, and there have been different standards for different groups of students.

For many years, students headed for selective colleges have known that they need to do well on courses labeled "college prep" by their high school, on their college entrance examinations, and on their Advanced Placement tests. The shelves of the bookstores they patronize are loaded with books showing examples of the kinds of questions they could expect and the kinds of answers they would be expected to give. The AP courses come with their own curriculum. There is no mystery about what one is supposed to study, learn, and know in the AP system. The college entrance exams and the APs are external exams. No one in the school can change them. That makes the students, teachers, and parents allies. Working as a team, they can improve the student's performance on the exam.

Below the college track, however, the standards are lower, less external, and less explicit—less explicit, that is, until we reach the bottom track, where it is still true in many states that a high school diploma depends only on getting a D- or better in one's courses, and getting a D- depends only on turning in homework most of the time (quality does not count), not causing too much trouble, and showing up with reasonable frequency. In no state does graduation require more than an 8th grade level of demonstrated literacy.

Outside of the AP system, getting a better grade has been mostly a matter of the parent jawboning the school to get the principal to make the teacher raise a grade already given to the student, rather than a matter of the student working harder in the course. What we propose is an external standard for the school—not for one or two courses and only a few students, but for the whole core curriculum and for all students. Not different standards for different groups of students, but the same standard across the board.

This is not the place for a detailed treatment of the issue of standards, but it is important to go beyond what has already been said to make a few points about the nature of what is most important to learn, irrespective of subject. The first point has to do with the coverage and sequence of the curriculum. Most nations that have high performance at the top end of the distribution and a relatively narrow gap between the highest and lowest performing students have a more or less fixed curriculum for the first 9 or 10 years of schooling. Everyone takes the same courses in the same sequence, with very few choices along the way. This makes it possible for teachers to be certain about what the students know and can do coming into their classrooms at the beginning of the year. It makes it possible for textbook publishers to cover only what needs to be covered for a particular year and to cover it in depth, rather than covering a vast range of topics in the hope that there will be something for everyone. It makes it possible for students who move from school to school and town to town to be sure that they will be able to pick up where they left off. More important than anything else, it makes it possible to deliver a curriculum that progresses in an ordered sequence through the most important topics, each covered in depth and each leading in a logical way to the next step in the progression. All of this can be captured in a set of standards for student performance that progresses through the grades.

The second point has to do with the character of the curriculum. What is needed now is a curriculum that attends in almost equal measure to skills and knowledge, conceptual mastery and the ability to apply what one knows to complex, real-world problems. Individuals must know a lot and be able to think with what they know. There are those who are insisting that schooling ought to be about skills and knowledge of the facts and only that. And there are those who are insisting that there is so much to know now that it is pointless to try to teach it to our children—all that is important is to teach them how to learn and how to apply what they learn in an "interdisciplinary" context.

This argument between the advocates of the "basics" on the one hand and the advocates of "problem solving," the "interdisciplinary curriculum," and the process approach to education on the other hand seems to us to be very sterile. It is patently the case that people who cannot decode the language and who have an inadequate command of spelling, diction, grammar, vocabulary, arithmetic, and fractions are going to have a tough time. The basics are absolutely necessary. But it is no less necessary for students to understand the concepts underlying the disciplines, because it is only by understanding the conceptual underpinning that students will be able to apply what they know to problems that are not exactly like the ones at the end of the chapter in the

31

textbook. Conceptual mastery, in other words, is the key to understanding, "learning how to learn," thinking, and "problem solving." It is not possible to really understand the subject, in the sense of being able to use what one has learned, without grasping the concepts underlying the disciplines.

That said, we can now describe the key characteristics of an instructional system to meet the requirements of the beginning of the next millennium:

Required Curriculum
- Agreed-upon subjects that will constitute a required curriculum for the first 9 or 10 years in school; a curriculum with few options.

Performance Standards
- Standards for that curriculum that are comparable to the standards met by students in those nations where performance is highest; standards that clearly indicate how good is good enough by including examples of student work that meets the standard.

Curriculum Map
- A curriculum map that lays out the sequence of topics and concepts that will be studied in each subject through the grades.

Curriculum Materials
- "Concept books" and "practice problem books" for students, matched to the standards and curriculum maps, that present the underlying concepts in straightforward terms, provide problems to practice on, and contain needed reference material (such as grammar rules and mathematical formulas and tables).
- "Core assignments" designed to provide modules of instruction for students keyed to the standards and curriculum maps; a series of these assignments will constitute the core of the syllabus for a standards-based course.
- New forms of teachers guides that contain syllabi for courses matched to the standards and curriculum maps, as well as a wealth of material designed to help the teacher reach students from many different backgrounds as they work on the core assignments.
- In the upper grades, courses of study that go beyond the syllabi to constitute the full design for the courses that will get the students to the school-leaving standards.

Assessment System
- Reference examinations matched to the standards to be given at

the end of elementary school and middle school and in high school as
the key element in determining whether the student has met the
school-leaving standard; these exams to be called "reference examinations" because they are referenced to the standards.

• End-of-course examinations for each course, to determine
whether the student has learned what he or she had to learn to go on to
the next course in the sequence.

• A new grading system that aims to help teachers produce
grades for courses and for student work that are very close to the same
from teacher to teacher for the same piece of student work.

• A portfolio system that enables students to make sure that they
are producing the array of work that is needed to let the teacher judge
whether the student has met each component of the standards.

• Rules for assembling the scores obtained in the courses and the
examinations into an overall score that determines whether or not the
school-leaving standard has been met.

Safety Net
• A special set of curriculum materials designed for students who
enter the stream of the regular curriculum significantly behind where
the standards say they should be; these materials to be designed so that
the student, by putting in some extra time and effort, can vault ahead
and catch up to classmates who are on track.

• Time before school, outside the regular curriculum during
school, after school, on Saturdays, and during the summer when students who are behind can go to school to catch up, using the safety net
materials just described. The object is to make certain that no student is
left behind, and all can catch up if they start behind.

Master Schedule Keyed to Results
• A school day structured to make sure that every student meets
the standards by allocating time in response to a careful analysis of the
student body's strengths and weaknesses in relation to the standards.

Instructional Technology Linked to the Curriculum and Tied to the Standards
• Technology used not as a teacher but as a powerful tool for
analysis, production, graphical representation, and access to information, all in support of the standards-based curriculum.

What ties these elements together is a commitment to get every
student to high standards. The instructional system is fully aligned.
Every element in it is tied to the standards. The curriculum reflects the
balance between basic skills and knowledge, concepts and applications,

and is consciously constructed step-by-step to match the standards. The nature of the materials as well as their content matches the standards. The courses are sequenced to match the standards. They leave nothing out that is needed and include nothing that is not needed. Extra time during the day, week, and year allows students who are behind to catch up. The time during the regular school day is scheduled in light of student performance against the standards, so that available resources can be used in the most efficient manner to get all students to the standards. Instructional technology is harnessed to the curriculum, which in turn is tied to the standards. A fixed curriculum assures that everyone's attention is focused on what is most important: getting everyone to reach a set of explicit, high standards. The focus throughout is on the standards and on getting results as defined by the standards. In this design, nothing else counts.

LEADING, MANAGING AND ORGANIZING THE SCHOOL

We are describing schools in which nothing and no one falls through the cracks. Everyone succeeds. That will take real leadership—of several kinds.

At the dawn of the next millennium, schools will look a lot more like professional partnerships and a lot less like factories. Law firms are headed by lawyers who practice law, not by administrators. Much the same can be said of medical practices and of engineering and architectural practices.

The principal will have to be a head teacher, a true instructional leader. Student success in these schools will depend on the teachers having a full repertoire of sound, research-based strategies for teaching students from a wide range of backgrounds. If that is going to happen, the principal (teacher) will have to know whether the teachers have actually mastered that repertoire and will have to be able to model good teaching in the classroom, judge whether the work on the classroom walls meets or does not meet the standard, and help the teachers figure out how to solve student performance problems that they cannot solve unaided. In that sense, the principal will have to be a master teacher, or arrange to have one or more other people in the school play that role. In an institution that is "keeping school," it is enough to have a principal who is a politician and administrator. In an institution devoted to quality results, the principal must first and foremost be a principal teacher.

There is another sense in which the principal will have to be a leader, and leadership in this sense cannot be delegated. The principal

34

will constantly have to make tough choices, and those choices will have to demonstrate an unwavering commitment to results before everything else—results defined by the academic standards. This is and always will be hard.

In most communities, sports take precedence over academics. Schools spend more on football helmets than on science labs. Priority goes to the sports schedule rather than the English class when the demands of the two collide. Almost everywhere, the employment needs of the faculty come before the academic needs of the students. Getting all students to high standards can be done, but it will not happen unless priority goes to academics first, last, and always. That will require personal leadership from the principal.

But principals cannot manage the school alone. Nothing will happen unless people make it happen. The principal will have to decide what is most important to get done over the long haul and then appoint people who will be responsible for making those things happen. A number of these people will serve in a sort of school cabinet, sharing the burden of managing and leading the school. Each of these people will be responsible for involving others in their work, until everyone is involved. This, too, is very similar to the way a professional partnership works.

This kind of leadership structure is one way that the faculty can take collective responsibility for what happens to the students. Another way involves arranging the master schedule so that teachers of the same subject can meet regularly to adjust the curriculum to the needs of the students and to work together to produce more effective lessons than individual teachers can produce on their own. Such a schedule also allows teachers of the same students to get together regularly to share their perspectives on each student to make sure that their collective knowledge and observations contribute to fully informed decisions as to what program will most likely get the student to the standards.

In the traditional "egg crate" school, each teacher has each student for a year. In many other countries with high student performance, some teachers follow the students through the grades, sometimes through as many as six grades. This is called the "class teacher" system. It fosters a close relationship among teachers, students, and their families and enables teachers to plan ahead and take personal responsibility for students in a way that is virtually impossible in the U.S. system.

Everywhere you look in a standards-based school, you see the standards, pieces of student work that exemplify the standards, hints to keep in mind when trying to produce work that meets the standards, and rubrics that can be used to judge whether a piece of work meets the standards. The standards, the production of work intended to meet the standards, and the judging of work against the standards are the leitmotifs of the standards-based school.

Standards-based schools are also schools that are immersed in student performance data, the analysis of that data, and the use of the products of that analysis to plan programs that will get students to standards. In such an environment, planning takes on a new and much more urgent centrality. When teachers know what the standard is and how far their students are from achieving it, it becomes terribly important to diagnose the problems correctly, search for the most effective solutions available, plan carefully for implementation, and then actually do it! How different this is from the more usual environment in which plans are typically produced to meet some external requirement and then shelved soon afterward.

So far, we may have conveyed the idea that we believe that the only thing that matters is standards-based instruction. Although it is true that attention to instruction is long overdue, the fact is that other things count very much. Instruction cannot take place if there is no order in the school. And it is very hard, sometimes impossible, to bring order to a school if the students in that school do not feel that they matter very much to the adults there. It is also true that when both parents and students feel alienated from the staff, it is very unlikely that student performance will improve. Involvement begins with respect, but it does not end there. The staff of the school need to listen to the students, parents, and the larger community. Listening is the key to warm relations and to the support that is so vital to success.

These comments apply to the leadership, organization, and management of both elementary and secondary schools. Before we get to comments that apply only to one or the other, a word is in order on the division between elementary and secondary education.

It is time to abandon the idea of the middle school. It is hard to remember why we thought it was a good idea in the first place. It is even harder to see why it is needed now. Student learning proceeds apace through elementary school, levels off or even goes into reverse in middle school, and then resumes in high school. Few other nations have separate school organizations for the middle years. Middle school students get neither the warmth and sense of family of the elementary school nor the attention to academic rigor characteristic of the best of our high schools.

Most of the rest of the world has variations of the K–8 school. The students in the upper grades seem to benefit from the reflected warmth of the lower grades, and the students in the lower grades seem to get a little more academic rigor than they otherwise would. Most important, the students going into the upper grades do not get the cold bath that the students leaving elementary grades now get when they leave their neighborhood school for middle school. We would have a system composed only of K–8 schools and high schools.

The overriding priority of K–8 schools should be the development of literacy. The research is now clear. If a student is not fluent by 2nd grade, he or she will never catch up to the other students, mainly because the initial lack of fluency makes it more difficult to acquire new vocabulary, lack of vocabulary slows down reading, which further retards the development of comprehension, and so on. Literacy is, of course, the key to competence in all the other subjects. So schools must pay great attention to carefully monitoring the literacy development of the student in the early years and to addressing the problem quickly when the student starts to fall behind.

This will take considerable expertise on the part of the teacher—more than many now have. Producing that expertise would be easier if we stopped expecting elementary school teachers to be jacks of all trades and asked some teachers to specialize in English language arts and social studies and others to specialize in mathematics and science. Schools will have to find ways to organize very high quality, sustained technical assistance and professional development programs for teachers in the primary grades to help them take advantage of the wealth of information that has been gained in recent years about the most effective strategies for teaching literacy to students from different backgrounds.

Given the goal we have set for our elementary and secondary schools, the high school will have to undergo a major redesign. The object, you recall, is to get all students to an internationally benchmarked level of accomplishment that qualifies them to do college-level work without remediation. No high school that we know of has ever attempted this. And no comprehensive high school is likely to achieve it, because comprehensive high schools, by virtue of trying to accomplish so many different things for so many, end up doing nothing very well.

The first and by far the most important goal of the new U.S. high school should be to make sure that all its students get the new U.S. diploma attesting to their ability to do college-level work without remediation. That will require a continuation in high school of the fixed curriculum we advocated in the K–8 school. The standards will determine the curriculum. The curriculum may offer some choices, but they should be very few. Many students will reach the diploma standard by the time they are 16. But many will not, and they should have the rest of their time in high school, if necessary, to reach it.

Figure 2.1 depicts the structure of the new, standards-based U.S. high school and shows how the new system would work. All students

FIGURE 2.1

The U.S. High School—Redesigned

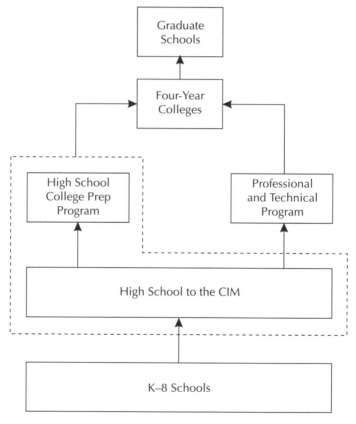

Source: M. S. Tucker & J. B. Codding. (1998). *Standards for our schools: How to set them, measure them, and reach them.* (San Francisco: Jossey-Bass), p. 194.

would work toward the new diploma standard until they reach it. Then they would have several choices.

One choice would be to stay in high school for a demanding college preparatory program designed to prepare students to do as well as possible on competitive college entrance examinations. This could be the International Baccalaureate program or a program made up of a coherent set of Advanced Placement courses or the state equivalent—for example, the Golden State exam courses in California or the Regents in New York.

Another choice would be to begin a program of professional and technical education designed to prepare the student to take the exams leading to industry certification for a cluster of professional and technical careers. These programs would culminate in the awarding of the industry certificate, college credit, and, in most cases, a two-year college degree. Many of these programs would involve a combination of class work and structured training at the work site. The programs would be offered by community colleges and, in those states that have them, technical colleges.

Some students who had their diploma in hand would decide to enter a community college to pursue a two-year degree in an academic area, usually with the intention of transferring to a four-year institution. And a few might decide to enter the job market, probably continuing their education later.

This plan turns the high school into a single-purpose institution, and that purpose is academics alone. The demands of technical education now far outstrip the capacity of most high schools, which cannot attract teachers with the necessary skills, build the capacity to forge the necessary partnerships with employers and industry groups, or purchase and replace the very expensive equipment that is needed.

This plan places those responsibilities in a small number of institutions that have the necessary resources and that are located within commuting distance of most of the population. That leaves the high school to do one thing very well.

Doing well would require other changes in the high school structure, not least of which would be breaking the high school down into a "house" system of not more than 400 students per house. Each house would have its own faculty, administrative structure, and student body, thus creating a much more intimate setting than most high schools currently offer.

LEADING, MANAGING, AND
ORGANIZING THE SCHOOL DISTRICT

So far, we have been describing high-performance schools—that is, schools that are designed to get virtually all of their students to explicit, high standards in the most efficient way possible. But schools do not exist in a vacuum; they are managed by the central offices of school districts. It is simply not possible to operate successful standards-based schools in districts that are not themselves organized and managed for results, defined by student performance against high standards.

Districts that are managed in the context of the sorting paradigm will inevitably defeat schools that are managed to abandon the sorting paradigm in favor of getting all students to perform at high levels. The two goals are antithetical; either one or the other will prevail.

Many school people have assumed that the role of the central office in the new U.S. school district will be to decentralize everything. That is not so. Modern management is not about the democratization of the workplace. It is about the professionalization of the workplace. There is a world of difference.

The mass production management model assumed that the people in the central office were to do the thinking and the workers were to do as they were told, leaving their heads at the factory gate. The people at central would design the machines, which would produce the goods. They would also design the jobs of the people who tended the machines and figure out the one best way to do those jobs. Having done that, they would tell the people on the front line exactly how to do their jobs the one best way. Front-line workers could expect a fair day's pay for an honest day of work. That is the management model that public education adopted in the early part of this century. It has not changed much since then.

The model works fairly well if the goal is to produce a flood of products at low cost and of indifferent quality. It simply will not work if the object is to produce products and services of consistently high and ever improving quality. When our elementary and secondary schools were in a situation in which a majority of students did not have to perform above an 8th grade level of literacy when they left school, the mass production organizational scheme worked quite well. But it will not work any more.

If the object is quality, and if getting consistent quality depends on making innumerable judgments "on the ground," then one must

40

(1) make sure the professional on the ground—the person actually rendering the service—has the information needed to make the best judgment, (2) provide incentives to reward good work and hard work, and (3) trust the professional to make the right judgment in any given situation.

Since the early 1980s firm after firm in the United States has decided that corporate survival requires going for quality. Having decided that, they discovered that they had no alternative but to abandon the factory model in favor of a professional model of organization. Their staff, they came to realize, is their most important asset.

Roughly speaking, they concluded that success depended on (1) being very clear about the goals of the enterprise and communicating those goals very clearly to everyone in the organization, (2) finding a way to accurately measure progress toward those goals, (3) setting up accountability systems so that everyone in the organization had strong incentives to make substantial progress toward the goals and strong disincentives to sit on their hands, (4) providing appropriate information and effective help to the people on the front lines to enable them to do the best possible job, and (5) letting the people on the front lines decide how to use the available resources to get the job done.

This approach to organization and management is the antithesis of the way school districts have been organized and managed for decades. If school districts were to adopt these principles in the interest of embracing a results-oriented, standards-based system, here is what the board and central office would have to do:

Goals and Indicators
   • Adopt a short set of goals for the district and decide on indicators of progress for each goal.
   • Establish targets for each goal in terms of progress against each indicator to be made by set dates.

Structure
   • Establish a standards-based, rather than time-based, standard for graduation.
   • Adopt the organizational design pictured in Figure 2.1 for post-diploma studies.
   • Create an institutional structure of K–8 schools and high schools.

Standards and Curriculum Framework
   • Adopt standards for earning the new diploma and for benchmarks in each subject on the way to earning the diploma, making sure

that the standards include examples of student work that meet the standards.

• Decide whether to have a required curriculum for the program leading to the diploma, and if so, what that program (in terms of content and sequences of courses) will be.

Assessment

• Fix the assessments for the diploma and for the courses in the required curriculum.

• Decide on a uniform grading system.

Resource Allocation

• Give each school at least 85 percent of its pro rata share of the district's total resources and authorize the schools to spend those resources as they wish, purchasing necessary services from the central office or elsewhere, establishing their own staffing patterns, selecting their own staff, and designing their own program—within the constraints, however, of the required curriculum and assessment regime.

• Base the allocations on a formula that provides a standard amount for students at each level of the system (primary, upper elementary, high school to diploma, high school beyond the diploma), and includes additional factors for students who are more expensive to educate (because of low-income background, limited English proficiency, need for special education, etc.). Use the formula to determine the allocation for the school, not the student.

Staff Incentives

• Create a system of financial rewards for schools that do a better job from one year to the next in getting their students to the standards. In this system, a school competes not against other schools, but against itself. The rewards go not to individual teachers but to the whole staff. Rewards are based on the performance of all the students, not just some of them.

• Create a system of consequences for schools that fall below a level of performance established by policy. The consequences should include first the possibility of no raises until school performance reaches the minimum acceptable level and then, if the school fails to improve within a reasonable time, the possible reconstitution of the school and ultimate dismissal of staff members whom no other school wished to employ after a reasonable time following reconstitution.

• Make sure that the compensation of every staff member in the district, including that of the superintendent, is related in some reasonable way to results.

Personal Accountability for Results
  • Make sure that everyone in the district reports to one and only one person.
  • Make sure that the "line" is defined as those people directly responsible for student performance, and that the line consists of the principals, the superintendent, and, if necessary, only one person between the superintendent and the principal. Define every role as a support role, and make sure that only people in the line can say no to the principal.
  • Make sure that everyone knows what results he or she will be held accountable for.

Getting Out of the Way and Providing Help to the Schools
  • Let the line do its work. Do not let the board or the central office staff get involved in addressing the problems at individual schools. That should be work of the principals, their staffs, and, when necessary, the principal's immediate supervisor.
  • Make sure that only the people in the line can say no to a principal. Everyone else is an advisor whose advice can be sought or ignored.
  • Make sure that there is a steady flow of high-quality information to the schools about what works best in what circumstances. The schools should be required to use this information, but it must be made available.

Getting High-Quality Data to Everyone Who Needs It
  • Make sure that concentrated attention goes to the establishment of the district's capacity to collect, store, analyze, and distribute timely, accurate information on student performance against the standards and to relate that information to a wealth of other information needed to identify promptly which students need what kind of help and what kinds of help are likely to be most effective in any given situation.

This approach to the design of a new kind of central office essentially places the board and the central office in the position of establishing the goals, measures, and incentive and accountability structures, letting the schools figure out how to get the job done, and then handing out the rewards and consequences.

Thought about this way, the system could as easily be used to manage charter schools as regular public schools. Whether this is a distinction without a difference depends on your views as to how much autonomy charter schools should have. Many advocates of charter schools would bridle at the idea that the central office should establish the curriculum framework and the structure for the sequence of courses in a required curriculum. Some would object that central should retain no role at all in the employment of teachers.

These are arguable points. But we would argue that no school supported by public money should have the option of rejecting applicants on a discriminatory basis, and every school supported by public funds should be accountable for results against the same standards that apply to students in the public system. If you accept those propositions, the overall organizational and management plan just described could be applied to a system of charter schools with only a few modifications.

If there is one quality that best characterizes what will be needed to accomplish the goals we have described here, it is the quality of relentless dedication to high-quality results. Leadership, as always, is the key. There is nothing new here. It has always been true that major institutional changes require courageous leaders. But it has also been true that changing times have created opportunities for new leaders to surface. We rise to the occasion.

The times are without doubt changing. The sorting system is producing incipient social disaster. That disaster can be averted only if we somehow convince ourselves that most of our children can do much better than we have expected them to do in the past, that they can do as well as children anywhere in the world can do. We expect you, dear reader, to argue with many of the specific proposals in this chapter. But we hope that when you do, you feel compelled to substitute your own ideas about how to achieve the goal we have described, and that you campaign relentlessly on behalf of that goal and those ideas.

REFERENCES

Commission on the Skills of the American Workforce. (1990). *America's choice: High skills or low wages!* Rochester, NY: National Center on Education and the Economy.

Tucker, M. S., & Codding, J. B. (1998). *Standards for our schools: How to set them, measure them, and reach them.* San Francisco: Jossey-Bass.

3

Education for the Public Good: Strategic Intentions for the 21st Century

Brian J. Caldwell

B y any criterion, the public school is one of the most successful organizations of the modern era. Most organizations created a century ago no longer exist; yet many public schools of that time may still be found on the same site, with the same name, serving the same community. The public school is an important factor in accounting for the United States as a world power. In addition to creating an educated citizenry, it molds the nation's athletes and nurtures those who have created and sustained the arts.

Despite these achievements, *Education Week*'s 1997 "Report Card on the Condition of Public Education in the 50 States" asserted that "public education systems in the fifty states are riddled with excellence but rife with mediocrity" and suggested that, if public education does not soon improve, either democracy and economic strength will erode or "alternative forms of education will emerge to replace public schools as we have known them" ("The State of the States," p. 1). Recent events suggest that the second possibility may not be fanciful. Already the entire system of one state (Kentucky) has been reengineered; in several urban school districts, mayors have assumed control or the private sector has been granted contracts for part or all of their operation; momentum for charter schools is building; voucher plans are edging closer to realization; and home schooling is expanding. In the midst of these developments, some of the finest designs for learning and teaching have been implemented, with the challenge being how to achieve scale-up so that all students can reap the benefits.

The United States is not alone in this search for an approach to public schooling that will ensure success in the next century. Beginning in 1988, under Conservative governments led by Margaret Thatcher and John Major, Great Britain experienced the most far-reaching transformation of its public school system in modern times, and the Labour government elected in 1997 and led by Prime Minister Tony Blair has kept most elements in place, vowing to focus on standards as never before, with its top priorities being "education, education, education." In Australia, where more than 30 percent of students are already attending private schools, there is a sense that public education is in transition, and the search for a form that will suit the third millennium is under way. Comprehensive reforms such as Schools of the Future in Victoria lay the groundwork (Caldwell & Hayward, 1998).

A review of developments in these and other nations suggests that there are three different movements under way, and they are occurring simultaneously. The image of a "track" seems appropriate, because the three movements are under way at the same time in most places; schools, school systems, and nations vary in the distance they have moved down each track. Track 1 is the shifting of significant authority, responsibility, and accountability to schools. Track 2 is an unrelenting focus on learning outcomes. Track 3 is the creation of schools for the knowledge society. Developments on Tracks 1 and 2 underpin a new view of "professionalism." Developments on Track 3 suggest a new concept of "school."

This chapter contains three sections. The first and second deal with the new professionalism and the new school, respectively. In each instance a vision is derived from accounts of emerging practice. The third section employs the technique of "backward mapping" to describe what a system of schools will look like under the conditions implied by the new professionalism and the new school. I conclude that public education, narrowly conceived as a system of schools publicly owned and publicly resourced, must be reconceptualized. It is necessary to form a broader view of "education for the public good" to admit such concepts as "voluntarism," "civil society," and the "third way," for these are critical elements of the vision for schooling in the 21st century.

THE NEW PROFESSIONALISM

It appears that the shift of significant responsibility, authority, and accountability to the school level within a curriculum and standards framework, with new alignments of personnel and other resource functions (Track 1), is becoming the norm for the management of public schools. At first sight this is school-based or school-site management, but it is actually much more. School-based management and school-site management were structural rearrangements of the 1970s and 1980s that simply realigned in a relatively minor way some of the responsibilities of the central office, with provision for a local school-based decision-making body. In the new order, significant authorities are shifted to the local site, including responsibilities for most of the budget and staff, but there are substantial accountability requirements in terms of targets and standards within a clearly defined curriculum framework.

There is rarely a proposal for school reform that does not call for extending the capacity for the self-management of schools. The movement is well advanced in nations such as Australia and Great Britain, and the evidence suggests that no system that has moved in this direction is likely to return to arrangements that provided good service over much of the last century but are now obsolete.

It is sobering to note the consistent finding in research over many years that there appear to be few if any direct links between self-management or school-based management and gains in learning outcomes for students (Whitty, Power, & Halpin, 1998; Summers & Johnson, 1996; Malen, Ogawa, & Kranz, 1990). Some observers have noted that such gains are unlikely to be achieved in the absence of purposeful links between capacities associated with school reform—in this instance, school-based management—and what occurs in the classroom in terms of learning and teaching and the support of learning and teaching (Bullock & Thomas, 1997; Hanushek, 1996, 1997; Levacic, 1995; Smith, Scoll, & Link, 1996). According to Wirt (1991), the absence of impact may be due to preoccupation with an "adult game" rather than a "children game." Some researchers have developed models for achieving these linkages, with promising work in Hong Kong by Cheung and Cheng (Cheng, 1996; Cheung & Cheng, 1996; Cheung & Cheng, 1997).

Reform on Track 1 will have an impact on learning only if momentum builds for reform on Track 2—that is, if explicit linkages are made between new responsibilities, authorities, and accountabilities at the school level and what occurs in the classroom. Evidence of how this has been accomplished is emerging (Bryk, 1998; Caldwell, 1998; Caldwell & Spinks, 1998; Cooperative Research Project, 1998). Significant change depends on schools taking up and applying knowledge about school and classroom effectiveness and improvement. Fortunately, this body of knowledge is richer and deeper than ever. There are several imperatives around which consensus is building, including early literacy, adoption of approaches that smooth the transition from elementary to secondary school, and managing increasingly complex arrangements in programs at the senior secondary level. *Unrelenting* is an appropriate word to describe the commitment that is required to ensure that all students learn well. Governments in a host of nations are endeavoring to set targets for improvement in at least the areas of literacy and numeracy.

What can be expected for teachers, given the agenda for further change that is starting to emerge on Tracks 1 and 2? Will it be more of the same, depressing even further any hope of gaining or regaining the elixir of "being professional"?

The word *new* is becoming a cliché, as in "New Labour" in Britain and "New American Schools" in the United States. Its suitability is, however, worth testing, because the context and expectations for teaching are so different now. Peter Drucker (1993) believes that the world is going through one of the great social transformations that come along every few hundred years. He suggests that schools will be affected more than any other social institution and will face the greatest challenge. A consequence is surely a profound change in the role of the teacher. Except in ways that will be readily accepted, this does not mean abandoning the traditional tenets of professionalism; indeed, they are extended and enriched. The new view of the professional calls for the shedding of many aspects of the role that have recently become tiresome or distasteful or, at least, more appropriate for others to perform.

The starting point for constructing a view of the new professionalism is to examine the ingredients for success in learning and teaching under these conditions. Darling-Hammond (1997); A. Hargreaves (1997); MacGilchrist, Myers, and Reed (1997); and McLaughlin (1997) provide broadly based accounts. More detailed accounts appear in reports of developments in particular learning areas, such as early literacy (Crévola & Hill, 1998).

A number of important dimensions of professional practice emerge from these accounts. Teachers acquire new knowledge and skill in a learning area they are already qualified to teach. They need to be skillful in using an array of diagnostic and assessment instruments to identify precisely what entry levels and needs exist among their students, and the resultant approaches to learning and teaching are different in each classroom. Each child is treated as an individual, in reality as well as in rhetorical terms. Teachers work as part of a team, and they devote much time out of class to preparation, and in briefing and debriefing meetings to assess the effectiveness of approaches and to plan new ones. Cross-cultural communication and the effective involvement of parents as partners in the enterprise are also required. There is an appreciation that existing approaches, though good enough to get by on in the past, are no longer good enough; and there is a shared expectation that all children can succeed. Professional development is continuous.

These are the hallmarks of the new professional in teaching. To repeat, none of these capacities calls for abandonment of the traditional tenets of professionalism. Rather, the tenets are reinforced, extended, and enriched. The effective professional in the past will likely be well-suited to the new circumstances, albeit with an updating of knowledge and skill. But there should be no doubting that the new professional has a more sophisticated body of knowledge and skill than was common in the past, and a new and very demanding set of expectations to live up to.

One contrast with past practice in the profession is in order, as is a comparison with professional practice in other fields. With respect to the former, it is clear that the isolation of the past has gone. The new professional is not a teacher working alone, who is expected or expects to teach her or his class behind closed doors. The new professional is at ease working in a team and at ease sharing complex sets of data about student entry points, progress, and outcomes. There is a willingness to be vulnerable as well as a willingness to share.

Comparisons with other professions, particular the caring professions, are immediately apparent. One expects doctors—general practitioners and specialists—to use an increasingly sophisticated battery of tests and to select the right treatment. There is distress at the prospect that doctors might not keep up-to-date with the latest developments in their fields, through private reading and successful participation at regularly organized programs of professional development provided as a matter of course by professional associations. At a place where there is a concentration of doctors, such as a clinic or a hospital, there is an expectation of regular conferences involving a sharing of information about what does or does not work. We expect full accountability.

This comparison of education with the health care field is not new. David Hargreaves, professor of education at Cambridge University, has employed it to good effect (1994, 1997). The comparison is not perfect, because education involves concern about students who are learning, whereas medicine involves dealing with patients who have an ailment. It is, however, appropriate to show that the new professionalism for teachers can be as thorough as that of doctors, whose status in society in this regard is held to be unquestionable.

THE NEW PROFESSIONALISM IN ACTION

What will the new professionalism be like in practice at the school level? It is difficult to provide a detailed account or to formulate a strategic plan to guide its development, given the turbulent school environment. However, the concept of "strategic intention" is helpful.

> Strategic intention describes a process of coping with turbulence through a direct, intuitive understanding of what is occurring in an effort to guide the work of the [school]. A turbulent environment cannot be tamed by rational analysis alone so that conventional strategic planning is deemed to be of little use. Yet it does not follow that a [school's] response must be left to a random distribution of lone individuals acting opportunistically and often in isolation . . . . Strategic intention relies on an intuitively formed pattern or *gestalt*—some would call it a vision—to give it unity and coherence. (Boisot, 1995, p. 36)

The notion of *gestalt* is employed in several places in this chapter. It refers to an organization of ideas or constructs, the total of which is greater than the sum of its parts. In the case of the new professionalism, the gestalt is presented below in a list of 10 strategic intentions drawn from a set of 100 in an extended account of leadership and change in schools (Caldwell & Spinks, 1998). A gestalt for the new school appears later in this chapter, first as a diagram of constructs and then in a second list of 10 strategic intentions. Finally, a gestalt for the reconceptualization of "education for the public good" draws on emerging practice of international significance.

The 10 strategic intentions for the new professionalism are the following:

1. There will be planned and purposeful efforts to reach higher levels of professionalism in data-driven, outcomes-oriented, team-based approaches to raising levels of achievement for all students.

2. Substantial blocks of time will be scheduled for teams of teachers and other professionals to reflect on data, devise and adapt approaches to learning and teaching, and set standards and targets that are relevant to their students.

3. Teachers and other professionals will read widely and continuously in local, national, and international literature in their fields, consistent with expectations and norms for medical practitioners.

4. Teachers and other professionals will become skillful in the use of a range of information and communications technology, employing it to support learning and teaching, and to gain access to current information that will inform their professional practice.

5. Schools will join networks of schools and other providers of professional services in the public and private sectors to ensure that the needs of all students will be diagnosed and met, especially among the disabled and disadvantaged, employing the techniques of case management to ensure success for every individual in need.

6. Professionals will work within curriculum and standards frameworks, as well as other protocols and standards of professional practice, with the same level of commitment and rigor as is expected in medicine.

7. Staff will seek recognition of their work that meets or exceeds standards of professional practice, and will support and participate in the programs of professional bodies established for this purpose.

8. Schools will ensure a much broader agenda than is evident in much of public discourse, including literacy and numeracy, and shall, without sacrificing attention to these, build their capacity to address a range of "intelligences."

9. The notions of "the learning organization" and "the intelligent school" will be embraced, and strategies will be designed and implemented to ensure success.

10. Schools will work with universities and other providers in a range of programs in teaching and research and development that support and reflect the new professionalism in education.

THE NEW SCHOOL

Figure 3.1 presents in diagrammatic form a gestalt for Track 3 of change in education (Caldwell & Spinks, 1998, p. 13). It is a vision for schooling in the knowledge society, because those who manage information to solve problems, provide service, or create new products form the largest group in the work force, displacing industrial workers, who formed the largest group following the industrial revolution and who, in turn, displaced agricultural and domestic workers, who dominated in preindustrial times.

In the diagram, "Connectedness in Curriculum" (g1) suggests dramatic changes to come in approaches to learning and teaching as electronic networking allows "cutting across and so challenging the very idea of subject boundaries" and "changing the emphasis from impersonal curriculum to excited live exploration" (Papert, 1993). At risk is the balkanized curriculum that has done much to alienate children from schooling, especially in the years of transition from elementary to secondary school.

"Workplace Transformation" (g2) refers to schools as workplaces being transformed in every dimension, including the scheduling of time for learning and approaches to human resource management. This transformation will render obsolete most approaches that derive from an industrial age, including the concept of "industrial relations."

As represented by "School Fabric and Globalization" (g3), the fabric of schooling is similarly rendered obsolete by electronic networking. Everything from building design to the size, shape, alignment, and furnishing of space for the "knowledge worker" in the school is transformed. In one sense, of course, global learning networks mean that the school has no walls; in addition, much of the learning that the student acquires occurs in many places, including at home and—during the later years of secondary schooling and as part of lifelong learning—in the workplace.

"Professionalism and Great Teaching" (g4) suggests that a wide range of professionals and paraprofessionals support learning in an educational parallel to the diversity of support found in modern health care. The role of teacher is elevated, for it demands wisdom, judgment, and a facility to manage learning in modes more complex and varied than ever before. Although the matter of intellectual capital must be resolved, teachers are freed from the impossible task of designing from their own resources learning experiences to challenge every student: The resources of the world's great teachers will be at hand.

FIGURE 3.1
A Gestalt (Vision) for Schooling in the Knowledge Society

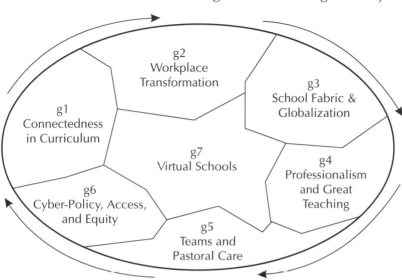

Source: B. J. Caldwell and J. M. Spinks, *Beyond the self-managing school* (London: Falmer Press, 1998), p. 13.

The component "Teams and Pastoral Care" (g5) indicates that a capacity to work in teams is more evident in approaches to learning, given the primacy of the team in every formulation of the workplace in the knowledge society. This, of course, will confound those who see electronic networking in terms of an outdated stereotype of the loner with the laptop computer. The concept of "pastoral care" of students is as important as ever for learning in this mode and in schools that quite literally have no boundaries.

As represented by "Cyber-Policy, Access, and Equity" (g6), the formulation of "cyber-policy of the future" is a priority (Spender, 1995). The issues of access and equity will drive public debate until prices fall to the point that electronic networks are as common as the telephone or radio. That may soon be a reality, given trends in networked computers.

"Virtual Schools" (g7) refers to the fact that the virtual organization or the learning network organization is a reality in the knowledge society. Schools take on many of the characteristics of such organizations, given that learning occurs in so many modes and from so many sources, all networked electronically.

The term "virtual school" is now widely used but rarely defined. Until now, school has been considered a place, and "a place called school" captures the traditional meaning, as in the book of that title by John Goodlad (1984). What changes a place called school to a virtual school is that learning does not necessarily occur at the place, nor at the time, nor in the style that traditionally characterized the place called school. The learning can occur anywhere. It need not occur between the hours of 9 and 4; it can occur at any time, 24 hours per day, 365 days per year. And it need not necessarily occur only between the ages of 5 and 16, but any time from birth to death. The style of schooling will include that of the traditional classroom, with traditional roles for teachers and students, but the repertoire will be much wider. The notion of school is maintained because the learning is coherent and contractual.

There will still be a place called school if the full range of intelligences, such as those proposed by Gardner (1983), are to be addressed. Those who expect or advocate the disappearance of a place called school are foreclosing on the achievement of such intelligences, including musical intelligence or emotional intelligence or interpersonal intelligence. Included in a place called school might be a home school, especially for young children, whose home can become the source of coherence and some learning opportunities, particularly when networked with other homes or institutions, even other places called school in the traditional sense.

Beare (1997) envisages "neighborhood educational houses" for young children, enriching the view of the home school movement now gaining momentum around the world. He describes the conception and the constraints in the following terms:

> At the very least, the very youngest learners—toddlers and children—need somewhere on their own (or the next) street where they can physically go to access programs; to learn with other groups of learners; to interact physically with their "teachers," "tutors," counselors, coordinating educators; to access richer learning materials than those they have online from their own home; and also to develop an identification with their neighborhood "storage house of learning." The same holds true of learners of all ages.

> The problem which educational authorities have always faced is that when neighborhood buildings are put up and labeled "primary school," their use becomes limited, they are reserved for only some learners, they become identified by age, territoriality sets in, and they are no longer considered a community or common resource. Furthermore, there is no guarantee in a mobile society that

we can predict accurately how permanent they need to be or how many rooms or spaces need to be provided. (p. 6)

Neighborhood educational houses can be established at the direction and with the support of a school authority. An example is the Foshay Learning Center, a K–12 public school in Los Angeles. Foshay set up eight satellite learning centers in low-income apartment complexes across the city so that, without leaving the building, students can obtain assistance with homework, gain knowledge and skill in technology, and participate in enriched learning activities. Consistent with the concept of the virtual school, Cynthia Amos, program coordinator for Foshay's satellite project, observes that "school is anywhere the equipment is. . . . We're trying to show the kids that you can learn anywhere" (cited in Zehr, 1997, p. 36).

Ellyard (1997) describes the learning culture of a virtual school in 2010 in a set of eight concepts. "Life Long Learning" reflects a view that learning will have to become "a pleasurable activity again" because

we had grown up with the idea that most of our education occurred early in life during the period of compulsory education. Under these circumstances we could force-feed learning into often unwilling consumers. This was education as a factory. (p. 1)

"Learner Driven Learning" applies to learning beyond the years of puberty, using learning technologies with the aid of teachers and mentors. "Just-in-Time Learning" recognizes that the best learning opportunities are created when interest and motivation are at their peak. "Customized Learning" is possible because

modern technology enables us to package learning modules to suit people with different preferred thinking and learning styles. . . . In this way the quality of learning has been dramatically improved for many people who were disadvantaged by the old system because their thinking and learning preferences were not fully catered [to]. (p. 2)

"Transformative Learning" reflects a commitment that transforms attitudes, values, and beliefs, including higher aspirations and expectations for self and society. "Collaborative Learning" uses learning technologies that have shifted from highly individualistic modes in the 1980s to those that allow teams at the same location or at different locations, indeed whole communities, to learn together. "Contextual Learning" accepts that "learning is most effective if it occurs in an environment which makes the learning relevant . . . to the experience and expectations of the learner" (p. 3). The final concept is the familiar "Learning to Learn."

THE NEW SCHOOL IN ACTION

Ten strategic intentions such as the following contribute to a gestalt, or vision, of the new school in action:

1. Subject boundaries will be broken, and learning will be integrated across the curriculum as the new learning technologies become universal, challenging rigidity in curriculum and standards frameworks, without removing the need for testing in discrete areas as well as in learning that spans the whole.

2. School buildings designed for the Industrial Age will be redesigned to suit the needs of the knowledge society.

3. Schools will establish a richer range of professionals to work with and support teachers. Many of these will be located on site, but increasingly more will be located in other places as the best services are located and made available to meet the needs of all students.

4. Teachers will have access to the best resources to support their work, with many of these resources accessed from CD-ROMs and the Internet. Teachers will have assistance from learning resource specialists who locate and advise on sources and help with financial and other arrangements to protect intellectual capital.

5. Students, teachers, and other professionals will increasingly work in teams, reflecting a pattern that is widely evident in workplace arrangements in other fields, with many parallels for professionals in education and medicine.

6. Schools will expand their policies and practices for the pastoral care of students, given the high expectations for all to succeed. As learning is dispersed, the maintenance of schools' duty of care will require cyber-policy on care in virtual schools.

7. Pastoral care for teachers will be important given the shift to the new professionalism and major changes in roles, responsibilities, and accountabilities, with professional development, individually and in teams, being one element in the strategy.

8. Issues of access and equity will be addressed in school cyber-policy, with a range of strategies including the sharing of resources among schools, partnerships with the private sector for donations and subsidies, and the creation of community-based learning centers.

9. Virtual schooling will be a reality at every stage of schooling,

but there will still be a place called school, with approaches to virtual schooling including neighborhood educational houses, especially for the very young.

10. New cultures for learning will take hold in schools for the knowledge society. Complementing such widely accepted concepts as "lifelong learning" will be approaches such as "just-in-time learning" that allows state-of-the-art approaches to learning and teaching to be designed and delivered on short notice in any setting for all learners.

EDUCATION FOR THE PUBLIC GOOD

How would a system of public education be constructed to support the overall vision suggested in the two interrelated sets of 10 strategic intentions, one for the new professionalism and one for the new school? This is an invitation to engage in a form of "backward mapping" (Elmore, 1979–80), free of intellectual constraint as far as current arrangements are concerned. The outcome challenges the current arrangements, especially in respect to matters of governance, resources, the relationship between the school and its community, and the concepts of public and private.

The level of professionalism required for a new system of public education suggests that success depends on attracting to the profession people with capacities of a high order, and providing a system of incentives, recognition, and rewards to match. There are major resource implications, not only for the system of incentives, recognition, and rewards, but also for the fabric of the workplace and the acquisition of information and communications technology. Resourcing schools in this image means capital investment of a kind that is customarily associated with state-of-the-art hospitals. Many schools are currently the antithesis, with staff struggling to maintain a sense of professionalism amidst buildings and equipment that were barely adequate in a previous era, let alone for what lies ahead. The synergy of these requirements calls for a new paradigm in the resourcing of public education.

This vision of schooling breaks boundaries. An unrelenting focus on learning outcomes means that teachers must network with other professionals within the schools and, especially, beyond. These professional networks will span the public and private sectors. Indeed, there may be scores of employers and contractual arrangements in a professionally networked school of the future. A similar situation can be expected in respect to the location and ownership of the physical facilities in which learning shall occur, with those for a particular student at a particular time including the home, at least one place called school, and at least one workplace other than a school, depending on the stage of schooling, the area of learning, and the level of resourcing. High levels of social cohesiveness or social capital (Coleman & Hoffer, 1987) are required to establish and sustain these arrangements. Virtually every agency in society is engaged, including the family, systems of schools, networks of professionals, providers of information and communications technology, business and industry, and churches or other volunteer organizations that provide service and support across the boundaries. There must be high levels of understanding of what is intended and what is at stake if the enterprise fails.

Public education as traditionally and, for the most part, currently conceived, refers to a system of schools that are publicly owned and publicly resourced. Although the boundaries have been breached in a number of places, they are still largely in place. In the United States, the divide between public and private schools is probably higher than in any other nation. Networking of professionals across sectors is evident to some extent but is still relatively constrained, indicated by the very small number of integrated or full-service schools, in which all of the services required to support students are brought to the school site, regardless of level of government or agency that provides them. The involvement of the corporate sector in funding schools is high by international standards, but much remains to be done to establish a coherent approach to the resourcing of schools along the lines implied in the vision. The advent of charter schools has widened the boundaries, but the notion that all students should have an entitlement to public funds that can be deployed in any setting where learning is advanced is far from realization. The battle lines have been drawn and extraordinary amounts of money are being spent in protecting them. It is unlikely that the forces for change will let up; so it is timely to propose a new view of public education that derives from the broader concept of "education for the public good."

THIRD-SECTOR THEORY

Growth in private, charter, and home schools and increasing dissatisfaction with public schools are to be expected under current conditions. Burton Weisbrod, described by Powell and Clemens as "perhaps the most sophisticated theorist of the 'third' sector," has argued that

> the more homogeneous the society, the less need there is for the nonprofit form. But when citizens' preferences are broadly heterogeneous, a government that meets only the desires of the majority will leave many dissatisfied, willing to pay more for collective services but unable to achieve them from government. As diversity increases and dissatisfaction with existing institutional arrangements increases, nonprofits are created as both a response and a complement to public and private enterprise. (Weisbrod as cited by Powell & Clemens, 1998, p. xv)

Weisbrod's theory seems to account for the variety of organizational arrangements in school education, with heterogeneity increasing exponentially as the vision outlined in this chapter is realized.

Mansbridge's (1998) tour de force on the contested nature of the public good merits close attention. She contends that the concept is "unendingly contestable," but that contest should be welcomed to help "retrieve the public good from platitude, disdain, and justifiable mistrust to rebuild it as a centerpiece of American politics." She observes that "moral language of the Western tradition has typically contrasted the public good with private goods," but that "Western thinkers [including Adam Smith] have also suggested that the opposition between public good and private benefits so prominent in ordinary language might conceal a deeper congruence" (p. 3). After reviewing a range of meanings since Plato, she proposes new tools and new solutions that involve "nesting" altruism or public spirit within "a return to self-interest," acknowledging that "several different institutional arrangements and mixes may be equally efficient" (pp. 13–17). It is time to apply this line of analysis to public education.

In political or ideological terms, a common feature of voluntarism, civil society, and the third sector is the contribution of all sectors of society to the public good, moving away from an exclusive reliance on government (Old Left) or exclusive reliance on the market (New Right). British Prime Minister Tony Blair describes "the third way" in terms of an absolute adherence to basic values and a key belief in a strong community for achieving individual advancement. With respect to how to get there, he says, "We should be infinitely adaptable and imaginative in the means of applying those values. There are no ideological preconditions, no pre-determined veto on means. What counts is what works" (cited by Midgley, 1998, p. 44).

THE THIRD SECTOR IN ACTION

Several approaches to the integration of public, private, and third-sector services are now evident. The gestalt in this instance is a constellation of international practices. A remarkable example of voluntarism in the United States, for example, is the NetDay initiative. NetDay was established in 1996 by Michael Kaufman, a senior director of digital learning for the Public Broadcasting System (PBS), and John Gage, a chief scientist for Sun Microsystems. It began as a one-day event to wire schools in California for access to the Internet. However, it was expanded at the urging of the White House and the U.S. Department of Education. By mid-1997, more than 250,000 volunteers had helped wire 50,000 classrooms across the United States (Zehr, 1997, p. 38). Systematic attention is now being given to voluntarism in support of schools (Brown, 1998).

The overall strength of the third sector in the United States is extraordinary, with the total of funds that support it exceeding the gross national product of all but seven nations, cutting "a wide swath through society (Rifkin, 1995, pp. 240–241). The issue raised here is that, except for instances such as NetDay and the direct involvement of the corporate sector through initiatives such as those by The Annenberg Institute for School Reform—initiatives in which the United States is a world leader—third-sector involvement has not penetrated public education to the extent that is possible and desirable.

The most interesting and potentially far-reaching initiatives in the public, private, and third sectors are in Britain, and they have international significance. Reform on Track 1 (building systems of self-managing schools) is virtually complete, with the Labour government reining in charter-type, grant-maintained schools but increasing to almost 100 percent the amount of funds decentralized to the school level (Department for Education and Employment, 1998). The great divide between publicly owned and privately owned schools that exists in the United States does not exist in Britain, because most church-owned schools are in the so-called aided sector, drawing public funds to almost the same extent as schools owned by a public authority. These structural arrangements help build the capacity of schools to make progress on Track 2, with schools required to set targets for improvement in the achievement of all students as part of national strategies in literacy and numeracy.

Of particular interest in the third sector in Britain are developments in Education Action Zones. These are communities in which there are clusters of schools where achievement levels are low and socioeconomic circumstances present difficulties in efforts to achieve improvement. There are 50 such zones, and the strategy for addressing the problem calls for a remarkable mix of public and private effort. School authorities, schools, businesses, industries, media organizations, cultural institutions, and even sporting clubs are working together in these endeavors, sharing expertise as much as contributing resources. Private support is matched by public support in the ratio of three to one. It is striking that in Britain, as in the United States, the major part of private effort is targeted at schools in these circumstances. This is building social capital in a new view of public education as "education for the public good."

An important issue is the extent to which funding entitlements from the public purse can be tracked in these new arrangements where boundaries between public, private, and third sectors are blurred. There are promising developments in several nations, including Australia, Britain, and the United States, in needs-based formula funding of students (Ross & Levacic, 1998); an extension of these efforts, aided by developments in technology, will ensure that this need not be a problem.

LEADERSHIP, ALIGNMENT, AND WILL

Bringing this gestalt, or vision, to realization in the three nations cited will be difficult. In Australia there is no tradition for the involvement of the private sector in publicly owned schools. The view of public education as publicly owned and publicly resourced is deeply entrenched, leaving weak roles for the private and third sectors. There is a broader view of public education in Britain, but only in recent years has a role for the private sector been embraced, with momentum building in the public-private initiatives of the Blair government. The use of public funds in private schools has been barred on constitutional grounds in the United States, but the boundaries have been breached in recent times with developments involving charters and vouchers.

Constructing a new view of "education for the public good" is a long-term project that requires leadership at all levels, the alignment of key institutions and organizations with an interest and stake in the venture, and, above all, the will to see it through.

REFERENCES

Beare, H. (1997, July). *Designing a break-the-mold school for the future.* Paper presented at a virtual conference of the Australian Council for Educational Administration.

Boisot, M. (1995). Preparing for turbulence: The changing relationship between strategy and management development in the learning organization. In B. Garratt (Ed.), *Developing strategic thought: Rediscovering the art of direction-giving* (pp. 29–46). London: McGraw-Hill.

Brown, D. (1998). *Schools with heart: Voluntarism and public education.* Boulder, CO: Westview Press.

Bryk, A. S. (1998, April). Chicago school reform: Linkages between local control, educational supports, and student achievement. Presentation with colleagues in the Consortium on Chicago School Research at the annual meeting of the American Educational Research Association, San Diego, CA.

Bullock, A., & Thomas, H. (1997). *Schools at the center? A study of decentralization.* London: Routledge.

Caldwell, B. J. (1998). *Self-managing schools and improved learning outcomes.* (Report on Autonomy and Quality in School Education). Canberra: Department of Employment, Education, Training, and Youth Affairs.

Caldwell, B. J., & Hayward, D. K. (1998). *The future of schools: Lessons from the reform of public education.* London: Falmer Press.

Caldwell, B. J., & Spinks, J. M. (1998). *Beyond the self-managing school.* London: Falmer Press.

Cheng, Y. C. (1996). *School effectiveness and school-based management: A mechanism for development.* London: Falmer Press.

Cheung, W. M., & Cheng, Y. C. (1996). A multi-level framework for self-management in school. *International Journal of Educational Management, 10*(1), 17–29.

Cheung, W. M., & Cheng, Y. C. (1997, January). Multi-level self management in school as related to school performance: A multi-level analysis. Paper presented at the International Congress of School Effectiveness and Improvement, Memphis, TN.

Coleman, J. S., & Hoffer, T. (1987). *Public and private high schools: The impact of communities.* New York: Basic Books.

Cooperative Research Project (Department of Education, Victorian Association of State Secondary Principals, Victorian Primary Principals Association, University of Melbourne). (1998). *Assessing the outcomes.* (Report of the Cooperative Research Project on "Leading Victoria's Schools of the Future"). Melbourne: Department of Education.

Crévola, C. A., & Hill, P. W. (1998). Evaluation of a whole-school approach to prevention and intervention in early literacy. *Journal of Education for Students Placed at Risk, 3*(2), 133–157.

Darling-Hammond, L. (1997). *The right to learn: A blueprint for creating schools that work.* San Francisco: Jossey-Bass.

Department for Education and Employment. (1998). *Fair funding for schools.* Consultation paper. London: Author. [Online]. Available: http://www.open.gov.uk/dfee/

Drucker, P. F. (1993). *Post-capitalist society.* New York: HarperBusiness.

Ellyard, P. (1997, July). Developing a learning culture. Paper presented at a virtual conference of the Australian Council for Education Administration.

Elmore, R. F. (1979–80). Backward mapping: Implementation research and policy decisions. *Political Science Quarterly, 94,* 601–616.

Gardner, H. (1983). *Frames of mind.* London: Heinemann.

Goodlad, J. I. (1984). *A place called school.* New York: McGraw-Hill.

Hanushek, E. A. (1996). Outcomes, costs, and incentives in schools. In E. A. Hanushek & D. W. Jorgenson (Eds.), *Improving America's schools: The role of incentives* (pp. 29–52). Washington, DC: National Academy Press.

Hanushek, E. A. (1997). Assessing the effects of school resources on student performance: An update. *Educational Evaluation and Policy Analysis, 19(2),* 141–164.

Hargreaves, A. (1997). From reform to renewal. In A. Hargreaves & R. Evans (Eds.), *Beyond educational reform: Bringing teachers back in* (pp. 105–125). Buckingham: Open University Press.

Hargreaves, D. (1994). *The mosaic of learning: Schools and teachers for the new century.* London: Demos.

Hargreaves, D. (1997). A road to the learning society. *School Leadership and Management, 17(4),* 9–21.

Levacic, R. (1995). *Local management of schools: Analysis and practice.* Buckingham: Open University Press.

Malen, B., Ogawa, R. T., & Kranz, J. (1990). What do we know about site-based management: A case study of the literature—A call for research. In W. Clune & J. Witte (Eds.), *Choice and control in American education, volume 2: The practice of choice, decentralization and school restructuring* (pp. 289–342). London: Falmer Press.

MacGilchrist B., Myers, K., & Reed, J. (1997). *The intelligent school.* London: Paul Chapman.

Mansbridge, J. (1998). On the contested nature of the public good. In W. W. Powell & E. S. Clemens (Eds.), *Private action and the public good* (pp. 3–19). New Haven: Yale University Press.

McLaughlin, M. W. (1997). Rebuilding teacher professionalism in the United States. In A. Hargreaves & R. Evans (Eds.), *Beyond educational reform: Bringing teachers back in* (pp. 77–93). Buckingham: Open University Press.

Midgley, S. (1998, June 26). Third way: A challenge for all in education. *Times Educational Supplement,* pp. 44–45. [Published by The Times in London.]

Papert, S. (1993). *The children's machine: Rethinking school in the age of the computer.* New York: Basic Books.

Powell, W. W., & Clemens, E. S. (1998). Introduction. In W. W. Powell & E. S. Clemens (Eds.), *Private action and the public good* (pp. xiii–xi). New Haven: Yale University Press.

Rifkin, J. (1995). *The end of work: The decline of the global labor force and the dawn of the post-market era.* New York: Putnam.

Ross, K., & Levacic, R. (Eds.). (1998). *Needs-based resource allocation in education via formula-funding of schools.* Paris: International Institute for Educational Planning (UNESCO).

Smith, M. S., Scoll B. W., & Link, J. (1996). Research-based school reform: The Clinton administration's agenda. In E. A. Hanushek & D. W. Jorgenson, (Eds.), *Improving America's schools: The role of incentives* (pp. 9–27). Washington, DC: National Academy Press.

Spender, D. (1995). *Nattering on the net: Women, power and cyberspace.* North Melbourne: Spinifex.

State of the States. (1997, January). Editorial in *Education Week* supplement, "Quality Counts," p. 3.

Summers, A. A., & Johnson, A. W. (1996). The effects of school-based management plans. In E. A. Hanushek & D. W. Jorgenson (Eds.), *Improving America's schools: The role of incentives* (pp. 75–96). Washington, DC: National Academy Press.

Weisbrod, B. (1975). Toward a theory of the voluntary nonprofit sector in a three sector economy. In E. S. Phelps (Ed.), *Altruism, morality, and economic theory* (pp. 171–195). New York: Russell Sage.

Whitty, G., Power, S., & Halpin, G. (1998). *Devolution and choice in education: The school, the state and the market.* Buckingham: Open University Press.

Wirt, F. M. (1991). Policy origins and policy games: Site-based management in the United States and the United Kingdom. In G. Harman, H. Beare, & G. F. Berkeley (Eds.), *Restructuring school management: Administrative reorganization of public school governance in Australia* (pp. 27–45). Curtin, ACT: Australian College of Education.

Zehr, M. A. (1997, November 10). Partnering with the public. In Information Age, *Education Week* Special Report, pp. 36–38.

Rethinking Civic Education for the 21st Century

Todd Clark

S hortly after the 1992 Los Angeles civil unrest, I had occasion to discuss the importance of civic education with a prominent business leader. It was clear that the frustration among nearly everyone in the community regarding local government was a factor in causing the unrest. In Los Angeles at that time, the conflict between the chief of police, the mayor, and the police commission played a role in the events that followed the jury verdict in the Rodney King case. Yet, expectations regarding the city, the police, and the justice system were based more on passions of the moment than on an understanding of how the system functioned or was organized. Public rancor replaced reasoned argument. Without a better understanding of the system, I argued, we remained susceptible in the future to the same uninformed public reaction to controversy with the same potentially disastrous result.

The business leader, who was very involved in efforts to rebuild Los Angeles and who understood many of the other causal factors responsible for the unrest, dismissed me by saying that once we had reformed our schools so that young people had the skills needed to meet business standards and hence become employable, we could perhaps then give attention to frills such as citizenship education, music, the arts, and other nonbasic subjects.

The Los Angeles incident illustrates the need for four guiding assumptions about civic education in the 21st century. First, citizenship education is not a frill; it is an essential. It is, however, much more than strong, substantive courses in history, geography, and government. Although the knowledge base of those subjects and the skills that can be learned through their study are important, they do not prepare young people to be citizens. Unless those subjects are presented as part of a well-developed plan of citizenship education, they do little to encourage students' engagement in public life.

Second, if citizenship education in our schools does not help students recognize that they are members of a community with institutions and conflicting interests and issues that affect their lives, they will learn about local government through their own random experience. Because we presently make no effort to prepare students to know about and understand local government, we are living with the result, at least in part, of our own failure to recognize and address the most important reason for civic education: the creation of a sense of membership in one's local community, a knowledge of its institutions, a willingness to participate, and a passion to solve its problems.

Third, the focus of civic education should be on the local setting. Former Speaker of the House of Representatives Thomas P. (Tip) O'Neill said, "All politics is local." As important as this insight is, neither local politics nor governance receives much attention in the traditional civic education curriculum of U.S. schools. To satisfy O'Neill's dictum, civic education should focus on local government. As educators, we should help build the muscle of democracy by teaching our children how to be effective citizens, beginning in their own communities.

Finally, civic education needs to be integrated with other socializing forces in the community and society. Schools socialize young people in direct and indirect ways. They are one part of a complex process of educating citizens who are the sovereigns in a democracy.[1] Barber (1984) describes the challenge in powerful terms: "The literacy required to live in civil society, the competence to live in democratic communities,

---

[1] It is not the purpose of this chapter to discuss the range of socializing institutions and their impact on young people. A useful reference for that wider subject is *Character Building for a Democratic, Civil Society*, Task Force Reports (1997), The Communitarian Network, 2130 H St. NW, Suite 714J, Washington, DC.

the ability to think critically and act deliberately in a pluralistic world, the empathy that permits us to hear and thus accommodate others, all involve skills that must be acquired" (pp. 4–5).

THE TRADITIONAL CIVIC EDUCATION CURRICULUM

Unfortunately, the typical civic education curriculum is not constructed to help young people acquire such skills. The traditional curriculum presents several problems. First, there is little consensus as to what it should include. Civic educators have spent the last century of the old millennium arguing among themselves over whether or not civic education should emphasize traditional content or the processes and skills of civic involvement. Today, history and geography dominate the social studies curriculum. Over the years, the same debate has raged in every content field. Should it be "old" or "new" math? Whole language or phonics? And so on and so on. In civic education, we must try to bring the arguing parties together. We must get on with the task of educating citizens who understand both the substantive base of U.S. political, economic, and social history and geography, including the structure and function of our government, and who also have the tools, the skills, and the civic passion needed to apply their knowledge to the world we live in.

Second, the goal of the traditional social studies curriculum does not include much emphasis on civic involvement. Rather, it focuses on content knowledge with heavy emphasis on world and U.S. history, geography, and the structure of our national government. Although most frameworks of instruction discuss the importance of civic engagement, such documents actually focus on content (California Department of Education, 1997). This focus suggests that knowledge and the academic skills needed to manipulate information are sufficient to prepare individuals for civic action at some later time in their own communities, or that such preparation is not a goal of the curriculum. Whatever the reason, the present curriculum simply does not go far enough. It fails to provide young people with the skills and the practice needed to apply knowledge of history and government to local issues or to identify and solve local problems.

Third, the traditional U.S. government courses focus on the structure and function of the national government. Although most frameworks of instruction such as the one cited above advise giving attention to state and local government, almost all the teachers that I talk to acknowledge that formal instruction ignores these levels of government. It is encouraging that the National Standards for Civics and Government, developed by the Center for Civic Education (1994) under a contract with the United States Department of Education, do call for the development of participatory skills that can be gained only through local activity. It is hoped that this important standards document will encourage schools to focus on this task. However, unless U.S. government courses shift away from their present emphasis on national government, it is doubtful that the standards' call for students to have "opportunities to practice these skills and to interact with those in their community who are adept in exercising them" will receive more than lip service. It is also doubtful that students will have the opportunities to "perform service in their schools or communities directly related to civic life, politics, and government" called for by the standards (pp. 5–6).

Fourth, the traditional curriculum looks backward, without a connection to the future. A substantial portion of the curriculum should, quite properly, focus on the nation's past and the philosophy and institutions basic to the U.S. governmental system. However, it should also make strong connections between the past and the present and between the institutions and experiences of national government and local communities. The traditional curriculum provides no useful strategy for connecting general information and ideas to the examination of issues of power and politics at the local level. Even when programs do focus on appropriate skill development, without a bridge to local content there is simply no way for students to make the connection to the vital issues all local communities now face.

Finally, the traditional curriculum provides for little development of skills and strategies that are essential to democracy in the United States. We need programs that use acquisition of content as a means of teaching skills that are transferable to a study of local affairs. Basic research and problem-solving skills, learning how to find information and evaluate the reliability of sources, formulating and testing hypotheses, and drawing conclusions from evidence all contribute greatly to the job of citizen. The unfortunate reality is that these skills will remain largely academic as long as the traditional curriculum continues to give little attention to their application in local public affairs. Without such a bridge between the academic and the practical, students cannot understand the importance of civic issues to their lives as citizens.

WHY CHANGE THE PRESENT CURRICULUM?

Unfortunately, most indicators suggest that the traditional curriculum provides neither the information, the skills, nor the civic commitment needed to stimulate rational and capable involvement at the local level (National Assessment Governing Board, 1997; Sax, Astin, & Korn, 1997). The impact of the present focus on history and geography is hard to measure with precision. However, the National Assessment of Educational Progress (NAEP) reported national results for its U.S. history assessment at the 4th, 8th, and 12th grades most recently in 1994. In addition to the categories of Basic, Proficient, and Advanced, the test results forced NAEP to create a fourth indicator, Below Basic; and NAEP reported that 36 percent of 4th graders, 39 percent of 8th graders, and 57 percent of 12th graders fell into that category. These results hardly provide a strong endorsement for the status quo. In 1998 NAEP will survey educational progress in civics. The assessment in civics will cover only the knowledge and intellectual skills categories of the testing framework, leaving out civic dispositions—those factors that might come closest to predicting the inclination to take part actively in the affairs of U.S. society.

To further underscore the problem, a recent survey of college freshmen indicated that their interest in political life is at an all-time low, based on 32 years of polling, even though their interest in volunteering for community service continues to increase (Sax, Astin, Korn, & Mahoney, 1997; "Community Activism," 1998). These findings provide an ironic insight; students have little interest in politics, the domain in which policies affecting our society are made, but they do wish to take part actively in helping to solve problems at the community level. Perhaps their understanding of the relationship between politics and participation might be greater if school programs focused on the connection.

CIVIC EDUCATION AND THE NATIONAL REFORM MOVEMENT IN EDUCATION

School reform is high on the national agenda, but civic education and concern for establishing a civil society are not a major part of that effort. When U.S. governors pledged in 1989 to implement a series of national school reform goals, Goals 2000, they included citizenship education as part of Goal 3. Unfortunately, there are no examples of new precollegiate initiatives in civic education sponsored by the government or by private foundations either as a part of the Goals 2000 effort or elsewhere. In fact, my experience suggests that the federal government currently spends more money, through the U.S. Information Agency and the U.S. Department of Education, on education for democracy in other countries than it does in the United States.

That schools should play a major role in building strong communities and helping to create a civil society has always been a major justification for public education in the United States. To achieve this goal, I believe our schools must follow Tip O'Neill's advice on politics and link their curriculum to local issues and institutions. To connect the classroom to the real world, educators must also become part of the civic renewal efforts in their own communities. As preparation for the new millennium, or at least its first century, schools must create civic education programs that appropriately prepare young people for the work of citizenship in their neighborhoods, communities, and states. Developing citizenship at those levels is both the most neglected and the most important task in terms of the health of our democracy.

CIVIC EDUCATION IN THE 21ST CENTURY: GOALS AND CHOICES

The goals of civic education in the 21st century will not be new. John Dewey (1916) said:

> Popular suffrage cannot be successful unless those who elect and who obey their governors are educated. Since a democratic society repudiates the principle of external authority, it must find a substitute in voluntary disposition and interest; these can be created only by education (p. 31).

That statement powerfully declares the importance of the task. Policymakers at all levels must view the work more seriously, and it must be undertaken through partnerships with the larger community. Civic education must respond to this challenge by working to build essential civic dispositions—namely, support for the common good, support for inclusion, and support for liberty.

U.S. citizens have always felt a tension between their individualism and their concern for the common good. They make choices that benefit themselves and then worry about others. This conflict between

70

self-interest and the common good explains why it is important for schools to develop in students the acceptance of civic responsibility—the formal practices of civic engagement such as voting, serving on juries, serving in the military, and paying taxes, as well as informal acts such as voluntary engagement in civic improvement efforts and other forms of action intended to benefit the larger community.

Well-informed citizens know enough of U.S. history to understand how hard it has been for those who went before to win the widespread opportunity so many citizens now enjoy. Even though expanding opportunity for increasingly large segments of the population has been a theme running through U.S. history, the goal of inclusion has not always been fulfilled, and many have been left out. People need to address the reality that they still have a long way to go before they are able to provide "liberty and justice for all" (Banks, 1996, pp. xi–xii).

History also demonstrates that U.S. citizens must be wary of the power of the majority and the power of all large institutions to overwhelm the national commitment to individual liberty, especially in times of crises. Students must come to understand the importance of protecting individual and minority rights.

Although the goals of civic education are not new, some choices about the direction of the civic education curriculum need to be made.

Should the focus of civic education be on the local community, its institutions and problems? To understand the importance of civic dispositions, U.S. citizens must understand the impact of such dispositions on individuals at the local level. In addition to having knowledge of U.S. history, traditions, and institutions at the national level, U.S. citizens must feel a part of and understand the local community—its government, politics, and problems. This sense of membership in one's community makes the use of civic knowledge and dispositions important. Members of communities—geographic, ethnic, or cultural—must first care about what happens, have an interest in and almost a sense of kinship and concern for the welfare of their fellow citizens. A citizen must have the knowledge and skills to know how to act on local issues *and* the concern for the general welfare needed to be willing to work to solve local problems within the context of national civic dispositions. Civic education programs do not now focus on making this connection.

This failure to prepare students for local civic life is one explanation for the negative attitude citizens share in communities all over the United States. In his book *Strong Democracy* Ben Barber (1984) describes the grim result:

> Empower the merely ignorant and endow the uneducated with a
> right to make collective decisions and what results is not democ-
> racy but, at best, mob rule: the government of private prejudice and
> the tyranny of opinion—all the perversions that liberty's enemies
> like to pretend (and its friend fear) constitute democracy. (pp. 4–5)

What should the goal of civic education be? It is not my purpose to
describe an alternative scope and sequence for citizenship education;
there could be many acceptable variations. It is useful to call attention
to the National Standards for Civics and Government developed by the
Center for Civic Education (1994). These standards, part of the effort
funded by the United States Department of Education to develop standards across the disciplines, provide exit standards (not curriculum
outlines) describing what students should know as they complete the
4th, 8th, and 12th grades. The standards also serve as the basis for the
1998 NAEP testing framework in civics, the results of which will be reported in the year 2000. Focusing on content to be mastered and "what
students should be able to do in relation to that content," the standards
specify what intellectual and participatory skills students should acquire. The content specified and the academic skills described are, for
the most part, similar to many traditional programs in civics.

The emphasis of the standards on participatory skills is *not*
traditional, however, and deserves special mention. As stated in the
standards:

> Education in civics and government must not only address the ac-
> quisition of knowledge and intellectual skills; it also must focus
> specifically on the development of those skills required for compe-
> tent participation in the political process. These include such skills
> as
>
> • the capacity to influence policies and decisions by working with
> others
> • clearly articulating interests and making them known to key deci-
> sion and policy makers
> • building coalitions, negotiating, compromising, and seeking con-
> sensus
> • managing conflicts. (pp. 5–6)

To help students develop participatory skills it is important to
provide them with opportunities to practice the skills and to observe
and interact with those in their community who are adept in exercising
them. The National Standards for Civics and Government suggest various learning opportunities useful in fostering students' participatory

skills, including the following:

1. Monitoring politics and government
   - Track an issue in the media
   - Perform research tasks in the community
   - Report and reflect on their experiences
2. Influencing politics and government
   - Take part in the politics and governance of their classrooms and schools
   - Take part in simulations of the activities of government and private sector agencies
   - Observe governmental agencies and private sector organizations at work
   - Learn how members of government and private organizations attempt to influence public policy
   - Present positions to student councils, school administrators, and school boards
   - Write letters to newspapers
   - Meet with members of government to advocate
   - Testify before public bodies
   - Perform service in their schools or communities directly related to civic life, politics, and government. (p. 6)

These standards are essential to the development of a civic community in the 21st century.

EXAMPLES OF THE NEW PERSPECTIVE ON CIVIC PARTICIPATION

Creating the new perspective on civic participation described above is only half of the needed change; helping schools create civic education programs that are linked to the new perspective is the other half. All of the programs described below give substantial emphasis to the development of these participatory skills. Most traditional programs do not. By providing the following descriptions of programs that are not now part of the mainstream curriculum, I hope to bring useful models to the attention of educators trying to connect their present curriculum to the life in the communities they are a part of. Several of the examples are community-based programs that focus on stimulating adult engagement in civic life. They have materials and sources of information that are transferable to a school setting. Others are school

73

based but provide nontraditional ways to connect students to their communities through a focus on service, which grows out of the curriculum, and on character development as a task related to civic education. There is no single answer to the need to connect young people to the concept of citizenship; but whatever the answer, it must be local.

PROGRAMS TO REENGAGE ADULTS

Today, the most ambitious efforts to stimulate civic engagement are not part of education reform. Instead they are efforts to build communitywide citizen involvement. There is substantial national concern regarding the declining involvement of citizens in public life, whether it be voting, support for public education, considering vital national issues, or involvement in the voluntary associations that have played an important part in the development of the character of the United States. In response to these concerns, several national initiatives have been created in an effort to engage citizens in their communities.

Because these initiatives do not focus on schools and because the work they are doing is intended to offer civic education not to students but primarily to adults, the work of these groups may go unnoticed by educators. Although these models address the need to prepare adult citizens to engage in local affairs, they also provide examples and even some curriculum materials that could form the basis for units or courses on local government.

Civic Practices Network. Probably the best source of information on a number of these initiatives is the Civic Practices Network (CPN) Web site, which is a collaboration of at least 50 affiliated organizations, all linked through this Internet site. The CPN is operated by the Heller School of Public Administration at Brandeis University and is supported by grants from the Surdna Foundation, Inc.[2]

For information: www.cpn.org; e-mail: cpn@cpn.org.

Pew Partnership for Civic Change. The Pew Partnership for Civic Change is a large, broad-based effort funded by the Pew Charitable Trust, headquartered in Philadelphia. The partnership was launched in 1992 and has offices in Charlottesville, Virginia. Programs include a

---

[2]The Surdna Foundation, located in New York City, is a family foundation that has made a special commitment to civic renewal activities through its Effective Citizenship and Community Revitalization initiatives. The two initiatives make dozens of grants annually. Some precollegiate programs receive funding from the foundation.

grant initiative involving 14 cities. The research and communications component of the partnership produces research reports that examine strategies for civic change, available in the "Framework Series"; and *Civic Partners,* a journal that reports on the activities of the 14 partnership communities.

The mission of the partnership is to "work with local and national partners to: design and implement new solutions to tough problems; catalyze local civic leadership for action; and research and disseminate cutting-edge urban strategies" (Civic Partners, 1997). The partnership publications describe a wide range of activities, all dedicated to the reengagement of citizens in the affairs of their communities. The emphasis on efforts to strengthen local government demonstrates the realization by this important national foundation that without strong local institutions and widespread local involvement, U.S. democracy cannot function effectively in meeting the needs of citizens and improving the quality of civic life.

The partnership has developed a set of discussion materials and a guide called the *Leadership Collaboration* series. These materials are designed to encourage and help create a capacity for continuing dialogue between those engaged in civic change. The titles are "Building Healthy Communities," which discusses healthy civic life; "Building Deliberative Communities," on the role deliberation can play in community decision making; "Building Diverse Communities," a case study on leadership training and economic development; and "Building Collaborative Communities," on encouraging dialogue and building community collaboration.

These materials could well form part of a curriculum for examining the government and civic activity of any community and could serve as helpful guides to introducing young people to skills vital to civic engagement. If accompanied by a community profile that included current issues and the structure and operations of the local institutions, these materials would be a useful starting point in engaging students in a study of local civic action and decision making.

For information: Pew Partnership for Civic Change, 145-C Ednam Dr., Charlottesville, VA 22903; phone: 804-971-2073; fax: 804-971-7042; e-mail: mail@pew-partnership.org.

Center for Democracy and Citizenship. Harry Boyte, head of the Center for Democracy and Citizenship at the Humphrey Institute of Public Affairs at the University of Minnesota, has broad national influence through his research, training, and dissemination programs in civic renewal and education. The center's Project Public Life initiative in Minnesota and its offspring in other areas, and the Public Achievement program involving youth in the political process are important examples of an integration of academics with community organizing. The center has a number of useful publications. Of particular interest to civic educators is *Making the Rules: A Public Achievement Guidebook,* designed for "young people and adult coaches involved in Public Achievement or other community building and public problem-solving projects."

For information: Humphrey Institute of Public Affairs, University of Minnesota, Twin Cities Campus, 301 19th Ave. South, Minneapolis, MN 55455; phone: 612-625-0142; fax: 612-625-3515.

National Civic League. The National Civic League, sponsor of the well-known All-American City awards, created the Alliance for National Renewal, a collaboration of 120 organizations and a number of efforts designed to encourage greater citizen involvement in local civic life. Chaired by former senator Bill Bradley, this initiative works to call attention to the importance of local civic engagement. Its publications are also helpful sources of information. Its magazine, *Governing,* and newsletter, *The Kitchen Table,* provide ongoing information on local renewal; publications such as *The Community Resource Manual* and *The Community Visioning and Strategic Planning Handbook* would be useful resources for teachers and students.

For information: Alliance for National Renewal, National Civic League, 1445 Market Street, Suite 300, Denver, CO 80202-1717; phone: 303-571-4343.

Kettering Foundation. The Charles F. Kettering Foundation of Dayton, Ohio, has long focused attention on civic engagement and concern for the health of civil society. Through its journal, the *Kettering Review,* the foundation encourages the discussion of ideas that promote a healthy democracy. The foundation also sponsors the National Issues Forums (NIF) founded in 1982. The forum creates nonpartisan materials on three major public issues each year that are designed to be used as the basis for discussion. Used widely by civic and educational organizations, including precollegiate schools, service groups, and religious organizations, the NIF materials are of high quality and model an exemplary process for public discussion. The forum also sponsors training for group leaders to encourage a high level of discussion.

For information: National Issues Forum, 100 Commons Road, Dayton, OH 45459-2777; phone: 1-800-433-7834.

CORPORATE PROGRAMS

Farmers' Insurance provides a major corporate example of promoting civic engagement through its television series, *The American Promise*. These programs, featuring more than 200 people working at the grassroots level of civic involvement, illustrate the importance of local engagement. The company makes available a teaching guide to accompany the series videotapes, which are available free of charge to schools and community groups as a resource on local civic action. Thousands of teachers request these materials each year, indicating educators' recognition of the important effect that practical examples can have in stimulating young people's involvement in local affairs. *The American Promise* project also collects and circulates case studies of student actions inspired by their materials. This major U.S. insurance company has invested heavily in the series as a way of demonstrating its concern for the health of U.S. public life. The company has made a 10-year commitment to the distribution of these materials.

For information: 1-800-204-7722.

The Prudential Insurance Company of America sponsors a community service awards program for young people and distributes a guide, "Catch the Spirit: A Student's Guide to Community Service." Each year, two young people from each state are chosen to receive awards, presented in Washington, D.C. Through this effort to focus on the outstanding contributions young people make to their communities, Prudential illustrates the high levels of achievement many youth accomplish. These awards provide models, but not formal materials, that could be useful in designing activities related to curriculum.

For information: The Consumer Information Center, The Prudential Insurance Company of America, Dept. 506E, Pueblo, CO 81009.

SCHOOL-BASED PROGRAMS

Several school-based programs focus student attention on communities—their problems and policy choices—as part of either civic education or other reform strategies. These efforts are also consistent with the National Standards for Civics and Government and connect the community with the classroom in ways that are academically rigorous.

City Youth. The Constitutional Rights Foundation, with support

77

from the Carnegie Corporation of New York, has developed the City Youth curriculum, designed to be a key element in the middle school reform effort first advocated by Carnegie in 1989 in their *Turning Points* report. City Youth focuses student attention on the idea of community and the responsibilities of citizens. The curriculum contains interdisciplinary lessons and service learning opportunities that can involve students in the school community and beyond.

Student projects cover a wide range of issues affecting school and community life. This program, being implemented through the Carnegie middle school reform network in 15 states, is now being used in hundreds of middle schools and has spawned a wide range of student service learning projects. In New York City, as an outgrowth of a unit on health and well being at Intermediate School 302, students conduct an annual winter coat drive for the benefit of children in a nearby elementary school. At South Gate Middle School in Los Angeles, students concerned with crime and safety organized a public forum and dinner that brought police officers, fire fighters, and representatives of city government together with students and their families for a discussion of community issues. In Providence, Rhode Island, students working with their local police as a part of their study of crime and violence in their community simulated police patrol activities as a way of improving mutual understanding.

Active Citizenship Today. The Active Citizenship Today (ACT) curriculum was also developed by the Constitutional Rights Foundation, in cooperation with the Close Up Foundation and with the support of the DeWitt Wallace/Reader's Digest Fund, to provide resources for teachers. The ACT materials for students and teachers focus on participation skills cited in the National Standards and were designed to be integrated into the existing curriculum by social studies teachers at the middle school and senior high school levels. The goal of the program is to teach students how to gather information about community issues, examine them critically, make decisions that lead to action, and undertake and evaluate projects intended to improve the quality of life in the community. Developed with the involvement of several communities nationally, the program has successfully engaged teachers and students in a wide array of projects.

In Omaha, Nebraska, ACT students studied the problem of drugs in the United States, including their community. They focused on their own school, conducting a student survey. Concluding that students with a substance abuse problem did not know where to go for help,

78

they set up a before-and-after-school help group. The group researched and created a list of community resources and made referrals so that students with a problem could contact professionals for assistance.

In Jefferson County, Colorado, as part of the ACT process, students concluded that a busy residential street was hazardous because it had no street lights. The students contacted the local homeowners associations and got their support. In only two weeks, students gained county government approval for installation of street lights. The developer who had built the residential area was contacted and agreed to pay half the cost for the lights. Student-organized teams made up of a student and an adult went door to door and raised $34,232 to match the developer's funds, and the lights were installed.

In Jackson, Mississippi, after focusing on the community problem of violence, ACT students joined with community organizations and created a long-term program, "Taking Back the Neighborhood Block-by-Block." Targeting a 10-block area around their high school, students worked to reduce crime in the area. Their initial effort focused on building a community center. They are now in the process of raising money and seeking support from the city for the center.

Robinson Mini-Grants. The Constitutional Rights Foundation also sponsors the J. R. Robinson Mini-Grant program, which annually funds 30 small-scale teacher and student programs designed to address community problems. The program supports a broad array of activities throughout the nation, each costing between $200 and $800. All involve a process of planning and conducting research to identify needs—essential skills for sound civic action.

For information on City Youth, ACT, and Robinson Mini-Grants: Constitutional Rights Foundation, 601 S. Kingsley Dr., Los Angeles, CA 90005.

Project Citizen. Sponsored by the Center for Civic Education, developers of the National Standards for Civics and Government, Project Citizen is designed to engage middle school young people in the study of policy issues affecting their communities. Students research and develop policy proposals that are then presented to adults from the community who provide critical reaction to the students. Used as the basis for a competition, the objective of the program is to teach students a process for examining community issues.

For information: Center for Civic Education, 5146 Douglas Fir Rd., Calabasas, CA 91302-1467.

CHARACTER EDUCATION AND SERVICE LEARNING: TWO ESSENTIAL COMPONENTS OF CIVIC EDUCATION

Character education and service learning are closely related elements of the new civic education. Fortunately, considerable momentum for each of these elements is developing across the nation through efforts that are already well underway. These two important national movements should be integrated into civic education, both as part of the formal curriculum and as part of the school culture. The City Youth and ACT programs illustrate this connection between the curriculum and community involvement.

CHARACTER EDUCATION

Curriculum-based character education is not new—McGuffey practiced it in his famous reader. Neither is the controversy that surrounds it. Discussions about human nature and its relationship to character formation abound. Concern that education for character may simply be another form of religious or conformist indoctrination is part of the argument against introducing character education in the schools (Kohn, 1997). It is true that some approaches to character education are thinly veiled efforts to establish conformity and increase unquestioning obedience to authority. Nevertheless, there are strong proponents of character education who point out that character development takes place in young people whether it is planned for or not. They argue that planned programs are better than leaving character development to chance. In U.S. society, that would depend on whether or not the values taught build support for democratic citizenship (Etzioni, 1998; Kohn, 1998).

The democratic values that are part of the national tradition in the United States and that grow out of the Constitution and the Bill of Rights make up the most widely accepted list of values of good character. This view is illustrated by the recent position statement of the National Council for the Social Studies, which defines character as "a reasoned commitment to fundamental principles, such as popular sovereignty, rule of law, religious liberty, and the like." The statement asserts that the citizen must also "demonstrate a reasoned commitment to fundamental values such as life, liberty, pursuit of happiness, equality, truth, and promotion of the common good." The "position statement calls for a renewed effort by social studies educators, schools, and com-

80

munities to teach character and civic virtue" (National Council for the Social Studies, 1996, p. 1).

A study by Lynn Nielsen (1997) of state education standards demonstrates broad support for this view of character education. Nielsen concludes that, in the standards completed or in the process of being completed in 48 of the 50 states, "character education was defined in terms of general democratic values around which most communities would claim consensus" (p. 22). Even though broad agreement appears to exist for this approach, much work remains in designing curriculum materials that effectively integrate these values in a way that links them to behavior and that helps young people understand their explicit meaning.

Other groups, such as the Character Education Partnership, "a nonpartisan coalition of organizations and individuals concerned about the moral crises confronting America's youth," also describe a broad-based role for character education that weaves conscious efforts to develop character throughout schooling in a way that involves both the formal and informal curriculum (Character Education Partnership, 1997, p. 1). In its Eleven Principles of Effective Character, the partnership describes character education as core ethical values: caring, honesty, fairness, responsibility, and respect for self and others. The partnership publishes a newsletter, serves as a clearinghouse of information, holds a national conference, encourages research, and promotes activities by other organizations nationally.

Whether defined in terms of individual ethical values or broad-based U.S. values, character education represents an important link to educating youth for citizenship in a democratic society. It contributes to the creation of a civil society by identifying characteristics required of individuals in their relations with other members of a group and encouraging adults in their work with children to emulate as well as advocate the values they represent. As a part of the curriculum, character education helps by connecting content with civic behavior and participation.

SERVICE LEARNING

Service learning, the thoughtful integration of community service within the curriculum (as illustrated by the City Youth and ACT programs), is another potentially powerful way to connect civic education to a larger reform strategy, and it also is receiving much national attention. Not all service learning is civic education. If service is not explicitly linked to civic education, it may provide communities with useful help but do little to develop either the civic knowledge or the values needed to stimulate active citizenship. As Ben Barber (1992) has noted:

> Service to the community by itself can teach altruism and charity, but to become a tool of civic education it needs to be explained and combined with serious classroom work. Classroom civic education by itself can teach the theory of citizenship, but its practice depends on engagement in the real world. (p. 1)

Service learning can become a formal part of civic education only through programs such as City Youth, ACT, and Project Citizen, in which the civic knowledge and skills are made explicit.

Although the social studies in general and civic education in particular have always proclaimed civic engagement to be a major goal, there is little evidence that the traditional curriculum, focusing today largely on history and geography, provides students with much opportunity to take what they have learned and apply it outside of the classroom. Although the link between content and application is potentially greatest in the study of U.S. government, it does not appear that much effort is being made to develop opportunities for students to engage in civic action or to use the community as resource or laboratory. As Barber notes, one without the other fails to take advantage of an important learning opportunity for students.

If civic educators were to use service learning to create increasing opportunities for community involvement, it would represent an important milestone in achieving the civic education goal of public education. The Improving America's Schools programs of the United States Department of Education provide many opportunities to create service learning programs as a part of Title I, School to Work, and other titles that are part of that legislation. Service learning programs also can be developed and funded through the Learn and Serve division of the Corporation for National Service. Almost every state now receives funding from the corporation for programs selected and administered through state departments of education. Many programs now being funded do not have the conscious connection needed to maximize their potential as vehicles for civic education. It is also disappointing to note that civic educators have not yet been drawn to service learning in large numbers. However, service learning remains an important and promising approach to more engaging citizenship education.

Both character education and service learning move students

from the abstract discussion of principles or structures of a democracy to the level of individual responsibility and action. How concerned should the *individual* be for the common good or general welfare? How does that responsibility apply to practical questions and concerns of local civic life? Those are the central questions facing U.S. democracy and the individual citizen. If we do not focus the curriculum on those questions, what we teach remains abstract; important perhaps, but unrelated to the central questions of democratic citizenship.

COALITION BUILDING FOR A CIVIL SOCIETY

Two promising initiatives have the potential to foster the integration of character education and service learning into both civic education and broad-based efforts at education reform. The first is a series of reports on character building that grew out of meetings convened by the Communitarian Network. The second is the work of the National Partnering Initiative on Education and Civil Society. Both of these groups are large coalitions of education and community-based organizations concerned with the preparation of young people for membership in U.S. society.

THE COMMUNITARIAN NETWORK

Beginning in 1994, the Communitarian Network convened several task groups to examine and make recommendations regarding the integration of character education into various aspects of schooling and youth development. Each task group has issued separate reports; they are "The Schools as Moral Communities," "Building Character Through Sports," "Education for Interpersonal Relationships," "The Role of Family Involvement," "The Role of Civic Education," and "The Role of Community in Character Education." A newly formed task force is also developing recommendations for service learning. Because of the broad range of educational groups and leaders who have served as members of the task groups, the impact of these recommendations could be considerable if they are widely distributed by their members and used as guidelines for change. These recommendations provide valuable reference points for schools looking for guidance in assessing current programs and planning new ones designed to more consciously encourage the development of democratic values by young people (Communitarian Network, 1997).

83

In particular, the task force on the role of civic education strongly endorses the importance of creating new initiatives to revitalize the preparation of young people for citizenship:

> The goal of civic education is to prepare citizens who are informed and competent to take part in local, state and national civic and political life. Such participation requires (1) the acquisition of a body of knowledge and understandings, (2) the development of intellectual and participatory skills, (3) the development of certain dispositions or traits of character, and (4) the reasoned commitment to the fundamental values and principles of American constitutional democracy. (p. 77)

The report goes on to recommend that

> the formal curriculum should be augmented by learning experiences in both school and community that enable students to reach decisions about participation in their own governance and to determine how to take an active and constructive role in the betterment of the civic life of their schools, communities, and nation. (p. 80)

THE NATIONAL PARTNERING INITIATIVE

The National Partnering Initiative on Education and Civil Society views civil education (defined as the integration of service learning, character education, civic education, and democratic schooling) as a necessary and vital step toward reinvigorating our democracy. Growing out of ideas advanced by Jeremy Rifkin, the economist, the National Partnering Initiative is seeking to advance that perspective on school reform through a number of initiatives at the state and national levels. The members of the coalition include more than 60 national education and community-based organizations, including the National Education Association, the Association for Supervision and Curriculum Development, the National Association of Secondary School Principals, and the American Association of Higher Education.

The National Partnering Initiative's goal is to

> 1) make education relevant to young people by basing it in experiential learning in neighborhood and community based organizations; 2) prepare youth for the opportunities and challenges that go hand and hand with civic engagement; and 3) strengthen and enrich community-based organizations and local neighborhoods by making civil education a community responsibility. (1998, p. 1)

If the resources now being sought by the Partnering Initiative were made available to launch a significant implementation effort, it could have great impact because of the breadth of the initiative's membership. The initiative's plans include creating state partnering initiatives made up of local affiliates of national partners, and influencing textbook publishers to include material that supports the development of a civil society.

Taking Up the Challenge

Even as we move into the first century of a new millennium we must recognize democratic government to be a new phenomenon—one that is, in the modern world, only slightly more than 200 years old. The United States is prosperous economically but has a population that is relatively indifferent to public life and active civic engagement. Perhaps the Partnering Initiative is correct in identifying the development of a civil society as the most important national goal for education.

If that is so, our present efforts show little evidence of success. Ask almost any college freshman about their interest in political life, as UCLA does each year, and discover how minimal it is. Look at the NAEP results in U.S. history and anticipate what the results will be when the subject is civic understanding. Present school programs do not seem to be strengthening young people's commitment to democratic citizenship, and only a few citizens seem to be concerned. The informal curriculum is a vital part of the process of socializing youth and should be reviewed for the important role it plays in encouraging civic engagement. The impact of the varied social forces that affect the development of youth attitudes should also receive significant attention.

The focus here is on the absence of any link between the current curriculum, local affairs, and local government. Some students of U.S. life find evidence that fewer citizens are involved in voluntary associations identified as vital to the development of civic leadership. Many organizations are taking steps to reverse that trend among adults. Much that they are doing appears transferable to the school curriculum. Individual programs and larger initiatives involving many groups are advocating approaches that ask young people to reflect upon their own attitudes toward civil society and become actively involved in strengthening communities. How powerful the impact of these efforts will be is uncertain.

The United States is a nation where citizens are sovereign. If citizens make uneducated judgments, what follows is "mob rule: the government of private prejudice and the tyranny of opinion" (Barber, 1984, pp. 4–5). If citizens are indifferent, who runs the nation? Special interests, bureaucrats, and politicians—not citizens!

It is vital that we reexamine how we educate youth for citizenship. We must add participation and individual responsibility, key objectives of both service learning and character education, to the knowledge base of present programs and engage students in considering their personal stake in the general welfare of other U.S. citizens, with a focus on the local community. We must make civic education a key element of all school reform because it is critical to the future of democracy.

REFERENCES

Banks, J. (1996). Foreword. In Parker, W. C. *Educating the democratic mind.* Albany, NY: State University of New York Press.
Barber, B. R. (1984). *Strong democracy.* Berkeley, CA: University of California Press.
Barber, B. R. (1992). *From classroom to community service: A bridge to citizenship.* Los Angeles: National Youth Service Network, Constitutional Rights Foundation.
California Department of Education. (1997). *History social science framework.* Sacramento, CA: California Department of Education.
Center for Civic Education. (1994). National standards for civics and government. Calabasas, CA: Author.
Character Education Partnership. (1997). *Character educator.* Washington, DC: Character Education Partnership.
Civic Partners. (1997). *Pew partnership for civic change report.* Charlottesville, VA: University of Richmond.
Communitarian Network. (1997). *Character building for a democratic society.* Washington, DC: Author.
Community activism on rise among students. (1998, May 10). *Los Angeles Times Supplement: Campus & careers,* p. 10.
Dewey, J. (1916). The democratic conception in education. In J. A. Boydston (Ed.)., *Democracy and education: John Dewey, The middle works, 1899–1924,* 1980, Southern Illinois University Press. (As cited in *Educating the democratic mind,* by W. C. Parker, Ed., 1996, Albany, NY: State University of New York Press)
Etzioni, A. (1998, February). How not to discuss character education, *Phi Delta Kappan 79*(6), 446–448.
Kohn, A. (1997, February). How not to teach values, *Phi Delta Kappan 78*(6), 428–433.

Kohn, A. (1998, February). Adventures in ethics versus behavior control: A reply to my critics, *Phi Delta Kappan 79*, (6), 455–459.

National Partnering Initiative on Education and Civil Society. (1998). *Strategic plan, partnering initiative on education and civil society.* Washington, DC: Author.

National Assessment Governing Board. (1997). *Civics framework for the 1998 national assessment for educational progress.* Washington, DC: NAEP Governing Board of the U.S. Department of Education.

National Council for the Social Studies. (1996). Position statement. Washington, DC: National Council for the Social Studies.

Nielsen, L. (1997). Search summary: The status of character education from the perspective of state departments of education. *Social Studies Review.* San Francisco, CA: California Council for the Social Studies.

The Partnership (1997). *Pew partnership for civic change report.* Charlottesville, VA: University of Richmond.

Sax, L. J., Astin, A. W., & Korn, W. S. (1997). *The American freshman: National norms for fall 1997.* Los Angeles, CA: Higher Education Research Institute, UCLA.

Sax, L. J., Astin, A. W., Korn, W. S., & Mahoney, K. M. (1997). *The American freshman: National norms for fall 1997.* Los Angeles, CA: Higher Education Research Institute, UCLA.

5

Diversity and Education for the 21st Century

BELINDA WILLIAMS

What I have called the "triple dilemma," or "trilemma," is the mutually damaging collision of individual human rights, cultural human diversity, and global human opportunities. Today the damage from that collision is suddenly all around us. . . . Finding ways to become unified despite diversity may be the world's most urgent problem in the years ahead.

Harlan Cleveland, 1995

Individual human rights, cultural human diversity, and global human opportunities—the "trilemma" defined by Harlan Cleveland, former U.S. assistant secretary of state and ambassador to NATO—bring focus and a sense of urgency to an awesome challenge for society and education institutions. Restated, the challenge embodies three broad elements. First is the need to build on the experiences of a past in which "cultural human diversity" has not been valued; the second is to adequately prepare the diverse population of students we are not successfully educating with recognition and respect for their individual human rights; and the third is to enable all students to participate in and contribute to the growth of the nation and the world community in a future that demands cross-cultural interdependence and new social interactions—global human opportunities.

These challenges invite us to rethink and reshape our traditional values, beliefs, and institutional arrangements, especially given the current and anticipated increases in racial and ethnic diversity in the United States. According to the National Center for Education Statistics, U.S. Department of Education (1997),

> In 1995, 67 percent of U.S. children aged 5–17 were white, 15 percent were black, 13 percent were Hispanic, and 5 percent were Asian/Pacific Islander, American Indian, and Alaskan Native. Between 2000 and 2020, the number of minority children aged 5–17 is projected to grow much faster than the number of white children. (p. 3)

Darling-Hammond (1997) restates and further elaborates on these demographic projections:

> . . . the growth in the U.S. population and its potential for social renewal is largely among immigrants and people of color, who will make up 40 percent of the [overall] public school population and over a third of the entering workforce by the year 2000 (Hudson Institute, 1987). This nation's ability to embrace and enhance the talents of those who have struggled for voice and educational opportunity will determine much of its future. . . . Meeting America's twenty-first-century challenge is not just a matter of improved teaching of academic content in schools that are now failing. . . . Repairing the torn social fabric that increasingly arrays one group against another will require creating an inclusive social dialogue in which individuals can come to understand diverse experiences and points of view. (p. 30)

Orfield and associates (1997) alert us to yet another perspective:

> The United States is a nation with a shrinking proportion of white students and a rising share of black and Latino students, groups which experience far less success in American public education and are concentrated in schools with lower achievement levels and less demanding competition. Recent court decisions approving a return to segregated neighborhood schools in various parts of the country will intensify the isolation. (p. 3)

How can we mend the "torn social fabric," the phrase used by Darling-Hammond to describe the conditions of racial and ethnic diversity in the society? What must we do to improve the achievement and options of populations of students experiencing increasing "isolation in the society"?

This chapter discusses the following challenges facing society and education institutions as a result of diversity: (1) the need to comprehend and accept the paradigm shift in conceptualizations of diversity supported by new understandings of human development, (2) the need to centrally position new understandings of human development in reform proposals introduced to increase the learning success of a diverse student population, and (3) the need to integrate available models and strategies to facilitate the deeper conversations in efforts to develop the abilities and attitudes necessary for current populations of diverse students to successfully participate in the global market economy of the 21st century. It is hoped that readers will gain some new insights about the current conceptualizations of human development and cultural diversity that will stimulate the creative thinking required to change existing traditional values, beliefs, and institutional arrangements; provide an informed challenge to current education reform proposals; and guide the dialogue and decision making in schools necessary to define and ensure educational success for all students in the 21st century.

NEW CONCEPTUALIZATIONS OF HUMAN DEVELOPMENT AND DIVERSITY: A PARADIGM SHIFT

Limited conceptualizations of the role of cultural diversity in human development contribute to the current failure to educate diverse student populations and to enable citizens who will live in the 21st century to successfully interact with diverse populations in the United States and the world community. How have the identified challenges of diversity come to exist? What dynamics contribute to the complexities? I offer two explanations: (1) what we know about diversity and human development has been shaped and therefore limited by inadequate theoretical assumptions and historical, political, and economic conditions (Banks & Banks, 1995; Cleveland, 1995; Orfield, Bachmeier, James, & Eitle, 1997; National Center for Education Statistics, 1997); and (2) rapid changes in the society have superseded an understanding and acceptance of the complexities of human development.

INADEQUATE ASSUMPTIONS

From the recorded philosophical assumptions of Plato (427–347 B.C.) to current conceptualizations of human development based upon information processing constructs, there have been hundreds of theories of human development and intelligence (Ceci, 1996). Modern psychological theories have been motivated by either genetic (Herrnstein & Murray, 1994; Jensen, 1973) or contextual (Cole, 1996; Levine, Resnick, & Higgins, 1993; Greeno, Collins, & Resnick, 1996; Wozniak & Fischer, 1993; Vygotsky, 1978) assumptions. The "nature/nurture" controversy has been thoroughly debated elsewhere (Ceci, 1996; Gould, 1994; Kamin, 1974) and need not be reviewed here. Kamin (1974) offers a brief summary and perspective on the debate that has revolved around assumptions and interpretations of I.Q. tests:

> The I.Q. test in America, and the way in which we think about it, has been fostered by men committed to a particular social view. That view includes the belief that those on the bottom are genetically inferior victims of their own immutable defects. The consequence has been that the I.Q. test has served as an instrument of oppression against the poor—dressed in the trappings of science, rather than politics. The message of science is heard respectfully, particularly when the tidings it carries are soothing to the public conscience. There are few more soothing messages than those historically delivered by the I.Q. testers. The poor, the foreign-born, and racial minorities were shown to be stupid. They were shown to have been born that way. The underprivileged are today demonstrated to be ineducable, a message as soothing to the public purse as to the public conscience. . . .These are, of course, political considerations . . . .To pretend that the two are separable is either naive or dissembling. (p. 2)

    Banks (1995) describes the tradition of perceptions of difference and inherent intellectual inferiority that define the fabric of the society. He highlights the fact that these perceptions of inferiority have not been limited to African Americans, Hispanics, and Native Americans:

> Late 19th and early 20th century nativists made important and invidious distinctions between various white "races." These distinctions grew sharper as thousands of Southern and Eastern European immigrants entered the United States near the turn of the century. About 15 million immigrants arrived in the United States between 1890 and 1914; most of whom were from Southern and Eastern Europe (U.S. Bureau of the Census, 1993). Nativists and scientific racists were deeply concerned about the negative influences these predominantly non-Anglo-Saxon, Catholic immigrants would have on the development of civilization and democracy in the United States (Higham, 1972). They were also concerned about the negative effects these immigrants would have, through interracial marriage, on the development of the Anglo-Saxon race. (p. 17)

Currently, the research and theories of scholars from diverse disciplines (Ceci, 1996; Cole, 1996; Dewey, 1938; Dobzhansky, 1973; Wozniak & Fischer, 1993) have converged to support a framework of human development that builds on developmental, cognitive, and social psychology; anthropology; sociology; and genetics. Ceci (1996) suggests: "One's cultural context is an integral part of cognition because the culture arranges the occurrence or nonoccurrence of events that are known to affect cognitive developments, e.g., literacy . . ." (pp. 95–96).

Cole (1996) offers a perspective of human development that explains the absence of the role of context and culture in its historical definition. He shares an illuminating quote from Theodore Adorno, an anthropologist: "Culture might be precisely that condition that excludes a mentality capable of measuring it" (p. 7).

In addition, to further illustrate the elusive nature of culture in current theory and educational research, Cole (1996) reveals the following:

> Discussion of cultural context was virtually absent from the developmental psychology of the 1960s and 1970s, when we first began to publish our cross-cultural research. But in the 1990s, even those cross-cultural psychologists who have most severely criticized us for our particularism straightforwardly adopt "the individual in context as the unit of analysis". . . . Interest in cultural approaches to development has now spread well beyond the core of people associated with cultural psychology. (p. 337)

What is culture? How and by whom is it defined? Culture is closely intertwined with concepts of race, ethnicity, and social class. Hence, conceptual confusion has contributed to the failure to formulate a clear definition and understanding of culture (Avery, 1992). I offer the following definition: *Culture is the lens, crafted by history, tradition and environmental conditions, through which groups view themselves, their environment, and their future, and shape their decision making, problem solving, and behavioral responses.*

RAPID CHANGES IN SOCIETY

Rapid changes in society that have superseded an understanding and acceptance of the complexities of human development provide the second explanation for the origin of the current challenges related to diversity. A condensed overview of these rapid changes reveals that within a span of 100 to 200 years we have made the transition from the

Agricultural Age through the Industrial Age and into the Information Age. Huitt (1997) observes:

We have lived most of our human history in the hunter/gatherer age. In that environment the person with the best way to kill an animal or select the correct items to eat was most successful; in the agricultural age, the person with the most land and best agricultural machinery was most successful; and in the industrial age the person with the best manufacturing process or the most capital was most successful. (p. 2)

Toffler (1990) and Resnick (1995) suggest that in the 21st century, success will be defined by access to information and the ability to process it. Those individuals, groups, communities, societies, or nations that have access to information and the ability to process it will be most successful. Ensuring success for all student populations—with success defined as access to information and the ability to process it—emerges as the central challenge for education institutions.

Given the current recognition of the limitations of reductionist perspectives of human development (as expressed through philosophy, cognitive psychology, genetics, etc.) and the historical and political influences on understandings of human development, what *is* the current knowledge about human development? How is it being defined and by whom?

THE CURRENT KNOWLEDGE OF HUMAN DEVELOPMENT

The 21st Century Learning Initiative, a transnational program of 40 researchers, educational innovators, thinkers, and policymakers from 10 countries, was established in 1996 to synthesize the best of research and development into the nature of human development/learning, and to examine its implications for education, work, and the development of communities worldwide. An interim report and summaries of the work of The 21st Century Learning Initiative (1997), a work in progress, present four findings:

1. **A crisis of perception**—Current conceptualizations of knowing and learning reflect a shift from a science of the *analysis of discrete parts;* that is, behaviorism/observable connections between stimuli and responses and the individual's (internal) construction of knowledge, toward a science of *organizing principles and dynamic, interactive relationships;* that is, social group (external) construction of knowledge, meaning

94

and connections. The shift is supported by an integration of disciplines (including cognitive science, biology, anthropology, and sociology) that have developed separately.

2. **New understandings of what it means to be human**—Recent research is defining the co-evolution of man with his environment; that is, *an interaction of biological and cultural evolution,* and the development of multiple forms of intelligence that help make sense of the environment in different ways.

3. **New understandings about the brain**—Traditionally the study of learning was largely limited to philosophers and psychologists and more recently cognitive scientists. Neurologists, as a result of functional MRI and CAT scans, are now able to watch specific patterns of activity within the brain light up on a computer screen, causing scientists to revise earlier assumptions about *how individual learning actually occurs.*

4. **Evolving ideas about learning**—The process of learning has passed from simple self-organization to a *collaborative, interpersonal, social problem-solving activity* dependent on conversation, practical, meaningful involvement, and real-world experience and application. Learning and schooling are no longer viewed as synonymous. Learning is a consequence of experience, thinking, and an integral part of living.

In summary, these findings represent a subtle shift in perspective: from teaching to learning *(focus on the learner)* and from the information transmission view of traditional learning environments to a *constructivist/cultural environment* view (Greeno, Collins, & Resnick, 1994). Though theses findings can be simply stated and are routinely identified in the literature and educational conversations, there is little evidence that the deeper meanings are understood and internalized in the conversations and decision-making processes in schools, communities, and government agencies. Attention to the implications is left to chance, resulting in superficial, fragmented efforts and educational change limited to deficit perceptions and attention to behavioral symptoms (i.e., discipline, tracking, retention, remediation, and special education).

Researchers are exploring the impact of social factors on both the content and the process of people's cognitions and cognitive activities (Levine et al., 1993). Perkins (1998) suggests a framework that recognizes three basic dimensions to the development of cognitive and intellectual ability: the neural (genetic) dimension, the experiential (experience) dimension, and the reflective (thinking about thinking patterns) dimension. He concludes that "the reflective dimension offers the best target of opportunity for education because reflective intelligence is the most learnable of the three."

Other research has identified elements found in most teaching and learning environments that, when combined, are most effective. A parallel shift in recognizing that learning and work are not separate has resulted in efforts to focus on the role of *motivation and effort* in learning and to incorporate some of the characteristics of work environments into school learning environments (Greeno, Collins, & Resnick, 1994).

Meece and McColskey (1997), in a review of the research on motivation, distinguish *intrinsic (internal standards) and extrinsic (external rewards, grades, parent approval, etc.) motivation* and conclude:

> Psychological research over the years has described motivation in different ways. Motivation was first studied as a personality trait, as something people had in more or less degrees, perhaps depending in part on their genetic makeup and their early childhood experiences. However, much of the recent motivational research contradicts this view and demonstrates that motivation is sensitive to contexts. For example, a student may be highly motivated in geography but not in algebra. Disadvantaged students may be very unmotivated in some school environments but very motivated in others. Some teachers put a higher priority on setting up a motivating classroom environment than others. Motivation also reflects cognitive factors such as the ways in which individuals differ in how they interpret their success and failure and their beliefs about how "fixed" their ability is. . . . Many schools have not focused on improving student motivation as an important outcome. Rather they have focused mainly on improving test scores or achievement, a subtle, but significantly different approach. . . . If, in addition to a focus on academic outcomes, school improvement teams focused on improving student motivation, they would be more likely to consider improvements in the learning environment and more likely to invite regular feedback from students about how they feel about school and learning. (pp. 7–8)

Other emerging research, the resilience literature (Rutter, 1987; Werner & Smith, 1992; Wang, Haertel, & Walberg, 1998) offers another opportunity to more adequately address the educational supports for learning necessary for populations of economically diverse students. Many children live in neighborhoods with high rates of violence, crime, poverty, and unemployment. Yet, in spite of these conditions, we find children who become healthy, self-supportive, responsible, productive adults. These kinds of children are called stress resistant, hardy, and in the currently used term, resilient.

Werner and Smith (1992) cite Rutter (1987), who describes these children, and suggests:

> . . . if we want to help vulnerable youngsters we need to focus on the protective processes that bring about changes in life trajectories from risk to adaptation. He includes among them (1) those that reduce the risk impact; (2) those that reduce the likelihood of negative chain reactions; (3) those that promote self-esteem and self-efficacy; and (4) those that open up opportunities. We have seen these processes at work among the resilient children in our study and among those youths who recovered from serious coping problems in young adulthood. They represent the essence of any effective intervention program, whether by professionals or volunteers. (p. 204)

Ron Suskind (1998), in his recently published *A Hope in the Unseen*, describes Cedric Jennings:

> . . . an ambitious fifteen-year-old, the poor son of a clerical worker and a jailed drug dealer, who desperately wanted to make it not only to college, but to an elite four-year institution. . . . Cedric was admitted to Brown's class of 1999. . . . [his] transition from inner city to Ivy League is predictably daunting. Academically, his self-confidence is shattered. Culturally, this product of an all-black neighborhood and a religious upbringing must learn to decode an alien world whose signposts, from Sylvia Plath to Jerry Garcia, are only dimly familiar. . . . Cedric must also bridge chasms of race and class to find common ground with people like Rob, the roommate with whom he spends much of the year feuding; Zayd, a fellow rap-music aficionado who becomes Cedric's first white friend; and Chiniqua, the only other black freshman in Cedric's unit (and his occasional date). (p. 37)

What enables a youngster like Cedric to persevere? Researchers (Rutter, 1987; Werner & Smith, 1992; Wang et al., 1998) have identified the following attributes as those that enable individuals to cope with risks in the environment: (1) social competence, (2) problem-solving skills, (3) autonomy, and (4) sense of purpose/future. Looking beyond individuals to their environments—their families, schools, and communities—the protective characteristics that appear to facilitate the development of resiliency fall into three categories: (1) caring and support, (2) high expectations, and (3) opportunities for children to participate.

HUMAN DEVELOPMENT: A VISION TO GUIDE REFORM

The challenge to the research and education communities is to identify and *integrate* the following, emerging shifts in our knowledge of human development and to consider the implications of the integration in reform efforts for diverse student populations (Greeno, Collins, & Resnick, 1996; Levine, Resnick, & Higgins, 1993; Wang, Haertel, & Walberg, 1998; Williams & Newcombe, 1994; Williams & Woods, 1997; Williams, 1996):

1. Cultural environments—the impact of daily experiences and interpersonal relationships within and outside of school on knowledge acquisition and learning;

2. Cognitive/intellectual ability development—the role of culture and social processes in the development and transmission of intellectual abilities, language, and communication interactions;

3. Motivation and effort—the role and impact of the relationships among cultural environments, motivation, and effort in ability development and learning;

4. Conditions that foster and support resilience—the power of caring relationships, and high expectations in developing a sense of autonomy and a sense of future for individuals experiencing adversity.

What evidence exists to suggest that the implications of an *integration* of available knowledge about human development, *a vision to guide schools in the 21st century,* is being considered in current reform efforts?

Reform initiatives involving school choice represent examples of attempts by educators to get a better understanding of the learning process. Carvin (1998) describes initiatives that include rewards for teachers and schools for involvement in peer competition, attempts to raise the stature and confidence of teachers through professionalization, and dramatic changes in the role and structure of the school itself. Shokraii (1998) summarizes the progress of school choice reform proposals:

> In the academic arena, choice continues to gain credibility. Calls for additional research have replaced the traditional summons to keep all hands off the so-called common school ideal of the public school system. . . . In a study of Cleveland's program . . . 63 percent of the parents are "very satisfied" with the academic quality of their chosen schools, compared with less than 30 percent of public school parents. . . . [Students showed] improvements in both reading and math scores after only one year in attendance. (p. 5)

Other attempts to improve the educational outcomes for all students include the New American Schools Designs (Stringfield, Rossi, & Smith, 1996), e.g., Roots and Wings, Atlas, and Little Red School House. These designs attempt to incorporate some aspects of current thinking about learning (Newcombe et al., 1995). Achievement gains are impressive in some cases but uneven and not adequate to close the gap that limits the opportunities for culturally and linguistically diverse students to be competitive in the 21st century (Rossi & Stringfield, 1995; Walberg & Greenberg, 1998).

WHAT'S MISSING IN REFORM PROPOSALS: DEEPER UNDERSTANDINGS OF HUMAN DEVELOPMENT AND ISSUES OF EQUITY

In the late 1970s, less than two decades ago, the courses I took in preparation for certification as a school psychologist did not require an understanding of the impact of cultural environments on human development. Studying and learning to administer the Bender, a visual-motor perception test often administered to children experiencing learning difficulties, was a course requirement. Though *The Bender Gestalt Test for Young Children* (Koppitz, 1975) was a required text, Chapter 6, "The Bender Test and Social and Cultural Factors," was optional reading and was not discussed. In the chapter, several studies of Bender test patterns were reviewed, reporting on the performance of children from several cultures—African American, Chicano, Chinese, Native American, Japanese, and Anglo. In other words, a school psychologist could be certified to assess *all* students, including culturally diverse students, make critical recommendations about their educational experiences and programs—and, therefore, their lives—and not be required to understand the impact of cultural contexts on human development and learning.

I often speculate about education leaders and decision makers who have had similar professional development experiences—administrators, federal and state department bureaucrats, college professors, and researchers who have not studied or valued the available knowledge about cultural diversity and human development. Examples that come to mind include the principal I recently interviewed who proudly reported having used available funds to obtain state-of-the-art technology in a school with low reading scores, disproportionate numbers of special education classes, and 35 students in 1st grade; or another principal who proudly described to me all that is being done in his school to educate poor students while I observed a line of *only* African American males outside of the nurse's office waiting for their daily dosage of Ritalin. And then there was the "comprehensive school reform" researcher/model developer who reported raising reading scores to the 50th percentile and later admitted not having considered what might need to be addressed to raise scores to levels comparable to those achieved by middle-class suburban students.

In spite of the gaps in our knowledge and understanding, somehow we must prepare all students to contribute to and thrive in a complex global society and economy.

THE NARROW ASSUMPTIONS THAT GUIDE REFORM

What evidence exists to suggest that current reform efforts are achieving success with diverse student populations? Astuto and colleagues (1993) conclude that the narrow assumptions that lie beneath current reforms limit the scope of change recommended for schools. In summarizing their research they state the following:

> The insidious effect of taken-for-granted assumptions is the way they inter-connect with and reify one another in a seemingly logical set of relationships. If one assumes that the maintenance of the social, economic, and political order be a priority for education, then attempts by schools to counteract the fragmentary effects of diversity through the support and promotion of a common cultural tradition are appropriate. . . . Subscribing to a deficit model of cultural, parental, and community resources and values further limits the allies educators believe they can call upon for support. . . . If, on the other hand, educators began with a belief in the transformative role of education, the value of accessing diversity, a faith in the potential success of every student, a commitment to collaborative and political linkages with parents and communities, then mustering the inventiveness to create new ways of organizing on behalf of children would be the logical, moral, and just thing to do. (p. 41)

Current major reform proposals that take up issues of decentralization, site-based management, curriculum and assessment standards, and schoolwide projects have not centrally positioned the new understandings of human development outlined by the 21st Century Learning Initiative. A review of reform proposals reveals that they have left important issues of human development to chance (Stringfield, Rossi, & Smith, 1996).

100

REFORM PROPOSALS AND TEACHERS' PERCEPTIONS

In his paper *Schools for the 21st Century,* Robert McClure (1988), the director of the National Education Association's Mastery in Learning Project, delineates three categories of educational reform proposals:

• **State departments**—Higher standards, a narrowing of curriculum to the essentials, an increase in graduation requirements, longer school days and years, and upgrading the knowledge and skills of the teaching force.

• **Business community**—Preparation of students for the current world of work and strong vocational and career emphasis in the curriculum; greater emphasis on skills of inquiry, independent learning, creativity, problem solving, and critical thinking.

• **Academic and professional education communities**—Improving curriculum, instruction, and assessment (i.e., what knowledge is worth knowing); improving teaching; and restructuring schools.

McClure further observes,

There is a universal theme underlying almost all of the reports: If schools are to be better, significantly better, then those who work in them must take the responsibility for their improvement. No longer will top-down mandates instituting a new course on top of all of the old ones, a new accountability system, or a new instructional device be enough. (p. 2)

There is an assumption that those closest to students will do what is best to improve academic outcomes for students. Lipman (1998) reports research describing teacher decision making that challenges this assumption:

An assumption made by proponents of restructuring is that teacher collaboration will facilitate critical inquiry, reflection, and dialogue essential to educational change. . . . In general, there was little reflective conversation about beliefs and practices or school policies. Issues at the core of many African American students' experiences in school—deficit models, misinterpretation of discourse (language, style, social interactions), academic tracking, negation of students' strengths, the exclusion of diverse students' experiences and histories in the curriculum, the problematic implications of an emphasis on individual competition—were not touched. Indeed, team meetings and steering committee meetings reflected little real engagement of substantive issues. (p. 284)

101

What additional evidence exists to describe how some teachers respond to diversity? The first large-scale, systematic study reporting instructional practices in approximately 140 1st through 6th grade classrooms located in 15 elementary schools serving diverse student populations reports a range of teacher responses to diversity (Knapp, Shields, & Turnbull, 1995):

> The cultural and social diversity of the classroom presented teachers with a difficult task, which they approached in a variety of ways. Responses to this diversity ranged from approaches that actively excluded children from learning opportunities because of their backgrounds (e.g., in one classroom, not giving Hispanic children the chance to read aloud because they "might be embarrassed" in front of the Anglo children, who were generally better oral readers) to attempts to use students' backgrounds as a positive basis for learning in the classroom (e.g., in another classroom in the same district, choosing a novel about Hispanic migrant children as the centerpiece of a month's work in English and building a variety of learning experiences around this theme). (p. 172)

Corbett, Wilson, and Williams (1997) describe another dimension of teachers' responses to diversity. A study designed to explore the ways in which teachers can promote greater academic success with culturally diverse and poor students revealed that teachers overwhelmingly agreed (79 percent of 50 teachers interviewed) that "all students could succeed in school and that the teachers themselves could make a difference." One segment of the teachers maintained that "all children can succeed and it is the teachers' responsibility to ensure that they do so." Another segment claimed that "all children can succeed if the students put forth the necessary effort."

These studies illuminate the central importance of requiring attention to these issues in current reform efforts to improve the learning and academic success of students who are culturally different and often poor. It is evident that federal, state, and local policies and policymakers must revisit the assumptions of current reform proposals. Teachers bring varying degrees of knowledge and skills to address the education of culturally diverse students. There is evidence that the differing perceptions of teachers who recognize and value the diverse experiences of students and those who perceive the responsibility for learning in school to reside in the student may contribute to how they approach their practice. A perception or assumption that all students should come to school ready to learn and that *it is the teacher's job to teach and treat them the same* raises questions about the understanding of equity.

ISSUES OF EQUITY AND INTELLIGENCE

Perceptions and definitions of equity in education are central to the education of culturally diverse students. If current reform proposals such as site-based decision making are to improve academic outcomes for all children, issues of equity must be clarified, defined, and scheduled for discussion. Boisvert (1998), in his recent interpretation of Dewey's thought and philosophy, cites a useful definition of equality offered by Dewey:

> . . . equality is a manner of regarding others which refuses any absolute scale by which to judge them. People are equal in the sense that life offers multiple contexts within which to evaluate others. Democratic equality is postulated on the denial of any single, atemporal universal context for judgment. (p. 68)

What is the "universal context" for judgment in public schools serving diverse populations of students? Williams (1996), in elaborating on the role of the *deficit hypothesis* in decision making about the education of children who are poor and culturally different, cites the conclusions of the 1992 Commission on Chapter I:

> Most Americans assume that the low achievement of poor and minority children is bound up in the children themselves or their families. "The children don't try." "They have no place to study. . . . Their parents don't care." "Their culture does not value education." These and other excuses are regularly offered up to explain the achievement gap that separates poor and [culturally diverse] students from other young Americans. (p. 3)

The most historically significant attempt to define and address *equity* in education is illustrated by the assumptions of *Brown v. Board of Education* (1954). The U.S. Supreme Court extended the equal protection clause of the Fourteenth Amendment of the Constitution to children of all races. It was the political, social, and ethical precursor to subsequent decisions mandating that students from diverse racial, cultural, and linguistic backgrounds and students with diverse abilities be educated in the same schools and classrooms. In the aftermath of the *Brown* decision, society and the schools accepted the determination that *equity* was simply defined as all children having equal access to the same schools, classrooms, teachers, and instruction.

In poor urban and suburban schools, however, tracking, disproportionate placement in remedial programs and special education programs, and underrepresentation in advanced placement and gifted programs are the strategies replacing between-school segregation (Oakes, Wells, & Associates). Oakes et al. (1996) further draw our attention to recent evidence suggesting that perceptions, definitions, and decision-making measures of intelligence undermine efforts to eliminate ability tracking in schools:

> . . . arguments that intelligence is multidimensional, fluid, and often misjudged based on culturally biased assessments lead educators to question the "smart" versus "dumb" labels that are inadvertently placed on students by virtue of their track. . . . In essence, as these educators struggle to create more meaningful learning opportunities for students by "releasing intelligence rather than quantifying it" and "nurturing effort rather than defining ability," they find that the rigid tracking system that became so popular in this century cannot meet the educational needs of students or our society in the next. (p. 2)

The evidence is clear. Current reform proposals and strategies and programs to improve academic achievement for culturally, linguistically, and socioeconomically diverse students must explicitly require attention to new conceptualizations, *a new vision,* of cultural diversity and human development, and issues of intelligence. Discussions must be *deliberately* and *systematically* scheduled to determine and ensure attention to these deeper implications.

Darling-Hammond (1997) suggests that by allocating resources of staff and time to the "central task of classroom teaching and teachers' learning, . . . restructured schools have managed to create democratic learning communities that succeed in ways not previously thought possible with diverse groups of students." She goes on to say that these schools

> . . . organize teachers' and students' work together in ways that get beyond bureaucracy to produce:
>
> • Active in-depth learning
> • Emphasis on authentic performance
> • Attention to development
> • Appreciation for diversity
> • Opportunities for collaborative learning
> • A collective perspective across the school
> • Structures for caring
> • Support for democratic learning
> • Connections to family and community (pp. 331–332)

The issues raised by new conceptualizations of cultural diversity and human development (i.e., knowledge of cultural experiences; perceptions and definitions of intelligence and ability development; motivation and effort; resilience; etc.) and the identification of the knowledge, abilities, and skills required for the 21st century global economy underscore the central importance of requiring explicit attention to and integration of these conceptualizations in *all* current reform proposals. *The evidence does not support the taken-for-granted assumption that issues of diversity are understood in educational decision making and will be addressed.* Current education reform proposals must deliberately require deeper conversations and attention to cultural diversity and human development in efforts to develop (1) new sets of creative, analytical, problem-solving skills; (2) collaborative work that includes respect for diverse populations and ideas; (3) sense of future/career options and flexibility; and (4) the independent entrepreneurial skills projected to be required into the 21st century. The challenges and responsibilities are tremendous.

The preservice and inservice support for teachers identified by Darling-Hammond (1997) requires broad, clear perceptions, restructuring, and shared responsibility. The implications are clear:

* Institutions of teacher preparation must revise the courses required for certification to include new conceptualizations of cultural diversity and human development integrated with the pedagogy required to develop knowledge and skills for the 21st century.
* Policymakers and educational leaders must identify opportunities to schedule and facilitate deeper conversations about the role of cultural diversity in human development and strategies to impact learning.
* Communities and parents must be informed and included in conversations about the role of cultural environments in human development and the implications for community, home, and school environments.

The current education reform proposals that aim to improve the academic achievement of all students have ignored the issues of cultural diversity and human development. *There is a large gap between research-based reform efforts demonstrating only improved learning outcomes for culturally, linguistically, and socioeconomically diverse students and efforts resulting in comparable results for all students.* Thus the challenge for reform proposals is to integrate the tenets of education reform with current knowledge about the impact of culture and cultural environments on learning (Berman et al., 1997). Research has identified a positive correlation between the higher achievement of culturally diverse poor students and teachers who demonstrate instructional strategies that are culturally responsive (Knapp, Shields, & Turnbull, 1995; Ladson-Billings, 1994). In addition, there are programs, tools, and strategies available that could contribute to reform efforts— tools and strategies that might be introduced with site-based management and school improvement efforts, or integrated with reform models such as the Coalition of Essential Schools, Accelerated Schools, and others.

INFORMING THE EDUCATION COMMUNITY AND ENGAGING STUDENTS

As previously outlined, rapid changes in society have transformed purposeful learning and its connections to perceptions of work. During the relatively recent agricultural era, children did authentic work. Their work, expectations, and necessary knowledge and skills were valued, considered meaningful, and supported. If all student populations are to be prepared for the 21st century, similar clear relationships between learning and future work must be explicit.

Following are brief descriptions of selected examples of meaningful programs, tools, and strategies available to (1) inform the educational community about current conceptualizations of human development and diversity and position current conceptualizations of human development within reform efforts, and (2) prepare diverse populations of students for the global market economy of the 21st century.

RESOURCES TO INFORM THE EDUCATIONAL COMMUNITY

Educating Culturally and Linguistically Diverse Students (ASCD Professional Inquiry Kit)—The inquiry kit is an active approach to learning for school study groups and improvement teams. The resources included introduce theories, research, and practice important for educating diverse student populations. Included are readings and activities to explore personal cultural perspectives and how they can affect classroom practices, brain-based research, multiple intelligences, language development, standards, assessment, and change strategies.

The Urban Learner Framework (Research for Better Schools/Northeast and Islands Regional Education Laboratory at

Brown University)—The Urban Learner Framework (ULF) is a research-based conceptual framework that specifically addresses the complex issues that must be dealt with in urban restructuring efforts. The major features of the ULF are (1) four research-based themes (cultural diversity, unrecognized abilities, motivation and effort, resilience) and (2) the ramifications of the research-based themes for decision making within the functional areas of school organization (curriculum, instruction, and assessment; professional development; management/leadership; community, home, and school environments).

PROGRAMS AND STRATEGIES TO ENGAGE DIVERSE STUDENT POPULATIONS

The Responsive Classroom (Northeast Foundation for Children)—The Responsive Classroom is a teaching approach used in classrooms from prekindergarten through 8th grade. It is one approach that helps to integrate the academic and social curriculum in a way that enables teachers and students to be more responsive to each other's needs. The Responsive Classroom has the following aims:

1. To create community (each day begins with a whole-group circle).

2. To foster responsive interactions—sharing, listening, inclusion, and participation.

3. To teach through daily rituals and patterns the skills needed to be a responsive member of a classroom and school.

Differentiated Instruction in Mixed Ability Classrooms (ASCD Professional Inquiry Kit)—Differentiated instruction in the classroom provides multiple options for taking in information, making sense of ideas, expressing what has been learned, and developing products. Differentiated instruction has the following features:

1. It is proactive—the teacher proactively plans a variety of ways to make meaning and express learning.

2. It is more qualitative than quantitative—adjusting the nature of the assignment not the quantity/quality of the assignment.

3. It provides multiple approaches to content, process, and product.

4. It is student centered.

5. It is a blend of whole-class, group, and individual instruction.

6. It is organic—students and teachers learn together.

Looping—Supporting Student Learning Through Long-term Relationships (Grant, Johnson, & Richardson, 1996)—This program has the following features:

1. Schools keep groups of students together for more than one year.

2. The teacher moves with the class.

3. Groups can stay together for two to five years.

Status Treatments in the Classroom (Cohen, 1994)—Status Treatments is a strategy for group work in heterogeneous classes that enables the following:

1. Students working together in a group small enough so that everyone can participate on a task that has been clearly assigned.

2. Students carrying out their tasks without direct and immediate supervision of the teacher.

3. Delegated authority.

4. Group/task interdependence.

5. Identification of the explicit abilities required by the task and the identification and articulation by the teacher of a related range of students' strengths.

MicroSociety: A Real World in Miniature (Richmond, 1997)— MicroSociety is a program structured to explicitly tie formal instruction to the daily experiences of students and the authentic world of work. It has the following features:

1. Children learn by playing, doing, and working. They become producers and contributors, both in the miniature community and in the world outside the school.

2. Children confront moral issues and dilemmas in theory and in practice.

3. Children, teachers, administrators, parents, and community partners come together to improve the quality of life in school. Children and adults form new relationships based on the work experiences that unfold.

Resiliency in Schools (Henderson & Milstein, 1996)—The authors have developed instruments and a process outline to foster resiliency for students, educators, and schools. Suggested strategies include the following:

1. Mitigating risk.

2. Setting clear and consistent boundaries.

3. Teaching life skills.

4. Providing caring and support.

5. Setting and communicating high expectations.

6. Providing opportunities for meaningful participation.

CONCLUSIONS AND IMPLICATIONS

An elementary principal in an urban city in the Midwest describes his staff's decision to attend a local church service to learn more about the cultural life of students and demonstrate respect for their cultural experiences. A principal in another district shares the details of a bus trip taken by his entire school staff to the neighborhood surrounding the school so that the teachers, who don't live there, could become familiar with the community and daily experiences of their students. They got off the bus to speak with individuals who live in the community and individuals who own the local businesses to identify available opportunities and knowledge that could connect the students' community experiences to instruction. In another school, parents and community individuals are interviewed and featured in the school newsletter to strengthen parental involvement. Scheduled student-led conferences in schools result in record increases in parental involvement. Teachers involved in looping (remaining with the same students for two to three years) report improved student attendance, parent participation, and knowledge of their students.

These descriptions of innovations being tried around the United States illustrate the efforts of many educators to strengthen the relationships between staff and culturally diverse students in order to improve learning. There is no single best way, but the occasional increased awareness of the need to *know the learner* and strengthen relationships can be identified in these efforts. The challenge is to *systematize* such awareness, as well as knowledge of human development and explicit attention to relationships, caring environments, and strategies to connect learners to instruction (by paying attention, for example, to daily experiences and cultural traditions, abilities, interests, opportunities to encourage effort, and the need for students to develop a vision for their future).

The challenges described in this chapter will require in-depth exploration and consideration by educators, colleges of higher education, researchers, communities, and government agencies. Defining human development and communicating the understandings and implications in the context of educational reform is the major challenge for addressing diversity in the 21st century. Cole (1996) quotes Alexander Luria:

> Scientific observation is not merely pure description of separate facts. Its main goal is to view an event from as many perspectives as possible. Its real object is to see and understand the way a thing or event relates to other things or events. (p. 326)

This quote from Luria reflects the logic that, *no matter how far you have gone down the wrong path, you must turn back.* Current reform proposals are well underway. Although much has been expressed about the increasing diversity in public schools and disparate achievement patterns, the issues outlined here have not been centrally positioned in reform proposals for educating *all* students.

Much still remains to be resolved. Brain research continues, and new knowledge will certainly influence perceptions of diversity and learning. For example, research recently reviewed by a *New York Times* reporter (Hall, 1998) and scheduled to be published by the American Psychological Association (Neisser, 1998) reveals the following:

> . . . if IQ scores are any measure, people are getting smarter. Researchers who study intelligence say scores around the world have been increasing so fast that a high proportion of people regarded as normal at the turn of the century would be considered way below average today. . . . Psychologists offer a variety of possible explanations for the increase, including better nutrition, urbanization, more experience with test taking and smaller families . . . that intelligence is much more flexible and more subject to environmental influences than anyone thought. (p. A8)

Technology continues to explode, and means of communication are changing rapidly. Populations continue to move and grow, and opportunities to adjust learning experiences to more successfully educate increasingly diverse populations continue to be ignored and resisted.

What can we conclude? The programs and strategies included here represent a limited list of what is available to inform and shape reform. Educators and education communities must constantly update and consider the implications of new knowledge about human development and learning and the implications of technology for skill development. New professional development strategies (e.g., study groups, action research) face an ongoing challenge to discover what will make a difference for *all* students. New definitions of "success," including who should define it and what is required to ensure it for all students who will live in the 21st century, must be the topics of discussion for communities of learners—educators, state departments, universities, parents, communities, governments, and politicians—if current reform efforts are to achieve the required results.

REFERENCES

Astuto, T., Clark, D. L., Read, A., McGree, K., & Fernandez, L. P. (1993). *Challenges to dominant assumptions controlling educational reform*. Andover, MA: Regional Laboratory of Educational Improvement of the Northeast and Islands.

Avery, M. B. (1992, February). Reflections on the intercultural encounter. *WEEA Digest*, 3-5.

Banks, J. A. (1995). The historical reconstruction of knowledge about race: Implications for transformative teaching. *Educational Researcher, (24)*2, 15–25.

Banks, J. A., & Banks, C. A. (1995). *Handbook of research on multicultural education*. New York: Macmillan Publishing USA.

Berman, P., McLaughlin, B., McLeod, B., Minicucci, C., Nelson, B., & Woodworth, K. (1997). *School reform and student diversity*. Washington, DC: U.S. Department of Education.

Boisvert, R. D. (1998). *John Dewey: Rethinking our time*. New York: State University of New York Press.

Carvin, A. (1998). Styles of education reform. In *EdWeb: Exploring technology and school reform* [Website]. http://edweb/gsn/org/edrel.sys.types.html

Ceci, S. (1996). *On intelligence: A bioecological treatise on intellectual development*. Cambridge, MA: Harvard University Press.

Cleveland, H. (1995, March–April). The limits to cultural diversity. *The Futurist (29)*, 23–26.

Cohen, E. (1994). *Designing groupwork: Strategies for the heterogeneous classroom*. New York: Teachers College Press.

Cole, M. (1996). *Cultural psychology: A once and future discipline*. Cambridge, MA: Belknap Press of Harvard University Press.

Commission on Chapter 1. (1992). *Making schools work for children in poverty: A new framework prepared by the Commission on Chapter 1*. Baltimore, MD:

Author.

Corbett, D., Wilson, B., & Williams, B. (1997). *Assumptions, actions, and perform-ance: First-year report to OERI and the participating school districts.* Philadel-phia, PA. Unpublished report.

Darling-Hammond, L. (1997). *The right to learn: A blueprint for creating schools that work.* San Francisco: Jossey-Bass.

Dewey, J. (1938). *Experience and education.* New York: Macmillan.

Dobzhansky, T. (1973). *Genetic diversity and human equality: The facts and fallacies in the explosive genetics and education controversy.* New York: Basic Books, Inc.

Greeno, J. G., Collins, A. M., & Resnick, L. B. (1996). Cognition and learning. In D.C. Berliner & R.C. Calfee (Eds.), *Handbook of educational psychology.* New York, Macmillan.

Gould, S. (1994, November 28). The bell curve, curve ball. *New Yorker, 28,* 139–149.

Grant, J., Johnson, B., & Richardson, I. (1996). *The looping handbook: Teachers and students progressing together.* Peterborough, NH: Crystal Spring Books.

Hall, T. (1998, April 1). A gray-and-white matter. St. Paul, MN: *Star Tribune,* p. A8.

Henderson, N., & Milstein, M. M. (1996). *Resiliency in schools: Making it happen for students and educators.* Thousand Oaks, CA: Corwin Press.

Herrnstein, R., & Murray, C. (1994). *The bell curve: Intelligence and class structure in American life.* New York: Free Press.

Huitt, W. G. (1997). Success in the information age: A paradigm shift. Paper pre-sented at the Georgia Independent School Association, Atlanta, GA.

Jensen, A. R. (1973). *Educability and group differences.* New York: Harper & Row.

Kamin, L. (1974). *The science and politics of I.Q.* New York: Lawrence Erlbaum Associates.

Knapp, M., Shields, P. M., & Turnbull, B. J. (1995). Academic challenge in high-poverty classrooms. *Phi Delta Kappan, 76,* 770–776.

Koppitz, E. M. (1975). *The Bender Gestalt Test for young children.* New York: Grune & Stratton.

Ladson-Billings, G. (1994). *The dreamkeepers: Successful teachers of African-American children.* San Francisco: Jossey-Bass.

Levine, J. M., Resnick, L. B., & Higgins, E. T. (1993). Social foundations of cogni-tion. *Annual Review of Psychology, 44( ),* 585-612.

Lipman, P. (1998). *Race, class, and power in school restructuring.* New York: State University of New York Press.

McClure, R. (1988). Schools for the 21st century. *Context (18),* 41–47.

Meece, J. & McColskey, W. (1997). *Improving student motivation: A guide for teach-ers and school improvement teams.* Greensboro, NC: SouthEastern Regional Vision for Education.

National Center for Education Statistics. (1997). *The condition of education 1997.* Washington, DC: U.S. Department of Education.

Neisser, O. (1998). *Rising curve: Long-term gains in IQ and related measures.* Washington, DC: American Psychological Association.

Newcombe, E., Eaton, J., Williams, B., & Kinney, D. (1995). *Urban learner framework research-based themes in programs recommended for increasing urban students' success.* Philadelphia, PA: Research for Better Schools.

Oakes, J., Wells, A. S., & Associates. (1996). *Beyond the technicalities of school reform: Policy lessons from detracking schools.* Los Angeles, CA: UCLA Graduate School of Education & Information Studies.

Orfield, G., Bachmeier, M., James, D. R., & Eitle, T. (1997). *Deepening segregation in American public schools.* Harvard University: Taubman Center for State and Local Government.

Perkins, D. N. (1998). Mindware and the metacurriculum. In D. Dickinson (Ed.), *Creating the future: Perspectives on educational change.* Seattle, WA: New Horizons for Learning.

Resnick, L. D. (1995). From aptitude to effort: A new foundation for our schools. *Daedalus, (124)4,* 55-62.

Richmond, G. (1997). *The microsociety school: A real world in miniature.* Philadelphia, PA: MICROSOCIETY.

Rossi, R., & Stringfield, S. (1995, September). What we must do for students placed at risk. *Phi Delta Kappan, 76*(1), 73-76.

Rutter, M. (1987). Psychosocial resilience and protective mechanisms. *American Journal of Orthopsychiatry, 57,* 316–331.

Shokraii, N. H. (1998, January 30). School choice 1998: A progress report. *The Heritage Foundation* [Website]. Http://www.heritage.org/library/categories/education/fyi172.html.

Stringfield, A., Rossi, S., & Smith, L. (1996). *Bold plans for school restructuring: The new American schools designs.* Mahwah, NJ: Lawrence Erlbaum Associates.

Suskind, R. (1998). *A hope in the unseen: An American odyssey from the inner city to the ivy league.* New York: Broadway Books.

Toffler, A. (1990). *Powershift.* New York: Bantam Books.

21st Century Learning Initiative. (1997). *Executive summary; initiative synthesis.* Washington, DC: Author.

Walberg, H. J. & Greenberg, R. C. (1998, April 8). The diogenes factor: Why it's hard to get an unbiased view of programs like 'Success for All.' *Education Week, 17*(30), 52.

Wang, M. C., Haertel, G. D., & Walberg, H. J. (1998). *Building educational resilience.* Bloomington, IN: Phi Delta Kappa Educational Foundation.

Werner, E. E. & Smith, R. S. (1992). *Overcoming the odds: High risk children from birth to adulthood.* Ithaca, NY: Cornell University Press.

Williams, B. (1996). *Closing the achievement gap: A vision for changing beliefs and practices.* Alexandria, VA: Association for Supervision and Curriculum Development.

Williams, B., & Newcombe, E. (1994, May). Building on the strengths of urban learners. *Educational Leadership, 51,* 75–78.

Williams, B., & Woods, M. (1997, April). Building on urban learners' experiences. *Educational Leadership, 54,* 29–32.

Wozniak, R. H., & Fischer, K. W. (Eds.). (1993). *Development in context: Acting and thinking in specific environments.* Hillsdale, NJ: Lawrence Erlbaum Associates.

Vygotsky, L. S. (1978). *Mind in society.* Cambridge, MA: Harvard University Press.

Section II.

Creating a New Era — Educational Reform for the 21st Century

The Role of
Standards in
Educational Reform
for the 21st Century

Peter W. Hill
Carmel A. Crévola

There are pressing reasons for educators to find ways to improve student performance. Doing well at school and college has never been more important for young people. High levels of educational attainment translate into improved life and career opportunities. The higher the level of education attained, the more choices the individual has and the lower the probability of ending up in a dead-end job or joining the ranks of the under- or unemployed.

At a collective level, society relies heavily on high levels of education. Values such as equality, fraternity, and democracy are hard to sustain without highly educated citizens. Moreover, high levels of education are essential for economic prosperity, particularly through the formation of a flexible, dynamic, and highly skilled work force. The demand for unskilled labor has almost disappeared in advanced economies as they have experienced the full impact of globalization and the technological revolution. The factors that once were critical in determining the wealth of nations—labor, capital, and resources—have given way to new factors, namely the knowledge, attitudes, and skills of the work force. No country that wishes to ensure social cohesion and ongoing economic prosperity is in a position to settle for anything less than a world-class education system.

In most English-speaking countries, including the United States, there is little cause for complacency with respect to student performance. According to several international surveys of achievement, such as the recent Third International Mathematics and Science Study (TIMSS, 1996a, 1996b, 1997a, 1997b), it is clear that performance levels of students in countries such as the United States are not in the first rank when benchmarked against those of other developed countries with similar levels of investment in education.

Looking at average levels of performance, however, masks the real picture. It is instructive to look instead at the increasing spread of achievement over successive years of schooling within a cohort of students.

THE LEARNING GAP

Although many students perform at a reasonable level and a few at an exceptionally high level, there is a significant proportion of students who do not reach minimally acceptable standards, who experience early failure in the classroom, and who fall further and further behind their peers. For example, a recent national literacy survey in Australia (Australian Council for Educational Research, 1997) found that around 30 percent of students failed to reach a nominated benchmark, or minimally acceptable standard. Although there has been considerable controversy over whether this standard was the correct standard, there was no denying the major finding of the survey: the existence of a "learning gap" of at least five years of schooling separating the top and bottom 10 percent of students in grades 3 and 5.

Another Australian study that collected longitudinal achievement data on five different cohorts of students in the State of Victoria (Rowe & Hill, 1996) found that although the gap between low- and high-achieving students in the first year of schooling was relatively small, it quickly became large. By 10th grade, students at the 10th percentile in reading were performing at the level of the average student in 3rd grade. Even by 3rd grade, the learning gap revealed in the two Australian studies was so large that for low-achieving students, catching up with their peers was virtually impossible.

These students face the prospect of an additional nine years of repeated failure in school and reduced opportunities thereafter, with all that such prospects mean for reduced self-esteem. A learning gap of this magnitude is of serious concern in a society that values equity and a "fair go" for all. It is also a serious issue for teachers. Managing learning and ensuring that all students make progress in classrooms with a five-year gap separating the top and bottom 10 percent become virtually impossible tasks.

In addition to the personal costs to the students and the professional frustrations for teachers, there are the social and economic costs that the community has to bear for its undereducated children and adults. These include higher probabilities of repeating grades (an expensive and generally ineffective response), dropping out, unemployment, conviction for criminal offenses, low tax contributions, and high dependence on social security and welfare benefits.

ZERO-TOLERANCE POLICIES

Awareness of these costs has caused political leaders in countries such as Australia, Canada, the United States, and the United Kingdom to mount an assault on low standards and to announce policies of "zero tolerance of educational failure." These policies involve setting standards that are challenging and that (almost) all students are expected to achieve. They also involve establishing targets for meeting these standards over a finite period of time, and national and/or state assessment programs to ascertain the extent to which the targets are being met. Finally, and most importantly, they involve refocusing the mission of schools and redesigning their operation so that meeting the standards comes first in everything that schools do.

Tucker and Codding (1998) note that in the United States, a defining moment for such policies was the first national summit on education, held in 1989, when President George Bush invited state governors to a meeting at which they agreed on a set of ambitious national education goals to be achieved by the year 2000. The debate quickly moved on, with the American Federation of Teachers, then under the leadership of Al Shanker, promoting the case for standards, examining practices overseas, and issuing its own report card on standards in the United States as a means of drawing attention to the need for challenging standards in all states (American Federation of Teachers, 1996). The national discipline associations, such as the National Council of

Teachers of Mathematics, became active in developing and publishing standards for their disciplines. Business leaders got behind the standards movement and sponsored the Second National Education Summit at the IBM Palisades Conference Center in New York, at which state governors agreed to produce standards for their states within two years. Partnerships were established involving charitable trusts and foundations, educators, discipline associations, academics, and states and districts to develop standards. One of the most productive of these has been that led by Professor Lauren Resnick of the University of Pittsburgh and Marc Tucker of the National Center on Education and the Economy to develop New Standards in English Language Arts, Mathematics, Science, and Applied Learning (National Center on Education and the Economy, 1997). Finally, states and districts across the nation have taken up the challenge by adopting new standards and new policies that embody zero tolerance of failure to meet these new standards.

Other countries have also demonstrated bipartisan support for zero-tolerance policies. In Australia, a defining moment was the so-called Hobart Declaration of the Australian Education Council (the standing council of federal and state/territory ministers for education), which endorsed "Common and Agreed National Goals for Schooling in Australia." The Hobart Declaration paved the way for another landmark decision in March 1997, when federal and state/territory ministers agreed to develop national educational benchmarks, or standards, and endorsed a new national goal—that every child commencing school from 1998 onward will achieve a minimum acceptable literacy and numeracy standard within four years. Both at the federal and state levels, substantial reshaping of funding, accountability, and school support arrangements are taking place to ensure that this national goal is achieved and that all students achieve the new standards.

THE PROMISE OF STANDARDS-BASED EDUCATION

Setting national goals that are based on world-class standards is commendable, but are zero-tolerance policies in education realistic? Or are schools being saddled with impossible expectations, and are they being "set up" by the politicians for inevitable failure?

A former prime minister of Australia, R. J. Hawke, once claimed that through the implementation of his government's policies "no child will live in poverty." The sentiment was noble, but it was also unrealistic, and before too long it was apparent to everyone just how unwise it is to promise too much. So the question must be asked: Is it wise to announce policies that assume that all children can achieve success at school?

Based on our experiences in working with many schools serving educationally disadvantaged students, we are optimistic that the war on low standards can be won. We also believe that our best prospects for winning the war lie in refining and implementing an approach to improvement that is referred to in this chapter as "standards-based education." So, the purpose of this chapter is to answer the question, What is standards-based education and what could standards-driven reform mean? In the chapter, we describe key elements of a standards-based model for improving student performance and illustrate these elements using a major project in early literacy. Then we share a perspective on the benefits of such a standards-based model and describe the system support that is needed for its success. Finally, we return to the overall theme of educational reform in the 21st century and discuss why we think this reform must have a standards-based core if it is to be successful.

A "DESIGN" APPROACH TO IMPROVEMENT

A highly readable account of the meaning and power of standards-based education is that of Tucker and Codding (1998). At the most general level, standards-based education refers to the search for ways of thinking about and operating schools and school systems that ensure that all students achieve defined and challenging standards of performance.

Paradoxically, standards-based education is both very familiar and very new. It is familiar in the sense that countless initiatives throughout the history of public schooling have focused on standards as a means of improving student learning outcomes. It is also familiar in the sense that most of the elements that make up standards-based education are well known to teachers and school administrators. They can be found to varying degrees in almost all schools and school systems.

What is new about standards-based education is (1) the degree of focus and commitment to the goal of ensuring that all students achieve defined and challenging standards of performance, (2) the coherence and depth of the beliefs and understandings that underpin the response, and (3) the rigor and sophistication with which every aspect of schools and school systems is examined, redesigned, and managed to ensure that high standards are achieved. Standards-based education is

121

not about incremental improvement of classrooms, schools, and school systems; it is about transforming the whole ecology of schooling to obtain the desired result. This means identifying all of the critical elements of the school and of the school system, working out what needs to change in order for them to operate effectively and in alignment with all the other elements, and then redesigning them accordingly. Wilson and Daviss (1994) describe the redesign process as follows:

> The redesign process is the integration of research, development, dissemination, and refinement by which innovations and the procedures that create them are originated, improved, and made affordable. . . . the redesign process is an institutionalized method of strategic, systemic change that works unceasingly to enact a vision of excellence as well as to redefine excellence itself when changing conditions make it necessary. (p. 22)

In the United States, there are now a number of designs that adopt a comprehensive, whole-school approach to improvement of learning outcomes. The best known are the nine designs promoted by the New American Schools Development Corporation (Stringfield, Ross, & Smith, 1996). Each design required many hundreds of hours of work by teams of educators all working to create a completely coherent and consistent approach to improvement, based wherever possible on best practice and findings from the research literature. These designs were then piloted in a small number of schools and subject to rigorous evaluation before being implemented more widely.

In this chapter, we illustrate the power of standards-driven reform by using a general design for improving learning outcomes (see Figure 6.1). This design emerged out of our experiences in working with a group of 27 disadvantaged elementary schools in Victoria, Australia, in the Early Literacy Research Project (ELRP), an attempt to bring about substantial improvements in early literacy outcomes. The model is relevant, however, for outcomes other than literacy and for students other than those in the early grades.

The design shown in Figure 6.1 has been heavily influenced by the research literature on educational effectiveness, which indicates that "proximal" factors—those closest to the instructional process, such as classroom practices—are much more important than "distal" factors, such as state and district governance and organization and school characteristics (Wang, Haertel, & Walberg, 1993) and that the impact of classroom effects on "value-added progress" greatly exceeds that of school effects (Creemers & Reezigt, 1996; Hill & Rowe, 1996; Monk, 1992).

122

FIGURE 6.1

General Design for Improving Learning Outcomes

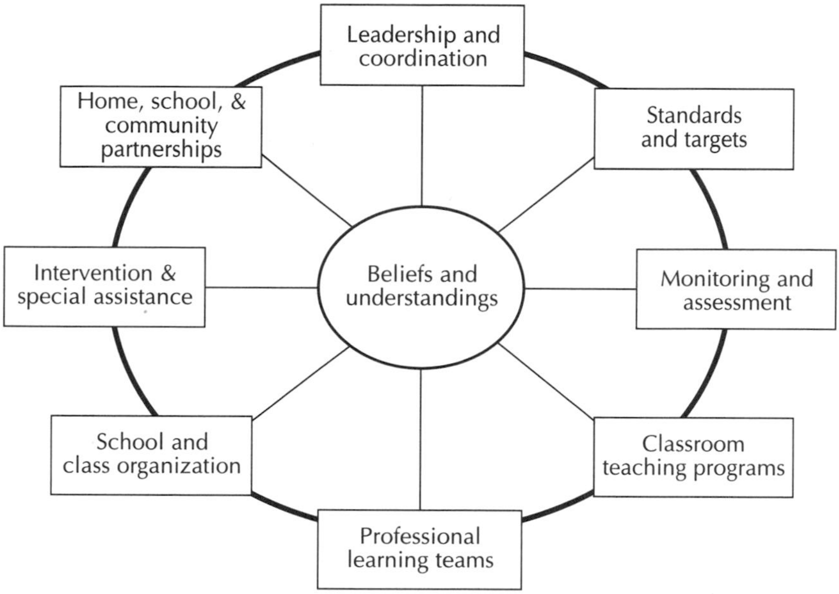

Source: Hill & Crévola, 1997.

The design is also influenced by the knowledge that a small number of factors are consistently shown to be associated with improved learning. Scheerens and Bosker (1997) conclude on the basis of meta-analyses of findings and best-evidence syntheses that the basic factors underlying instructional effectiveness are (1) time on task; (2) closeness of content covered to assessment instruments; (3) a structured approach with specific objectives, frequent assessment, and corrective feedback; and (4) types of adaptive instruction that can be managed by teachers. We would argue, on the basis of the same evidence, that the literature on effectiveness supports just three factors:

- High expectations of student achievement,
- Engaged learning time, and
- Structured teaching focused on the learning needs of students.

Improving learning thus involves focusing on those elements of the operation of systems, schools, and classrooms that determine whether expectations are high, whether students are engaged in learning, and whether teaching is focused on the learning needs of students. Those elements, we would suggest, are the ones depicted in Figure 6.1., p. 123. The following sections briefly describe each element and include illustrations based on our involvement in the Early Literacy Research Project.

BELIEFS AND UNDERSTANDINGS

Beliefs and understandings about teaching and learning occupy the central position in the design summarized in Figure 6.1. The literature on school effectiveness has consistently drawn attention to high expectations as a characteristic of effective schools (Mortimore, Sammons, Stoll, Lewis, & Ecob, 1988; Sammons, Hillman, & Mortimore, 1994; Scheerens, 1992). Unless teachers believe they can make a difference and have a commitment to doing so, the impact of the other elements is seriously diminished. Our general design is based on a belief in the capacity of the overwhelming majority of students to make progress, given sufficient time and support. This belief is supported by research in the field of cognitive science, which has confirmed that almost all students can engage in higher-order learning given the right conditions (Glaser, 1984; Resnick, 1998).

At the commencement of the Early Literacy Research Project (ELRP) it was evident that many of the trial schools had a culture of low expectations and a tendency to make excuses for low-achieving students, particularly those from educationally disadvantaged homes. These beliefs were challenged by referring to research findings regarding the power of good classroom teaching and the capacity of almost all students to learn. They were also addressed by collecting and analyzing detailed observational data that demonstrated that the majority of students began school with a sufficient base of knowledge (including oral language, concepts about print, and letter knowledge) to enable teaching to begin and for learning to occur.

STANDARDS AND TARGETS

High expectations of student achievement must be reflected in explicit standards that have been benchmarked against those of other systems to ensure that they reflect "best practice." Standards and associated targets drive the model summarized in Figure 6.1. They constitute the starting point for refocusing the mission of schools and redesigning how they operate so that meeting the standards comes first in everything that schools do.

When it comes to student achievement in core areas of the curriculum, it is useful to think in terms of two kinds of standards: content standards and performance standards. Content standards define the "what" and "when" of the curriculum: what is to be taught and in what order. Content standards provide a map of the curriculum that can be used to ensure that important content is covered and not overlooked and that students are not being retaught the same material at the same level of difficulty.

In addition to content standards, it is important to have performance standards and broad agreement as to what these might be. Performance standards attempt to define to what level students will progress and by which grade. Performance standards form the basis of longer-term goals for school systems and of shorter-term targets for individual schools and for individual students. They also provide the basis of system accountability, funding, and support arrangements.

For too long, many school systems have operated without adequate content standards or performance standards. This situation is changing as the result of concerted efforts by policymakers, legislators, and partnerships of interested groups.

At the commencement of the ELRP, schools had the benefit of content standards published by the State Board of Studies, but they lacked detailed performance standards and associated targets relevant to the first three years of schooling. This gap was filled by adopting a set of precise standards and targets derived from those of Clay and Tuck (1991) in their "three waves of teaching." Clay and Tuck argue that with good teaching in the first year of schooling, one can expect 80 percent of students to be under way as beginning readers and writers. During the second year of schooling, with good teaching and with appropriate one-on-one intervention, one can expect that a further 18 percent will be under way. This leaves approximately 2 percent who will need further referral and special support during their third year of schooling.

Minimum and target standards were developed to gauge the standard reached by students and in particular their level of performance in reading. The latter was established with a reference to student performance on a set of unseen, graded texts. Figure 6.2 (p. 126) summarizes the standards.

FIGURE 6.2

Literacy Standards for Kindergarten and Grade 1

Stage of Schooling	Target Percent of Students Meeting Standard	Minimum Text-Level Standard	Target Text-Level Standard
End of kindergarten	80	1 or above	5 or above
End of grade 1	98	15 or above	20 or above

It is worth commenting on three features of these standards. First, there is strong research evidence that they are achievable. For example, the minimum standard in grade 1 of a text level of 15 was chosen because this is the minimum level at which students enrolled in Reading Recovery (a one-to-one intervention for the lowest-performing students in a class) are discontinued from the program.

Second, the decision to identify both a minimum standard and a target standard was intended to ensure that the targets embodied a challenge for all schools and for all students and did not focus solely on the bottom end of the performance continuum. To specify only minimum standards is to run the risk of encouraging a culture of low expectations for the majority of students.

Third, the targets were specifically linked to an explicit level of performance and to a procedure for assessing whether students had reached that standard. This was achieved by using Reading Recovery Text Levels (which range from 1 to 26) and adding two additional levels, by using a set of benchmark texts that had been carefully leveled, and by keeping a running record of each student using these unseen texts.

These targets have provided the impetus for the ELRP with respect to setting appropriate expectations and have provided a benchmark for evaluating progress toward meeting the overall national literacy goal.

MONITORING AND ASSESSMENT

A standards-based approach implies regular monitoring and assessment. Assessment is important to establish whether targets have been met and whether progress has been made toward ensuring that all students meet the standards. But monitoring and assessment involve much more than establishing how far students have traveled. The most important function of monitoring and assessment within the design summarized in Figure 6.1 (p. 123) is to help the teacher find out as much as possible about each student, to establish starting points for teaching, and to use this diagnostic information to drive classroom teaching programs.

Effective teachers know that they must focus their teaching on the learning needs of each student and build on students' strengths in seeking to remedy their weaknesses. This implies finding out as quickly as possible what each student does and does not know. Effective teachers also make a habit of monitoring their students' progress so that they can ensure that each student is always working within his or her level of challenge or "zone of proximal development" (Vygotsky, 1978).

Assessment within the ELRP has focused on making teaching information driven. Assessment has guided decision making with respect to the identification of and intervention for "at risk" students and to ensure that teaching is matched to the learning needs of students. It has also been used to evaluate the effectiveness of the overall program. Consistent with the principle that instruction should be based on a detailed observation of each child as a learner, all classroom teachers within the ELRP trial schools keep daily running records of their children. They use the resulting information to establish dynamic instructional groups within the classroom and to ensure that students are working on texts at an appropriate level of difficulty. In addition, teachers carry out detailed, systematic observations of each child at the beginning and end of each year, based on Clay's *Observation Survey of Early Literacy Achievement* (1993) and *Record of Oral Language* (Clay, Gill, Glynn, McNaughton, & Salmon, 1983). Although this is a time-consuming process, it means that teachers have a detailed diagnostic profile of each student and the information necessary for making their teaching efficient and focused.

CLASSROOM TEACHING PROGRAMS

Effective teaching is structured and focused on the learning needs of each student in the class. This constitutes the most difficult challenge faced by teachers, particularly given the wide range of needs and abilities within the typical classroom. It requires teachers to have detailed understandings of how children learn, and well-developed classroom routines, structures, organization, and management related to the teaching of groups. It also requires teachers to motivate and engage students using a range of classroom practices and strategies.

The ELRP has looked to the good early literacy teaching practices operating in New Zealand classrooms as a basis for developing balanced and focused teaching programs (Department of Education, New Zealand, 1985). Within the ELRP, teachers combine the following strategies in their daily literacy programs:

- Oral language
- Reading to children
- Language experience (reading)
- Shared reading
- Guided reading
- Independent reading
- Modeled writing
- Language experience (writing)
- Shared writing
- Interactive writing
- Guided writing
- Independent writing

In each of the ELRP trial schools, the classroom literacy program consists of a reading and writing workshop conducted within a two-hour teaching block. Each session begins and ends with a teacher-directed, whole-class focus. Small-group activities make up the main part of each workshop. This allows for explicit teaching of instructional groups, while the rest of the class is engaged in self-regulated activities in learning centers. Wherever possible, volunteers help the students remain on task and free the teacher for small-group teaching. In this way, the expertise of the teacher is applied at the point of greatest need.

Figure 6.3 describes the structure of the two-hour literacy teaching block in greater detail. It is within this three-part (whole-class, small-group, whole-class) structure that each of the above strategies is integrated into effective classroom practice.

PROFESSIONAL LEARNING TEAMS

A crucial element in any design aimed at improved teaching and learning in schools is the provision of effective, ongoing, and practical professional learning opportunities for teachers. Improving student learning outcomes is utterly dependent upon improving the quality of classroom teaching. The general design summarized in Figure 6.1 (p. 123) not only assumes that good teachers make a difference, but that processes need to be in place to ensure that all classes are operating at the same level as the most effective classes in terms of improving student learning outcomes.

In our experience, the great majority of teachers are able to improve their effectiveness as professionals, given the right conditions and support. But achieving quantum improvements in teacher effectiveness is difficult if not impossible using traditional models of professional development and inservice training.

FIGURE 6.3

Structure of the Daily Two-Hour Literacy Teaching Block in the Early Literacy Research Project

Whole-Class Focus

The daily reading workshop begins with a whole-class focus based on the shared reading strategy. Shared reading may involve books, charts, poems, songs, etc. The daily writing workshop begins with a whole-class focus that consists of either modeled writing or shared writing. This element of the classroom program sets the scene for the workshop, providing an initial teaching focus and specific teaching of the visual information of print, including direct instruction in phonics. This is a teacher-directed time.

Small-Group Teaching Focus

This section of the reading and writing workshop focuses on the explicit teaching of small groups of students. During the reading workshop the teacher uses the strategies of reading to children, language experience, and guided reading, while other children are working in learning centers. During the writing workshop the teacher uses the strategies of language experience, interactive writing, and guided writing, while the remainder of the class is engaged in independent writing and various other activities included to extend understanding of grammar and spelling. During this segment students take responsibility for large sections of their learning time.

Whole-Class Focus: Sharing

This concluding section of both the reading and writing workshops is a time for reflection, when students articulate what they have learned and the teacher encourages the development of the students' oral language skills. Like the first part of the literacy teaching block, this is a teacher-directed time.

Effective professional learning assumes effective leadership to create the motivation and commitment to change and improve. It also involves intensive, sustained, theoretically based yet practically situated learning, with opportunities to observe good practice, to be involved in coaching and mentoring processes, and to take time for reflection (Fullan, 1991, 1993; Hargreaves & Fullan, 1991). Moreover, professional learning is most powerful when it occurs within the context of teachers working as members of a team and in pursuit of specific learning outcomes for students.

Teachers do not improve by remaining professionally isolated in their classrooms. We would argue that the establishment of "professional learning teams" is critical to "deprivatizing" teaching (Wehlage & Stone, 1996, p. 300) and to creating both a culture and a process for ongoing improvement in the quality of teaching in schools. As members of professional learning teams, teachers increasingly assume joint responsibility for the learning outcomes of *all* the students under their care, so that successful learning becomes a shared responsibility, not just a responsibility of the individual classroom teacher. They also assume responsibility for each other's professional growth and development so that successful teaching is also a shared responsibility in which the team provides individual members with both the pressure and the support to improve.

Within the ELRP, professional learning teams have been established comprising the classroom teachers of all students in the first three grades in each participating school. Each team has been placed under the leadership of a coordinator with a 0.6 to 1.0 time release. In addition, each team has been provided with eight full days of off-site, university-based professional development in the first year of implementation and four days in the second year. The coordinators have attended twice the number of sessions. On-site professional development has taken place through weekly meetings of learning teams, through opportunities created by the coordinators for modeling, demonstrating, coaching, mentoring, and observing each other, and through visits to professional learning teams operating in other ELRP schools.

A vital component of the professional learning program has been a full-day visit to each of the trial schools by the university-based professional development coordinator. These visits have been critical in making a direct connection between understandings gained during off-site professional development sessions and the actual working knowledge (classroom practice) of the teachers involved. They have also provided opportunities for the coordinator and the principal to raise leadership issues pertaining to a particular school.

SCHOOL AND CLASS ORGANIZATION

To maximize engaged learning time and focused teaching, it is necessary to ensure that

• Schools are organized around the learning needs of students (as opposed to, for example, the work conditions of teachers);
• Adequate time is allocated for core learning related to the standards, and that this time is free from external interruptions;
• Resources are allocated to support the coordination of professional learning teams and to provide time for these teams to meet regularly;
• The students who are most at-risk receive extra time and support; and
• Classes are organized in ways that facilitate focused teaching and minimize external interruptions and internal disruptions.

The above considerations give rise to a range of practical issues relating to school organization, staffing, scheduling, class size and composition, and classroom organization.

ELRP schools have had to confront a host of school and class organization issues. In the early stages, there were major challenges in ensuring an adequate allocation of time for specific literacy instruction. Although many schools had formerly provided for a daily two-hour literacy block, over the years new content had been added to the curriculum and more time had been allocated to areas such as the visual and performing arts, languages other than English, information and other technologies, and health and physical education. Invariably, these additions came at the expense of time devoted to direct literacy instruction. In other words, schools had reached the stage when it was necessary to reassess priorities and deal with the problems generated by an overcrowded curriculum.

Once schools had allocated adequate time to direct literacy instruction, the actual time available was still much less than the official time allocated, because of frequent interruptions. These included planned or semiplanned events such as school assemblies, which were often scheduled during prime learning time; and the withdrawal of students for special activities and programs, excursions, rehearsals, swimming lessons, and so on. They also included unplanned interruptions such as messengers entering the classroom during lesson time, public address system announcements, collections of monies, dealing with personal issues of individual students and teachers, and so on.

Although some of these interruptions were unavoidable or even desirable, it was also apparent that many were of the sort that should never happen. In a school culture that values the work of the classroom teacher and sees teaching as something of paramount importance, every effort should be made to respect the need for freedom from interruptions. Thus ELRP schools had to put in place simple rules or conventions to minimize interruptions to scheduled lesson time. There were also major issues relating to class composition and classroom organization. Many of the trial schools had established composite or multigrade classes to accommodate uneven numbers of students in different grade levels. Others had, for philosophical reasons and as a matter of choice, opted for multiage groupings of students. Reviews of research into multigrade and multiage grouping practices (Mason & Burns, 1997; Veenman, 1995, 1997) indicate that there are neither negative nor positive effects associated with these forms of class organization. On the other hand, positive effects are associated with those forms of class organization that facilitate teaching focused to the learning needs of students (Kulik & Kulik, 1992). Within the ELRP, some schools continue to use multigrade and multiage forms of class organization, but all have four or five dynamic instructional groups within each class and use learning centers and task management boards to ensure "on-task" behavior of students during the small-group focus of the two-hour literacy block.

INTERVENTION AND SPECIAL ASSISTANCE

Even with the very best classroom teaching, a significant proportion of students fail to make satisfactory progress. Among these students are those with disabilities and impairments, those who come from homes devoid of books and who see no purpose in school learning, those who may have severe emotional blocks that interfere with their concentration, and those who are frequently absent from school.

For such students, early intervention is essential to enable them to catch up quickly to their peers. Without timely and effective intervention, these students continue to fall further and further behind in their school work and experience diminished self-esteem and increased alienation from schooling. Schools have a narrow window of opportunity to help these students catch up, and the only real answer to narrowing the learning gap is to intervene quickly, relentlessly, and with all the resources at the school's disposal.

In the context of early literacy, Wasik and Slavin (1993) have found conclusive evidence to support the efficacy of various one-to-one tutoring programs. Of these programs, Reading Recovery has produced the most impressive evidence (Pinnell, Lyons, DeFord, Bryk, & Seltzer, 1994). Although one-to-one tutoring is relatively costly, Dyer (1992) has estimated substantial net cost savings as a result of its use. There is also a need for special assistance for students who continue to experience difficulties after intensive one-to-one intervention. This assistance might take the form of referral to specialists or placement in special settings. More generally, it involves individual learning plans devised in consultation with the school principal, the classroom teacher, specialists, and parents or caregivers.

At the commencement of the project, ELRP trial schools were required to commit to the implementation or maintenance of the Reading Recovery one-to-one tutoring program for at least three years. Reading Recovery has thus constituted the focus of intervention efforts for those grade 1 students making the least progress. Regrettably, resource constraints have meant that the number of Reading Recovery teachers available within the trial schools has fallen short of what has been required to serve the targeted number of at-risk first-year students. Nevertheless, schools have been able to provide coverage for 21 percent of the total cohort of grade 1 students. Furthermore, the average level of performance of students discontinued from the Reading Recovery program has been consistently at or above the average level of performance of the grade 1 students.

HOME/SCHOOL/COMMUNITY PARTNERSHIPS

Links with the home and the community are important at all levels of schooling. A strong body of research shows that when parents, caregivers, and the community support the work of the school and are involved in its activities, students make greater progress (Booth & Dunne, 1996; Cairney, Ruge, Buchanan, Lowe, & Munsie, 1995; Epstein, 1991). But effectiveness requires more than simply establishing links with the home. What is needed is comprehensive and permanent programs of partnerships with families and communities.

The way schools care about children is reflected in the way schools care about children's families. If educators view children simply as "students," they are likely to see families as separate from the school. That is, the family is expected to do its job and leave the education of the children to the school. If educators view the students as "young people," they are likely to see the family and the community as partners with the school in the children's education and development.

There are many reasons for developing school, family, and community partnerships. They can improve school programs and school climate, provide family support and services, increase parents' skills and leadership, connect families with others in the school and in the community, and help teachers with their work. However, the main reason to create such partnerships is to help students succeed in school and in later life. When parents, teachers, and students view one another as partners in education, a caring community forms around students and becomes one that supports learning.

Within the ELRP, successfully connecting with parents has been one of the schools' greatest challenges, given high proportions of students from non-English-speaking backgrounds. In some trial schools, more than 40 different languages are spoken in students' homes, and non-English-speaking students constitute up to 90 percent of the student population. This generates a communication gap that has to be dealt with in creative ways in order to address fundamental issues such as regular attendance at school.

In such schools it has also been difficult to recruit parent volunteers to help during school hours in classrooms. Schools have had to go into the wider community to forge new links with volunteers willing and able to act as classroom helpers.

LEADERSHIP AND COORDINATION

Leadership and coordination are critical ingredients in the general design summarized in Figure 6.1. Studies of effective schools have consistently drawn attention to the importance of strong educational leadership, and indeed it is often cited as their most important characteristic (Edmonds, 1979; Levine & Lezotte, 1990; Rutter, Maughan, Mortimer, Ouston, & Smith, 1979). Good teaching may be possible in a school with weak and ineffective leadership, but it is harder. Change and sustained improvement are extremely difficult, if not impossible, without good leadership, particularly where whole-school change is sought.

Standards-based education implies a renewed focus on instructional leadership. In the final analysis, how leadership is exercised in one school as opposed to another may vary considerably. Much depends upon personalities and individual strengths. In one school, the principal may play a very up-front, hands-on role; in another school, the principal may play a low-key role and leave much of the leadership role to a coordinator or other staff members. The important thing is that there is strong leadership within the school, regardless of the level at which it is exercised and by whom, and that it is directed to ensuring that all is done that is necessary to enable all students to meet the standards.

Moreover, the leadership role will change over time and depending on the phase reached in redesigning the school and in transforming teaching and learning. Miles talks about change as progressing through three phases, namely initiation, implementation, and institutionalization (quoted in Fullan, 1991). During each phase, the principal and the leadership team need to be able to provide an appropriate balance of pressure and support. Pressure is necessary to provide a stimulus and an incentive to change and improve. Low expectations and complacency are unavoidable consequences of lack of pressure. At the same time, pressure needs to be balanced with the kind of support and assistance that staff need in order to change and improve. Improvement in schools rarely happens simply by raising the level of challenge or by exhorting teachers to work harder or more effectively. It happens because the right mix of pressure and support are in place.

Within the ELRP, the critical role of the principal in ensuring the success of the program has been recognized in the form of regular meetings with the project team to discuss progress, share concerns, and participate in shaping the ongoing direction of the project. Principals have been key players at every stage of implementation, even though they have been able to delegate much of the work associated with the project to a coordinator.

As part of the initial conditions of entry to the project, trial schools were required to appoint a project coordinator. The coordinators have proved crucial to success within the ELRP schools by ensuring the right mix of pressure and support. Their role has been to assist in the development of classroom materials; provide direction, support, and assistance to classroom teachers; develop, implement, and coordinate the program elements in consultation with the school principal; coordinate data collection; provide in-school professional development for teachers; and disseminate information to the school community.

THE POSITIVE EFFECTS OF A WELL-DESIGNED PROGRAM

Incorporating the above general design elements into a specific whole-school approach to improvement and reform implies a massive investment of time and other resources. Staff are more likely to make such a commitment if there is strong empirical evidence that implementation of the reforms is likely to lead to the desired outcomes. Slavin (1997) has argued that it is important that there be multisite evaluations of the effectiveness of specific designs, using matched control groups of schools. Undertaking rigorous evaluations of whole-school designs is a costly and technically demanding business, but if the outcomes are positive and produce firm evidence regarding the efficacy of a particular design, that evidence is likely to be powerful in leveraging additional resources and in influencing policies regarding the allocation of existing resources.

The ELRP is designed around annual pre- and post-testing over a three-year period (1996–1998) in the 27 trial schools and a matched sample of control or reference schools. The results of an initial evaluation of the first year of implementation (1996) are presented in Crévola and Hill (1998). Using 10 separate measures of literacy progress and following adjustment for a range of background characteristics, effect sizes for participating schools in excess of 0.6 of a standard deviation were achieved. Unpublished data indicate that over the two-year period of 1996 through 1997, the proportions of students meeting the defined minimum standards increased from 49 percent to 75 percent in the preparatory grade, and from 70 percent to 91 percent in grade 1. In other words, although the ELRP schools had not reached the targets of 80 percent (preschool) and 98 percent (grade 1) by the end of 1997, they were expected to do so by the end of 1998.

Already results from the project have had a major impact on funding policies. In May 1998, the state government announced significant additional funding to assist all Victoria, Australia, government primary schools in implementing its *Keys to Life* program (Department of Education, Victoria, 1997). This program is based on the design elements summarized in Figure 6.1, p. 123. The additional funds have been specifically targeted to cover the appointment of a literacy coordinator and the implementation of Reading Recovery in every state primary school. The approach to making the extra funds available represents one of the first attempts by an Australian education system to specifically link additional resources to improved learning outcomes of students: The state will provide the funding on the condition that schools submit plans that commit them in an ongoing way to meeting challenging, predefined standards and to implementing a design approach based on the elements described above.

A SYSTEM POLICY AND SUPPORT FRAMEWORK

The general design of Figure 6.1 (p. 123) assumes that when it comes to improving teaching and learning, the most important action happens at the level of schools and classrooms. There is, however, a vital role for states and districts in implementing policies and in establishing a framework of support for schools. Within a standards-based approach to reform, the primary tasks of states and districts are to do the following:

• Determine standards and set systemwide and school-specific, year-by-year targets,

• Focus school support services and available funds on achieving the standards and targets,

• Put in place accountability and incentive arrangements linked to performance against standards and targets,

• Conduct periodic full-cohort testing to monitor performance against the standards and targets, and

• Conduct or sponsor research and evaluation of those programs and designs that have been identified as most useful in meeting the standards and targets.

These tasks should be the main priority of states and districts. In some cases, making such tasks the main priority implies a reduced emphasis on controlling and administering schools and related bureaucratic activities, and a rebuilding of the center around those roles that only the center can and should do.

In Victoria, Australia, the state government has pursued a policy known as Schools of the Future involving radical reforms of educational administration structures at the central and regional levels. Schools have been given substantial autonomy aimed at improving the quality and responsiveness of local decision making and hence the quality of the education provided to students. The intentions of the Schools of the Future program reflect a general trend both within Australia and in other English-speaking countries to decentralize educational administration and to devolve responsibility, authority, and accountability directly to the school level (Caldwell, 1993; Caldwell & Spinks, 1992).

Along with this increased autonomy, government schools have implemented new arrangements for ensuring accountability for the delivery of educational services and especially for improved student learning outcomes (Caldwell & Hayward, 1998). A curriculum and

137

standards framework has been developed, and schools are required to make the achievement of nominated standards the main priority in their school charters and to report publicly on their progress toward meeting these standards in their annual reports.

LOCKING IN IMPROVEMENT

The final phase in a standards-based approach is institutionalization, in which reform initiatives are no longer regarded as discrete projects with a defined beginning and end, and the key elements of the reforms are embedded in the ongoing structures, processes, and practices of the school. This institutionalization of reform does not always happen. All too often, at the end of a project that has resulted in significant improvement, when there is no longer the same focus on the reform process, people gradually revert to the old ways of doing business. Key personnel become exhausted or move on, and the school becomes preoccupied with new priorities and issues.

To prevent this from happening, schools and school systems must lock in the changes that have led to improvement. Indeed, it is important to go a stage further and incorporate continuous improvement processes into daily operations so that the gains achieved during the implementation phase are not only sustained but progressively extended. This is a challenge that ELRP schools and the wider state school system in Victoria, Australia, will confront over the coming years. At this stage, although the reforms have led to impressive improvements, they remain fragile and could easily dissipate.

TRANSFORMING OUR SCHOOLS

We began this chapter with the view that achieving high student performance must be the number-one priority of schools in the 21st century. However, narrowing the learning gap and ensuring that all students meet high standards will not happen given existing practices and structures. The answer lies in refocusing the mission of schools and school systems and redesigning how they operate so that meeting the standards comes first in everything that schools do.

In the 21st century, standards-based education will involve adopting a design approach to transforming the whole ecology of schooling so that everything is directed at meeting high standards. This means identifying all of the critical elements of schools and of school systems that have an impact on reaching the standards, working out what needs to change in order for the elements to operate effectively and in alignment with one another, and then redesigning the elements accordingly. We have described a general design that is based around these critical elements and illustrated it with references to the Early Literacy Research Project, which has involved implementing reforms within a sample of schools serving mainly educationally disadvantaged students to ensure that all students achieve early success in literacy.

The good news emerging from the ELRP in Australia and from many other standards-driven reform initiatives in the United States and elsewhere is that quantum improvements in student learning *can* be achieved on a relatively large scale and in a relatively short time. Within the ELRP, not only have levels of student performance increased dramatically, but there has also been an equally dramatic improvement in the morale and feelings of efficacy and achievement among teachers and school administrators. Moreover, the impact has been felt well beyond the sample of trial schools as the system has responded quickly to enable the reforms to penetrate all schools.

In our view, and in light of such evidence, all students should have a right to an education system that ensures high standards for all. The responsibility for ensuring that this happens rests not with one person, but with everyone with an interest in the future.

REFERENCES

American Federation of Teachers. (1996). *Making standards matter.* Washington, DC: Author.
Australian Council for Educational Research. (1997). *Literacy standards in Australia.* Canberra, Commonwealth of Australia.
Booth, A., & Dunne, J. (Eds.). (1996). *Family-school links: How do they affect educational outcomes?* Hillsdale, NJ: Erlbaum.
Cairney, T. H., Ruge, J., Buchanan, J., Lowe, K., & Munsie, L. (1995). *Developing partnerships: The home, school and community interface.* Canberra: Department of Employment, Education and Training.
Caldwell, B. J. (1993). *Decentralizing the management of Australia's schools.* Burwood, Victoria, Australia: National Industry Education Forum.
Caldwell, B. J., & Hayward, D. K. (1998). *The future of schools: Lessons from the reform of public education.* London: Falmer Press.
Caldwell, B. J., & Spinks, J. M. (1992). *Leading the self-managing school.* London: Falmer Press.
Clay, M. M. (1993). *An observation survey of early literacy achievement.* Auckland, New Zealand: Heinemann Education.

Clay, M. M., Gill, M., Glynn, T., McNaughton, T., & Salmon, K. (1983). *Record of oral language and biks and gutches*. Auckland, New Zealand: Heinemann Publishers.

Clay, M. M., & Tuck, B. (1991). *A study of Reading Recovery subgroups: Including outcomes for children who did not satisfy discontinuing criteria*. Auckland, New Zealand: University of Auckland.

Creemers, B. P. M., & Reezigt, G. J. (1996). School level conditions affecting the effectiveness of instruction. *School Effectiveness and School Improvement, 7*(6), 197–228.

Crévola, C. A., & Hill, P. W. (1998). Evaluation of a whole-school approach to prevention and intervention in early literacy. *Journal of Education for Students Placed at Risk, 3*(2), 133–157.

Department of Education, New Zealand. (1985). *Reading in the junior classes*. Wellington, New Zealand: School Publications.

Department of Education, Victoria. (1997). *Keys to life early literacy program*. Melbourne: Longman & Education Australia.

Dyer, P. C. (1992). Reading Recovery: A cost-effectiveness and educational outcomes analysis. Spectrum: *Journal of Research in Education, 10*(1), 10–19.

Edmonds, R. R. (1979, September). Effective schools for the urban poor. *Educational Leadership, 37*, 15–17.

Epstein, J. L. (1991). Effects on student achievement of teacher practices of parent involvement. In S. Silvern (Ed.), *Advances in reading/ language research: Vol. 5. Literacy through family, community and school interaction* (pp. 261–276). Greenwich, CT: JAI Press.

Fullan, M. (1993). *Change forces: Probing the depths of educational reform*. New York: Falmer Press.

Fullan, M., with Stiegelbauer, S. (1991). *The new meaning of educational change*. London: Cassell.

Glaser, R. (1984). Education and thinking: The role of knowledge. *American Psychologist, 39*(2), 93–104.

Hargreaves, A., & Fullan, M. (1991). *Understanding teacher development*. London: Cassell.

Hill, P. W., & Crévola, C. A. (1997). *The literacy challenge in Australian primary schools*. IARTV Seminar Series No. 69. Melbourne, Australia: IARTV.

Hill, P. W., & Rowe, K. J. (1996). Multilevel modeling in school effectiveness research. *School Effectiveness and School Improvement, 7*(1), 1–34.

Kulik, J. A., & Kulik, C. L. C. (1992). Meta-analytic findings on grouping programs. *Gifted Child Quarterly, 36*(2), 72–77.

Levine, D. U., & Lezotte, L. W. (1990). *Unusually effective schools: A review and analysis of research and practice*. Madison, WI: National Center for Effective Schools Research and Development.

Mason, D. A., & Burns, R. B. (1997). Reassessing the effects of combination classes. *Educational Research and Evaluation, 3*(1), 1–53.

Monk, D. H. (1992) Education productivity research: An update and assessment

140

of its role in education finance reform. *Education Evaluations and Policy Analysis, 14*(4), 307–332.

Mortimore, P., Sammons, P., Stoll, L., Lewis, D., & Ecob, R. (1988). *School matters: The junior years.* London: Paul Chapman Publishing.

National Center on Education and the Economy. (1997). *New standards performance standards.* Washington, DC: Author.

New Standards. (1997). *Performance standards: English language arts, mathematics, science, applied learning.* Washington, DC: Author.

Pinnell, G. S., Lyons, C. A., DeFord, D. E., Bryk, A. S., & Seltzer, M. (1994). Comparing instructional models for literacy education of high-risk first graders. *Reading Research Quarterly, 29*(1), 9–38.

Resnick, L. B. (1998). *Education and learning to think.* Washington, DC: National Academy Press.

Rowe, K. J., & Hill, P. W. (1996). Assessing, recording and reporting students' educational progress: The case for "subject profiles." *Assessment in Education, 3*(3), 309–352.

Rutter, M., Maughan, B., Mortimer, P., Ouston, J., & Smith, A. (1979). *Fifteen thousand hours: Secondary schools and their effects on children.* Cambridge: Harvard University Press.

Sammons, P., Hillman, J., & Mortimore, P. (1994). *Key characteristics of effective schools: A review of school effectiveness research.* London: Office for Standards in Education (OFSTED).

Scheerens, J. (1992). *Effective schooling: Research, theory and practice.* London: Cassell.

Scheerens, J., & Bosker, R. (1997). *The foundations of educational effectiveness.* Oxford: Pergamon.

Slavin, R. E. (1997). Design competitions and expert panels: Similar objectives, very different paths. *Educational Researcher, 26*(6), 21–22.

Stringfield, S., Ross, S., & Smith, L. (Eds.). (1996). *Bold plans for school restructuring: The New American Schools designs.* Mahwah, NJ: Lawrence Erlbaum.

(TIMSS) Beaton, A. E., Martin, M. O., Mullis, I. V. S., Gonzales, E. J., Smith, T. A., & Kelly, D. L. (1996a). *Science achievement in the middle school years: IEA's Third International Mathematics and Science Study (TIMSS).* Chestnut Hill, MA: Boston College.

(TIMSS) Beaton, A. E., Mullis, I. V. S., Martin, M. O., Gonzales, E. J., Kelly, D. L., & Smith, T. A. (1996b). *Mathematics achievement in the middle school years: IEA's Third International Mathematics and Science Study (TIMSS).* Chestnut Hill, MA: Boston College.

(TIMSS) Martin, M. O., Mullis, I. V. S., Beaton, A. E., Gonzales, E. J., Smith, T. A., & Kelly, D. L. (1997a). *Mathematics achievement in the primary school years: IEA's Third International Mathematics and Science Study (TIMSS).* Chestnut Hill, MA: Boston College.

(TIMSS) Martin, M. O., Mullis, I. V. S., Beaton, A. E., Gonzales, E. J., Smith, T. A., & Kelly, D. L. (1997b) *Science achievement in the primary school years:*

IEA's Third International Mathematics and Science Study (TIMSS). Chestnut Hill, MA: Boston College.

Tucker, M. S., & Codding, J. B. (1998). *Standards for our schools: How to set them, measure them and reach them.* San Francisco: Jossey-Bass.

Veenman, S. (1995). Cognitive and noncognitive effects of multigrade and multiage classes: A best-evidence synthesis. *Review of Educational Research, 65*(4), 319–381.

Veenman, S. (1997). Combination classes revisited. *Educational Research and Evaluation, 3*(3), 262–276.

Vygotsky, L. (1978). *Mind in society: The development of higher psychological processes.* (M. Cole, V. John-Steiner, S. Scribner, & E. Souberman, Eds. & Trans.). Cambridge, MA: Harvard University Press.

Wang, M. C., Haertel, G. D., & Walberg, H. J. (1993). Towards a knowledge base for school learning. *Review of Educational Research, 63*(3), 249–294.

Wasik, B. A., & Slavin, R. E. (1993). Preventing early reading failure with one-to-one tutoring: A review of five programs. *Reading Research Quarterly, 28,* 179–200.

Wehlage, G. G., & Stone, C. R. (1996). School-based student and family services: Community and bureaucracy. *Journal of Education for Students Placed at Risk, 1*(4), 299–317.

Wilson, K. G., & Daviss, B. (1994). *Redesigning education.* New York: Henry Holt and Company.

7

Making Better Use of Resources for Educational Reform

ALLAN R. ODDEN

Dollars are important to the tasks of restructuring schools to meet the demands of the 21st century. Though schools may need more dollars to accomplish the goal of teaching most students to high standards, from the school perspective a focus just on obtaining more dollars may be short-sighted. Most education dollars are now spent at the school site—but district officials often make all those spending decisions. Principals and teachers often have little say in how dollars are spent but usually can identify many ways that they would rather spend their school resources. So one critical fiscal goal for the schools of the next century should be providing schools with more authority to spend site resources in ways that best meet site needs. Because site budgets usually total millions of dollars, this authority can literally transform current dollars into millions of "new" dollars from the site perspective.

A fiscal focus on the school site is quite different from the district focus that has existed for nearly the entire 20th century—states fund school districts, school districts decide how those funds are to be used, and fiscal systems report only on districtwide patterns of expenditure and resource use. A school focus for the purpose of creating and

143

funding an education strategy that can be effective in teaching students to much higher achievement levels requires three major changes in school finance: (1) a new state-to-district finance system, (2) a district-to-school system to budget dollars (as opposed to staff resources) to each school site, and (3) better use of education resources by the school site. This chapter addresses each of these topics.

REDESIGNING STATE-TO-DISTRICT FINANCE STRUCTURES

Commenting on state school finance systems at the close of the 20th century, Odden and Clune (1998) argue that state school finance systems are "aging structures in need of renovation." They identify several reasons for that assertion, including the ineffectiveness of such systems in improving fiscal equity across districts over the past several decades, and the need to link the finance system to the goals and strategies of standards- and school-based education reform. They also address the need for more *school*-based financing policies as well as performance incentives to spur higher results. In sum, they propose shifting school finance away from its traditional emphasis on fiscal equity and toward a focus on educational adequacy and the school site, combined with mechanisms that provide schools with authority to allocate and use dollars, and incentives to improve results.

In parallel, independent, but complementary lines of analysis, several economists new to school finance analysis also have identified faults with state school finance systems (Downes & Pogue, 1994; Duncombe, Ruggiero, & Yinger, 1996; Imazeki & Reschovsky, 1997/1998; Ladd & Yinger, 1994; Reschovsky, 1994). They also have suggested a shift to adequacy and in addition have developed a means to measure and implement an adequacy-oriented education funding system.

In short, state school finance systems have come under attack, not just because they are not doing the job they were created to do, but because these old systems are inadequate both for current finance problems and for the ambitious education and education finance challenges that states face at the dawn of the 21st century.

The traditional focus of school finance has been on fiscal equity—that is, assessing the degree of spending differences across districts. To be sure, large differences have historically been unfair and were caused by widely varying property tax bases across districts. School finance programs designed to remedy these tax base problems were effective in raising overall education spending but only modestly effective in reducing spending differences (Evans, Murray, & Schwab,

1997) and even less effective in reducing the linkages between spending and wealth (Odden, 1998b). Indeed, today in many states that have new school finance programs, significant spending differences still exist, and they are still strongly tied to local wealth (General Accounting Office, 1997). Further, many low-wealth districts have looked at the potential provided by new school finance programs to raise spending, and they have traded that potential for low school tax rates instead. In short, the traditional school finance strategies for reducing spending differences across districts caused by differences in the local tax base have not worked very well (Odden & Picus, 1992).

Further, such a policy focus at best addresses issues of fiscal fairness and does not address the more substantive issues of student performance and how to use resources more effectively to boost student achievement. Given that the driving education goal across the country is to teach students to high standards, the new focus of a state school finance system should be on this agenda. The goal should be first to determine a spending base that is "adequate" to fiscally support an education program that can teach the average student to those standards. This suggests a foundation type of school finance program (Odden, 1998b). And the critical educational element of a foundation program is the base spending level. To follow the new directions of school finance, then, the task is to determine an "adequate" base spending level.

DETERMINING AN ADEQUATE FISCAL BASE[1]

There are at least three major ways to determine an adequate spending level: (1) identify a set of inputs and cost them out; (2) link a spending amount per pupil to a level of student performance; and (3) build a number from the bottom up by identifying the cost of schoolwide programs, including strategies discussed in this volume, that produce desired outcomes.

Identify inputs and cost them out. The input approach began nearly two decades ago when the state of Washington essentially identified the average staffing (teachers, professional support staff, administration, etc.) in a typical district and, using statewide average costs, calculated a spending level. To a substantial degree, Washington still uses this approach. More sophisticated input approaches also have been developed

---

[1]This section draws from Odden (1998b).

(Chambers & Parrish, 1994; Guthrie et al., 1997). These approaches use groups of professional educator experts to identify (1) staffing levels for the regular education program, and (2) effective practices and accompanying staffing and resource needs for compensatory, special, and bilingual education. The cost of all ingredients are then calculated using average price figures and are then adjusted by a geographic education price index to determine the funding level of each district or school.

The advantage of the input approaches is that they identify a set of ingredients that an amount of dollars would be able to purchase in each school district, including additional resources for three categories of special needs students, all adjusted by a price factor. The disadvantage is that the resource levels are connected to student achievement results only indirectly or inferentially through professional judgment and not directly through actual measures of student performance.

Link spending to a level of student performance. The second approach seeks to directly link a spending level to a specified level of student performance. Two procedures have been used. The first determines a desired level of performance using state tests of student performance, identifies districts that produce that level of performance, selects from that group those districts with characteristics comparable or close to state averages, and then calculates their average spending per pupil (Alexander, Augenblick, Driscoll, Guthrie, & Levin, 1995; Augenblick, 1997; Hinrichs & Laine, 1996). Interestingly, in all three studies, the level of spending identified was approximately the median spending per pupil in the state. The other procedure uses an economic "cost function" approach. This approach seeks to identify a spending-per-pupil level that is sufficient to produce a given level of performance, adjusting for characteristics of students and other socioeconomic characteristics of districts; this method also can be used to calculate how much more is required to produce the specified level of performance by factors such as special needs of students, scale economies or diseconomies, input prices, and even efficiency. Using Wisconsin data, Imazeki and Reschovsky (1998) identified an expenditure level that was also close to the median of spending per pupil. Similar cost function research has been conducted by others (Duncombe, Rugierrio, & Yinger, 1996).

Identify the costs of a high-performance school model. The third approach to adequacy has been to identify the costs of a "high-performance" school model—a schoolwide design crafted specifically to produce desired levels of student academic achievement—and to determine a level of spending that would be sufficient to fund such a model. New Jersey has taken this approach, using the Roots and

146

Wings/Success for All school design (Slavin, Madden, Dolan, & Wasik, 1996). There are several other schoolwide models being developed across the country (Northwest Regional Educational Laboratory, 1998; Stringfield, Ross, & Smith, 1996), all with reasonable costs (Odden & Busch, 1998). Early results suggest that the schoolwide models show promise for accomplishing the goal of teaching students to higher standards (Edison Project, 1997; Slavin & Fashola, 1998). Odden and Busch (1998) analyzed the costs of two such models—the Modern Red Schoolhouse and Roots and Wings/Success for All—and found that they could be financed and implemented with the national median expenditure per pupil.

Much additional research is needed to identify "adequate" expenditure levels. Each approach discussed here has strengths and weaknesses, and none has been perfected. But at their core, these new approaches to school finance seek to link spending levels with student achievement results—the appropriate objective for a school finance system for the next century.

ADJUSTING FOR SPECIAL NEEDS

Because some students require more services to reach the standards, the foundation base should be augmented by some extra amount of money for at least three major categories of students—those from low-income backgrounds, the disabled, and those who need to learn English. Research shows that an extra $1,000 for each student from a low-income background is about the level needed for that category of student (King, 1994; Odden, 1998b). Research also shows that it costs about an extra 130 percent to serve all disabled students (Chaikind, Danielson, & Braven, 1993; Chambers, Parrish, & Hikido, 1996; Odden & Picus, 1992; Parrish, 1996).

All dollar figures also should be adjusted by an education price index to ensure that the dollar figures provide equal education purchasing power to districts and schools across the wide range of geographic regions and labor markets in a state. Fortunately, the National Center of Education Statistics (NCES) has developed different versions of such education price adjustments (Chambers, 1995; McMahon, 1994); any state could use these externally developed price adjustments. States have been reluctant to add education price adjustments to their school aid formulas, in part because developing them requires some complex econometric analyses and manipulations and in part because they substantially change the distribution of state aid. The existence of the

NCES price indices, however, would allow states to use a price adjustment factor that has been developed by the best experts in the country under the auspices of a neutral governmental body.

THE NEW STATE-TO-DISTRICT SCHOOL FINANCE STRUCTURE IN BRIEF

In short, the new type of school finance structure that aligns the finance system with the policy system goal of teaching students to ambitious proficiency standards would consist of five elements:

1. A base spending level that would be considered "adequate" for the average child.

2. An extra amount of money for each child from a low-income background—approximately $1,000 in a combination of federal Title I and state compensatory education dollars.

3. An extra 130 percent for each disabled student.

4. An extra amount for each student who needs to learn English.

5. A price adjustment for all dollar figures to ensure comparable spending power.

Although the foundation base level of spending might be approximated by the median spending level in many states, in many other states, particularly those in the South and West, the *state* median would be insufficient. Preliminary research suggests that the *national* median is the lowest level of current spending that would approximate an "adequate" spending level (Odden & Busch, 1998). Thus, the foundation base might be set at the national or state median, whichever is higher. Implementing this approach, however, would require a new federal role in school finance, focused on those states that cannot or do not now provide a level of fiscal resources for education that would allow their schools to select and implement a schoolwide strategy robust enough to teach their students to high and rigorous performance standards.

PERFORMANCE ENHANCEMENT ELEMENTS

Odden and Clune (1998) argue that this type of new school finance structure could be strengthened by performance enhancement elements. They suggest three major elements, all rationalized as both aligning the school finance system to the *school*-based element of education reform and providing incentives to spur higher performance:

1. Provide school sites substantial control over their resources, so they can reallocate funds to the needs of more effective, higher

performance school strategies (see Bodilly, 1998; Odden & Busch, 1998), an issue addressed in the next section.

2. Change teacher compensation to provide salary increases for the knowledge, skills, and expertise teachers need to teach a more rigorous curriculum and to engage in the required actions related to school restructuring and resource reallocation (Odden & Kelley, 1997).

3. Create school-based performance incentives that provide monetary rewards for schools that consistently improve student achievement from one year to the next (Kelley, 1997; Kelley, 1998; Heneman, 1998; Kelley, Milanowski, & Heneman, 1998).

In sum, state-to-district school finance systems are aging and in need of change. The traditional focus on fiscal equity did not improve equity all that much and now needs to give way to the issue of adequacy; education program and finance systems need to be reengineered to 21st century strategies that allow and provide incentive to schools to teach students to high standards. Though the details of all elements of such a strategy are not completely known, the broad outlines of the strategy are known, and states should move as quickly as possible to design and implement these new and more effective approaches to school finance structures.

CREATING DISTRICT-TO-SCHOOL FORMULA FUNDING SYSTEMS[2]

It is quite possible that school districts as we know them might be disbanded sometime in the next century. For the foreseeable future, however, they very likely will remain a core element of the education system. The suggestions in the previous section would improve current state-to-district school finance mechanisms by actually providing a level of dollars to each district that would be sufficient for each school in that district to teach its students to high achievement standards. The next necessary fiscal step in designing a new school finance system is to budget the dollars to the school site and provide sites with the authority to use those dollars in ways that support revised instructional and related organizational strategies.[3]

---

[2]This section draws from Odden (1998a).
[3]Ross and Levacic (1998) provide examples from several countries for how a needs-based formula system can be created to fund school sites equitably, adequately, and effectively. The various chapters in the book indicate how four English-speaking democracies, including Australia, England, New Zealand, and several large districts in North America, are beginning to accomplish this goal. The chapter on North America (Odden, 1998a) argues that the school-based funding formulas developed by five large urban districts were part of overall, comprehensive district strategies created explicitly to dramatically improve student performance, whereas the formulas in the other countries were created as elements for decentralizing school systems within more of an "economic rationalization" framework.

The first decision in creating a budgeting system using a site-based formula is to determine how much of district operating and capital revenues should be budgeted to the school site. Though this often has been just a political decision, the substantive approach is to determine which functions should be centrally provided, which should be site provided, and which might be provided by either depending on the context. Odden and Busch (1998) conduct this functional analysis for a typical U.S. state and suggest quite strongly that each U.S. state should create, as England has done, an overall school-based budgeting framework, including this functional allocation, that would guide districts in the processes of decentralizing their finances to school sites. They also suggest that the framework include the macro elements of the district site formula, thus allowing each district to identify the specific formula parameters but having all districts take the same general approach.

Drawing on the formulas from Broward County, Florida; Cincinnati, Ohio; Edmonton, Alberta; Pittsburgh, Pennsylvania; and Seattle, Washington, Odden (1998b) shows that once the amount that will be budgeted to school sites has been determined, the funding formulas have five general elements:

- A base allocation for the "norm" student,
- Adjustments for grade-level differences,
- Enhancements for curriculum purposes,
- Adjustments for different student needs, and
- Adjustments for different and unique school needs.

Overall these elements mirror the general categories of state-to-district funding formulas; the interesting fact is that each of the districts discussed had all of these elements and oftentimes several adjustments for each element. For example, under the category of curriculum enhancement, districts provided extra funds for magnet schools, vocational education, drop-out prevention, foreign language, and numerous small, targeted curriculum enhancements. In the category of different student needs, each district had multiple, elaborate, and extensive adjustments for students from low socioeconomic backgrounds, low-achieving students, students with disabilities, students with limited proficiency in English, and drop-outs. Under the category of unique school needs, each district had some type of or multiple augmentations for small school size; the most common approach was to provide each school, regardless of size, a flat "lump sum" that was sufficient to provide for a principal, an office secretary, and perhaps even core staffing. In short, the leading-edge districts in North America created relatively comprehensive and sophisticated mechanisms for formula funding their school sites, and the formulas addressed not only core educational needs but also additional educational needs related to curriculum, students, and school sites.

The most surprising finding for the formulas were the adjustments for different grade levels. The common practice across the world is to provide more funds for secondary than for primary schools (OECD, 1997), and the typical pattern in the United States is to provide about 25 to 30 percent more for high schools as compared to elementary schools (Odden & Picus, 1992). Indeed, one of the primary contentions that has emerged as governments have shifted funding to the school site has been the higher funding of secondary students (Odden & Busch, 1998, chaps. 4 and 5). The formulas in these five districts took very different approaches to this issue. Pittsburgh was the only district to provide such differential funding to secondary students. The other districts either provided no or very small distinctions between elementary and secondary students (Edmonton and Broward), or actually weighted the system in favor of elementary school students (Seattle). In this sense, the grade-level weights in the five school districts studied represented quite different decisions regarding resource allocation.

Although the grade-level weights adopted by these five jurisdictions cannot be taken as indicative of practice across North America, they nevertheless reflect a major fiscal value shift in the basic allocation of resources for these districts, away from the traditional bias of higher-funded secondary students and toward a new bias of greater funding for elementary students, particularly elementary students in grades K–3. The rationale for this shift in resource allocation is to develop the basic skills early in the elementary career of a child, under the assumption that if students can read, write, and do mathematics proficiently by grade 3, then teachers at higher grades have virtually an unlimited horizon of expectations for student achievement. Of course, this also reflects the obverse of this proposition—that late intervention for secondary students who have not developed good literacy and numeracy skills is not only inefficient but also very difficult to make effective.

The following is one example of a simple yet comprehensive version of a school-site funding formula. The proposed grade-level weights reflect those currently used in many states—0.5 for a half-day kindergarten student, 1.0 for each student in grades 1 through 6, and 1.3 for each student in grades 7 through 12.

A. Lump sum:
  - $100,000 for elementary schools
  - $150,000 for middle schools
  - $200,000 for high schools

B. Base allocation and pupil grade-level weights:
  - Base allocation = $3,500
  - 1.0 for grades K, 3–5
  - 1.2 for grades 1 and 2
  - 1.2 for grades 6–8
  - 1.3 for grades 9–12

C. Extra weights for special need:
  - 0.4 for compensatory education
  - 1.3 for all categories combined of disabled students
  - 0.2 for limited English proficient students

D. Special factors:
  - Square footage of buildings or land
  - Unique school needs
  - Special programs for the severely disabled

For a K–5 elementary school with 420 students (about 70 students in each grade), 50 percent of them low income and 10 percent disabled, the budget would be as follows:

$100,000 + $3,500[140(1.2) + 280(1.0) + 420(0.50)(0.4) + 420 (0.10)(1.3)] + unique factors, or

$100,000 + $3,500 (168 + 280 + 84.0 + 54.6) + unique factors. or

$100,000 + $3,500 (586.6) + unique factors, or

$100,000 + $2,053,100 + unique factors, or

$2,153,100 + any unique budget factors.

In short, this formula shows that the school would receive a lump sum of about $2.15 million plus any budgets for unique factors. Such a strategy provides schools with dollars rather than a set of specified staff, and would allow schools—indeed, would require schools—to determine how to allocate and use the dollars, thus empowering schools to engage in patterns of resource use different from current practice (Odden, Monk, Nakib, & Picus 1995).

There is another approach to providing schools with resources that represents a strategy in between current practice, in which districts essentially provide schools with a variety of different staff, and the above dollar budgeting. This strategy also allows the district to play a role in reallocating school resources. Furthermore, this approach reflects some of the strategies now being deployed in San Antonio, in which more than 50 percent of the district's schools have selected different comprehensive school designs. As an example of this approach, consider an elementary school with 500 students. The district could provide the following resources:

- 1 principal
- 1 instructional facilitator
- 20 regular classroom teachers for a class size of 25
- 4 more teachers for planning and preparation time
- 1 reading tutor
- $1,000 for each child from a low-income family (combination of any state compensatory education money and federal Title I dollars)
- $50,000 for professional development, not to be spent on permanent staff
- $100,000 for additional school design costs
- A sum appropriate for supplies, materials, etc.
- Funding for disabled students

This is a budget level well within current resources now provided to the average elementary, middle, and high school. Part of the rationale for this resourcing configuration is explained in more detail in the next section, but a few comments are in order here. First, each school is provided with a full-time instructional facilitator, in addition to the principal. This position is a part of nearly all comprehensive school designs (Stringfield, Ross, & Smith, 1996) and provides ongoing instructional leadership. Currently this kind of position is rare in schools and represents a clear reallocation of resources.

Second, the budget includes a total of 24 undesignated teacher professional positions, which is sufficient to have an actual class size of 25, plus an additional 20 percent allotment of teachers to provide all teachers with at least one planning period a day. If a district's overall expenditure level would allow for a more generous staffing (for lower class sizes), that would be fine; but such a staffing is what the average U.S. school is provided (Odden & Busch, 1998). The teachers for the planning and preparation time could be used for any purpose selected by the schools; in the Modern Red Schoolhouse design, for example, at least two of these teachers would be art and music teachers. Third, each school is provided with a full-time reading tutor, under the assumption that all elementary schools will have some students who need intensive early intervention in order to learn to read by the 3rd grade (Crévola & Hill, 1998). The funds from the category that provides $1,000 per low-income child could be used to hire additional tutors in schools with poverty concentrations above 25 percent to provide a reading program that includes more tutors, such as the Success for All program (Slavin, Madden, Dolan, & Wasik, 1996). The amount for professional development is high, but so is the level required to implement a higher-standards curriculum program that is part of nearly all comprehensive school designs (Odden, 1997a). Both of these latter two elements are also rare for a school budget, and also represent substantial departures from traditional allocations.

Finally, alternative school designs have different specific needs, which largely could be met with some combination of the $100,000 provided for school designs, additional compensatory education funds, or funds for students with mild disabilities. Again, such a use would represent additional resource reallocation.

The point of the second example is that providing a lump-sum dollar budget is not the only viable way to provide schools with resources and the ability to reallocate them to the needs of higher-performance school strategies. A more mixed model, which fits the general needs of many school designs, is also a possibility, and might even be more feasible as a first step toward moving more resources and decision making about use of those resources to school sites.

IMPROVING THE USE OF EDUCATIONAL RESOURCES AT THE SCHOOL SITE[4]

Once a school receives resources through a new funding system, the task of the principal and faculty is to determine how best to use the funds. Indeed, the authority to allocate site funds in ways that meet a school's identified needs often is seen as more important fiscally than actually receiving more money. After all, when it includes personnel expenditures, the budget of most schools is in the millions of dollars and thus provides numerous possibilities for deploying resources differently.

---

[4]This section draws from Odden (1997a, 1997b) and Odden and Busch (1998), Chapter 7.

Of course, the first question is whether schools want to or actually would engage in different resource behaviors if they were able to do so. Although research in the United States is equivocal on this question, research in places that have actually provided substantial budgetary authority to school sites (Caldwell & Hayward, 1998; Levacic, 1995; Odden & Busch, 1998, chap. 5; Odden & Odden, 1996) finds schools almost immediately engage in resource reallocation practices and want to retain this budget decision-making authority. Though the degree of reallocation is modest in the first year, over time, the magnitude of resource reallocation increases substantially, and most schools begin to align their budget with their school improvement priorities.

There is some research in the United States on the potential for resource reallocation to have a positive effect on student performance. The goal, of course, is not just different behaviors in use of resources but reallocation of resources to implement strategies that lead to higher performance. Miles and Darling-Hammond (1997) and Murnane and Levy (1996) studied several schools that used resources differently from traditional practice and improved student performance. The schools in these studies were able to do all of the following *without any extra funding:*

- Reduce class sizes,
- Create even lower class sizes for reading,
- Reduce the daily student-teacher contact numbers in the high schools from around 150 to fewer than 100,
- Personalize the teaching-learning environment,
- Provide common planning time, and
- Expand professional development.

Although all schools faced obstacles and challenges in implementing these different strategies in use of resources and continued to provide appropriate services to students with special needs, they nevertheless engaged in substantive resource reallocation. They also improved educational results for students, particularly in core academic subjects and including special needs students. In short, the schools improved the productivity of their existing educational dollars through restructuring of program, organization, and resources.

How was this possible? Essentially, schools restructured from a bureaucratic to a more high-performance organizational structure. Most schools reflect a bureaucratic form of organization. Jobs are defined narrowly—principals manage schools and teachers teach students, often with a fairly set curriculum and assumed teaching strategies. As

155

schools face new issues—e.g., desegregation; disabled, low-achieving, and limited English proficient (LEP) students; students with more emotional and psychological problems, etc.—programs are created that provide money to enable schools to hire "specialist" staff to deal with the problems largely outside of the regular classroom. Teachers remain in the regular classroom, and specialists teach handicapped, low-achieving, or LEP students in pull-out classrooms or counsel and help students with emotional/psychological needs. Earlier examples of this phenomenon were the specialists added to school staffs to teach vocational education, physical education, and even art and music. Growth by addition and specialization has characterized the education system for several decades.

Indeed, recent studies have shown that the vast bulk of new dollars provided to schools over the past 30 years were not spent on the core instructional program but on specialist teachers and other services provided outside of the regular classroom (Lankford & Wykoff, 1997; Rothstein & Miles, 1995). And many other studies have shown that these programs and services have produced modest if any long-lasting impacts on student achievement (Allington & Johnston, 1989). These dollars represent laudable values; poor, limited English proficient, and disabled students need extra services. The values that provide the extra dollars for these additional services should be retained, but the productivity of the expenditure of these dollars needs to rise.

As a result of the increase in specialist staff, regular classroom teachers—the primary service providers—constitute a declining portion of professional staff in schools. The National Commission on Teaching and America's Future (1996) found that regular classroom teachers as a proportion of all professional staff fell from 70 percent in 1950 to 52 percent in 1995, with 10 percent of the latter not engaged in classroom teaching. In one case study, Miles (1995) showed how the Boston Public Schools had sufficient funding to provide class sizes of around 15, but actually provided class sizes from 25 to 30 because so much money was used for specialist and other nonacademic services provided outside the regular classroom.

This additional staffing falls into three categories: regular education specialists, categorical program specialists, and pupil support specialists. Each category has become a "regular" part of most school programs and is assumed as "necessary" or "expected" for running schools. Specialists are not perceived as "fat" or "organizational slack." They have been provided to schools for many years because they have been assumed to be critical to accomplishing school goals. The reality for schools that choose to implement one of the many high-performance school designs that are emerging across the United States is that while they have these resources today, few if any of these resources are part of any high-performance school design (see Odden & Busch, 1998, for an elaboration of this argument).

Several national school reform networks now offer whole-school education designs that have a cost structure very different from traditional schools: the New American Schools (NAS), which offers seven school designs (Stringfield, Ross, & Smith, 1996); America's Choice Schools (Tucker & Codding, 1998); Core Knowledge Schools (Hirsch, 1996); Accelerated Schools (Finnan, St. John, McCarthy, & Slovacek, 1996); the Coalition of Essential Schools (Sizer, 1996); the School Developmental Program (Comer, Haynes, Joyner, & Ben-Avie, 1996); the Edison Project (1994); and several others. The cost structures of these schools have many similarities. In addition to a principal and one teacher for each classroom of 25 students, most have a full-time instructional facilitator and require substantial funds ($25,000 to $60,000) for ongoing professional development. Several designs include substantial computer technologies, some have reading tutors to ensure that all elementary students learn to read, and others have various additional design-specific elements (Odden & Busch, 1998; Odden, 1997a).

Figure 7.1 (p. 158) shows in concise form how the approach to staffing and resourcing taken by many of these high-performance school designs differs from the approach typical of most schools. In addition to the core staffing of one principal and 20 teachers for a school of 500 students (25 students in each classroom), districts typically hire a series of specialists—regular education specialists, categorical program specialists, and pupil support services specialists, with little or no money for training. The specialists are supposed to handle functions, duties, and student needs that are different from regular instruction. In contrast, most comprehensive designs for high-performance schools account for these functions by expanding teacher jobs to include instructional as well as other specialized tasks. They require an instructional facilitator (to help teachers continually improve the instructional program) and substantial investment in ongoing professional development to develop new skills and competencies.

These are key differences, with traditional schools representing a bureaucratic approach and the new school designs representing a high-performance approach to organization and management. Indeed, the reduction in the number of "specialists," the stronger emphasis on staff providing the core service of instruction, the expansion of the job

FIGURE 7.1

School Staffing Patterns

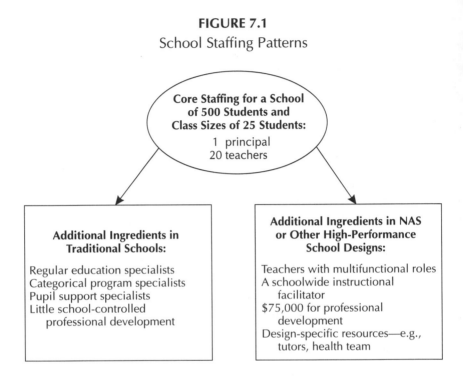

of the core-service provider to include multiple functions, and the emphasis on ongoing training and professional development are characteristic of most evolving high-performance organizations (Lawler, 1986, 1992, 1996) and particularly high-involvement, high-performance schools (Darling-Hammond, 1996; National Commission on Teaching and America's Future, 1996). This is how organizations restructure and reorganize for higher performance using current or even reduced resources.

Odden and Busch (1998) present several facts about these new school designs:

• They organize students within schools into smaller units, with 500 being about the largest student population. In this way, they provide a more personalized environment for all students.

• They are affordable for the average elementary, middle, and secondary school in the United States.

• They are affordable for all schools/districts with spending at or above the price-adjusted national median of spending per pupil.

- They are most easily affordable for schools with high concentrations of poverty and thus with many students eligible for federal Title I assistance; in many cases, the Title I dollars are sufficient to finance all of the design-specific ingredients.
- They require substantial resource reallocation at the school site, essentially reducing expenditures on specialist staff and increasing expenditures on regular classroom teachers, professional development, instructional leadership, and computer technologies.
- They take several years to implement fully (Bodilly, 1998) but can produce improvements in student achievement in the first or second year of the implementation process (Ross, Sanders, & Stringfield, 1998).
- Because they produce improved results with current resources, they represent one of the most powerful strategies for improving the productivity of the current education system.

To be sure, in the short run the restructuring and resource reallocation will be contained by federal, state, and local rules, regulations, and contract provisions, which would eventually need to be changed. Many districts and states are providing waivers for most schools and districts implementing designs offered by the New American Schools. To jump-start this restructuring and resource reallocation process, many districts provide "up front" money during the first couple of years to finance initial technical assistance and professional development costs. But even these costs are slowly transferred to the school over time, largely through a school-based budgeting process.

CONCLUSION

To be successful, the changes in curriculum, instruction, classroom and school organization, and management discussed in several chapters in this volume must also be accompanied by a redesigned school finance system. The goal of the redesign process should be to empower site professionals—principals and teachers—to use site dollars more effectively. This will put principals and teachers into the fiscal driver's seat and allow them to match budgets to school strategies. Rather than thinking only about how to use the hundreds of marginal new dollars they might (or might not) receive, they also will need to think about how to best use the millions of dollars they already have.

To make this strategy work, schools need to be provided with an "adequate" level of funds so they can teach the vast majority of their students to new, high, minimum achievement levels. This will require a change in state-to-district school finance systems, essentially shifting the focus away from fiscal equity across districts to ensuring that all districts have sufficient dollars to deploy strategies that teach all but their severely disabled students to high standards. Districts will then need to provide schools with resources on a fair, adequate, and effective basis so that schools will be empowered to deploy their resources for cohesive schoolwide strategies designed specifically for the students in the school and with the goal of having very high percentages of success at much higher performance levels. Finally, schools will need to engage in practices that substantially reallocate resources to finance their cohesive strategies. In sum, states need to redesign their finance systems, districts need to decentralize budgets to school sites, and school sites need to reallocate resources to higher-performance strategies and be held accountable for producing results.

REFERENCES

Alexander, K., Augenblick, J., Driscoll, W., Guthrie, J., & Levin, R. (1995). *Proposals for the elimination of wealth-based disparities in public education.* Columbus, OH: Department of Public Instruction.
Allington, R. L., & Johnston, P. (1989). Coordination, collaboration and consistency: The redesign of compensatory and special education interventions. In R. E. Slavin, N. L. Karweit, & N. A. Madden (Eds.), *Effective programs for students at risk* (pp. 320–354). Boston: Allyn and Bacon.
Augenblick, J. (1997). *Recommendations for a base figure and pupil-weighted adjustments to the base figure for use in a new school finance system in Ohio.* Columbus, OH: Ohio Department of Education.
Bodilly, S. (1998). *Lessons from New American Schools' scale-up phase: Prospects for bringing designs to multiple sites.* Santa Monica, CA: The RAND Corporation.
Caldwell, B. J., & Hayward, D. K. (1998). *The future of schools: Lessons from the reform of public education.* London: Falmer Press.
Chaikind, S., Danielson, L. C., & Braven M. L. (1993). What do we know about the costs of special education? A selected review. *Journal of Special Education, 26*(4), 344–370.
Chambers, J. G. (1995). Public school teacher cost differences across the United States: Introduction to a teacher cost index (TCI). In *Developments in school finance* [On-line]. Available: http://www.ed.gov/NCES/pubs/96344cha.html.
Chambers, J., & Parrish, T. (1994). State-level education finance. In *Advances in educational productivity* (pp. 45–74). Greenwich, CT: JAI Press.

Chambers, J., Parrish, T., & Hikido, C. (1996). Special education expenditures and revenues in a census-based funding system: Case study in the commonwealth of Massachusetts. *Journal of Education Finance, 21*(4), 527–554.

Comer, J. P., Haynes, N. M., Joyner, E. T., & Ben-Avie, M. (1996). *Rallying the whole village: The comer process for reforming education.* New York: Teachers College Press.

Crévola, C., & Hill, P. (1998). Initial evaluation of a whole-school approach to prevention and intervention in early literacy. *Journal of Education for Students Placed at Risk, 3*(2), 133–157.

Darling-Hammond, L., with Chajet, L., & Robertson, P. (1996). Restructuring schools for high performance. In S. Fuhrman & J. O'Day (Eds.), *Rewards and reform: Creating educational incentives that work* (pp. 144–192). San Francisco: Jossey-Bass.

Downes, T., & Pogue, T. (1994). Adjusting school aid formulas for the higher cost of educating disadvantaged students. *National Tax Journal, 47*(1), 89–110.

Duncombe, W., Ruggiero, J., & Yinger, J. (1996). Alternative approaches to measuring the cost of education. In H. F. Ladd (Ed.), *Holding schools accountable: Performance-based reform in education* (pp. 327–356). Washington, DC: The Brookings Institution.

Edison Project. (1994). *An invitation to public school partnership.* New York: The Edison Project.

Edison Project. (1997). *Annual report on school performance.* New York: Edison Project.

Evans, W., Murray, S., & Schwab, R. (1997). State education finance policy after court mandated reform: The legacy of Serrano. *1996 Proceedings of the eighty-ninth annual conference on taxation.* Washington, DC: National Tax Association–Tax Institute of America.

Finnan, C., St. John, E., McCarthy, J., & Slovacek, S. (1996). *Accelerated schools in action.* Thousand Oaks, CA: Corwin Press.

General Accounting Office (GAO). (1997). *School finance: State efforts to reduce funding gaps between poor and wealthy districts.* Washington, DC: Author.

Guthrie, J., Hayward, G., Smith, J., Rothstein, R., Bennett, R., Koppich, J., Bowman, E., DeLapp, L., Brandes, B., & Clark, S. (1997). *A proposed cost-based block grant model for Wyoming school finance.* Sacramento, CA: Management Analyst & Planning Associates.

Heneman, H. G. III. (1998). Assessment of the motivational reactions of teachers to a school-based performance award program. *Journal of personnel evaluation in education, 12*(1), 43–59.

Hinrichs, W. L., & Laine, R. D. (1996). *Adequacy: Building quality and efficiency into the cost of education.* Springfield, IL: Illinois Board of Education.

Hirsch, E. D. (1996). *The schools we need and why we don't have them.* New York: Doubleday.

Imazeki, J., & Reschovsky, A. (1997/1998). *The development of school finance formulas to guarantee the provision of adequate education to low-income students.* Paper presented at the annual conference of the Association for Public Policy Analysis and Management, Washington, DC, November 6–8, 1997. In W. Fowler, Jr. (Ed.), *Developments in School Finance 1998*, pp. 121–148, Washington, DC: U.S. Department of Education, National Center for Education Statistics.

Kelley, C. (1997). Teacher compensation and organization. *Educational evaluation & policy analysis, 19*(1), 15–28.

Kelley, C. (1998). The Kentucky school-based performance award program: School-level effects. *Educational policy, 12*(3), 305–324.

Kelley, C., Milanowski, A., & Heneman, H. G. III. (1998). *Changing teacher compensation: Cross-site analysis of the effects of school-based performance award programs.* Paper presented at the American Educational Research Association annual conference, San Diego, CA, and available from the Consortium for Policy Research in Education, University of Wisconsin–Madison.

King, J. (1994). Meeting the educational needs of at-risk students: A cost analysis of three models. *Educational evaluation and policy analysis, 16*(1), 1–19.

Ladd, H., & Yinger, J. (1994). The case for equalizing aid. *National tax journal, 47*(1), 211–224.

Lankford, H., & Wyckoff, J. (1997). The changing structure of teacher compensation 1970–94. *Economics of education review, 16*(4), 371–384.

Lawler, E. E. (1986). *High involvement management.* San Francisco: Jossey-Bass.

Lawler, E. E., III. (1992). *The ultimate advantage.* San Francisco: Jossey-Bass.

Lawler, E. E. (1996). *From the ground up.* San Francisco: Jossey-Bass.

Levacic, R. (1995). *Local management of schools: Analysis and practice.* Buckingham, England: Open University Press.

McMahon, W. W. (1994). Intrastate cost adjustment. In *Selected papers in school finance* [On-line]. Available: http://www.ed.gov/NCES/pubs/96068ica.html.

Miles, K. H. (1995). Freeing resources for improving schools: A case study of teacher allocation in Boston public schools. *Educational evaluation and policy analysis, 17*(4), 476–493.

Miles, K. H., & Darling-Hammond, L. (1997). *Rethinking school resources in high performing schools.* Madison, WI: Consortium for Policy Research in Education, University of Wisconsin–Madison.

Murnane, R., & Levy, F. (1996). *Teaching the new basic skills.* New York: The Free Press.

National Commission on Teaching and America's Future. (1996). *What matters most: Teaching for America's future.* New York: Columbia University, Teachers College, National Commission on Teaching and America's Future.

Northwest Regional Educational Laboratory. (1998). *Catalog of school reform models: First edition.* Portland, OR: Northwest Regional Educational Laboratory.

Odden, A. (1997a). *How to rethink school budgets to support school transformation. Getting better by design series: Vol. 3.* Arlington, VA: New American Schools.

Odden, A. (1997b). Improving the productivity of school resources. *School business affairs, 63*(6), 4–12.

Odden, A. (1998a). Case Study 3: North America (USA and Canada). In K. Ross & R. Levacic (Eds.), *Need-based resource allocation in education via formula funding of schools.* Paris: UNESCO, International Institute for Educational Planning.

Odden, A. (1998b). *Improving state school finance systems: New realities create need to re-engineer school finance structures.* Paper prepared for the Consortium for Policy Research in Education, University of Wisconsin–Madison.

Odden, A., & Busch, C. (1998). *Financing schools for high performance: Strategies for improving the use of educational resources.* San Francisco: Jossey-Bass.

Odden, A., & Clune, W. (1998). School finance systems: aging structures in need of renovation. Submitted to *Educational evaluation & policy analysis.*

Odden, A., & Kelley, C. (1997). *Paying teachers for what they know and do: New and smarter compensation strategies to improve schools.* Thousand Oaks, CA: Corwin Press.

Odden, A., Monk, D., Nakib, Y., & Picus, L. O. (1995). The story of the education dollar: No fiscal academy awards and no fiscal smoking guns. *Phi Delta Kappan, 77*(2), 161–168.

Odden, A., & Odden, E. (1996). Applying the high involvement framework to local management of schools in Victoria, Australia. *Educational research and evaluation, 2*(2), 150–184.

Odden, A., & Picus, L. O. (1992). *School finance: A policy perspective.* New York: McGraw Hill.

Organization for Economic Cooperation and Development (OECD). (1997). *Education at a glance: OECD indicators—1997.* Paris: OECD.

Parrish, T. (1996). Special education finance: Past, present and future. *Journal of education finance, 21*(4), 451–476.

Reschovsky, A. (1994). Fiscal equalization and school finance. *National tax journal, 47*(1), 185–197.

Ross, K., & Levacic, R. (Eds). (1998). *Needs based resource allocation in education via formula funding of schools.* Paris: UNESCO, International Institute for Educational Planning.

Ross, S., Sanders, W., & Stringfield, S. (1998). *The Memphis restructuring initiative: Achievement results for years 1 and 2 on the Tennessee value-added assessment system.* (A special report prepared for the Memphis City Schools.)

Rothstein, R., with Miles, K. H. (1995). *Where's the money gone?* Washington, DC: Economic Policy Institute.

Sizer, T. (1996). *Horace's hope.* Boston: Houghton Mifflin.

Slavin, R., & Fashola, O. (1998). *Show me the evidence! Proven and promising programs for America's schools.* Thousand Oaks, CA: Corwin Press.

Slavin, R. E., Madden, N. A., Dolan, L. J., & Wasik, B. A. (1996). *Every child, every school: Success for all.* Thousand Oaks, CA: Corwin Press.

Stringfield, S., Ross, S., & Smith, L. (1996). *Bold plans for school restructuring: The New American School designs.* Mahwah, NJ: Lawrence Erlbaum.

Tucker, M., & Codding, J. (1998). *Standards for our schools.* San Francisco: Jossey-Bass.

8

Leadership in the 21st Century: Using Feedback to Maintain Focus and Direction

Sherry P. King

The work of schools in the 21st century will be to create systems that are characterized by continuous improvement. The concept is not a new one; making it a reality, however, will require a different kind of organization. School systems will have to be much more dynamic, data-driven organizations that can be immediately responsive and that allow for learning at all levels. In the past, we boasted about our five-year strategic plans. In the context of uncertainty and rapid change that defines our era, those plans may be outdated before they are complete. Therefore, we must be prepared for continuous examination of our strategies. As educational leaders, we must help our organizations find stability and growth amidst enormous change.

The changing, complex nature of our times is seen in the debates about second-language instruction, in the proliferation of technology that outpaces our ability to integrate it into the curriculum, in the demand that we educate all students to a higher level than we used to reserve for a select few. Given these realities, there is no one reform we can adopt that will ensure that all students attain the skills they need to succeed in the complex world that awaits them. No change will be permanent. School schedules will have to be rethought many times; computer equipment and computer education requirements will have to be revised along with the changes in technology. Wheatley (1994) in *Leadership and the New Science* suggests that the old model of linear strategic planning is inadequate to the task at hand. Rather, organizations have to adopt models that can provide the continuous feedback that allows for ongoing transformation.

During my career in education, I have had the good fortune to work at what might be described as the cutting edge of school reform. My earliest work was in the area of democratic schools, when I had the opportunity to work with the late Lawrence Kohlberg of Harvard University. Later, when Ted Sizer was establishing the Coalition of Essential Schools, I found a set of principles that extended Kohlberg's work beyond the school culture to teaching and learning. During those years I became deeply immersed in assessment practices, but my understanding deepened as a result of my work with the National Center for Education and the Economy and one of its arms, New Standards. As a high school principal and superintendent, I have been committed to helping turn the lessons of these reform movements into reality. That goal has shaped my partnerships with teachers, students, administrators, and community members. This chapter will present some of the challenges we face in the future through the stories of real work in schools. The anecdotes are imperfect, but they are true. We didn't always see the purpose of our work; we didn't always make adequate time to reflect and then use our insights to rethink practice. We did do our best to improve student achievement for all of our students, often with heartening results.

THE FEEDBACK SPIRAL MODEL

A fundamental principle for all my work is my belief that the primary purpose of schools is to engage students in work that forces them to use their minds well and prepares them to take their place as responsible citizens in a democracy. The ways to help students achieve those goals are many. For me, a set of guiding principles, like those of the Coalition of Essential Schools, is a helpful way to maintain clarity of focus. Analyzing how those principles are being implemented requires the discipline of gathering data, making plans, implementing them, and analyzing the effects for modification. One image to support this model of continuous improvement is presented by Art Costa and Bena Kallick (1995). As Costa and Kallick explain (see Figure 8.1, p. 168), a feedback spiral helps create a learning organization by creating a situation in which people learn by

> building critique and assessment into their processes. Through those processes, they reexamine and clarify vision, values, purposes, and outcomes. Out of this clarity comes the capacity for individuals to communicate and share progress and to align the organization's goals with those of the individuals who compose the organization. Organizations and individuals who do not think and act in terms of feedback spirals remain oblivious to the data coming to them. (p. 28)

This cycle of inquiry, action, reflection, and inquiry is compelling in its simplicity but difficult to implement. Its potential reaches to many facets of organizational life; for schools, it takes on heightened power when grounded in examples of student work. Actual student achievement should be the focus of all the work of the school, whether examining data on student achievement, developing standards, making instructional decisions, or involving all stakeholders in the issues surrounding school life. Schools can identify multiple entry points for these discussions. In some of the schools in which I have worked, our look at student work led us to examine student achievement data. In another district, test score data provided the impetus for making student work more public. This chapter begins with student achievement data because that was the appropriate sequence for this school, not because there is a "right" way to begin.

EXAMINING ACHIEVEMENT DATA: THREE CASE STUDIES

Studying data on student achievement in schools that know students well is crucial to school improvement in the 21st century. Applying the feedback spiral to the examination of achievement data can support the kind of continuous change our students need. The term "results-driven organizations" may sound too businesslike to describe a system in which teachers know students as whole people and the ways each of their students make meaning. However, the three examples that follow illustrate that data analysis does not have to depersonalize, but can actually support schools in helping to identify problems, generate possible responses, and raise issues connected to student achievement.

FIGURE 8.1

Continuous Growth Through Feedback Spiral

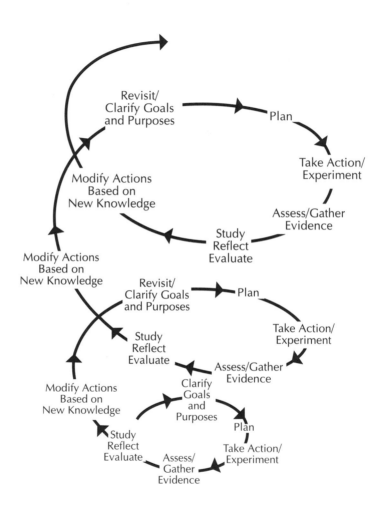

Source: Costa & Kallick (1995), p. 27.

168

In one situation, close examination of reading results had a significant impact on allocation of resources that led to enhanced student learning. A few years into my first superintendency, the high school principal explained that the 9th grade was the toughest group she had ever worked with. The high school had restructured itself in keeping with the principles of the Coalition of Essential Schools: Students were not tracked, grade levels functioned as teams, and there was an advisory program to ensure that students did not "fall through the cracks." The principal described the frustration of a team of veteran teachers with a long track record of commitment to kids. This group of students was not engaged in learning. Behavior problems were pronounced. Teachers who had fought hard to detrack now wanted students removed from their classes. Despite case conferences, team meetings with and without students and parents, and efforts to adapt the curriculum, everyone was at wit's end. No one imagined that the answer was hidden in the district data.

At the same time, a report on district results in reading showed a dip in 6th grade scores; nothing serious, but not the kind of achievement we had been used to. Because the district had low mobility rates, we decided to study the reading scores of the then 7th graders back through their elementary years to see what we would find. Tracing the students back to 3rd grade, we learned that students who were in the third quartile in reading while in the 3rd grade did not improve as they stayed in school. Those in the lowest quartile received adequate remedial help to raise their scores. Those at the top remained there. The students who were not needy enough for remediation and not secure in their reading skills were not making the kinds of gains teachers and administrators expected. When we asked ourselves whether this finding had any connection to the current 9th grade, we discovered that the freshman class was the first to go through the school system with the new language arts curriculum. An analysis of their high school scores showed that they were weak readers, particularly those in the same third quartile.

Applying the feedback loop had a profound impact on the school system. We had gathered and assessed evidence, studied our findings, and were prepared to modify actions based on the new knowledge. In the short term, the high school knew it had to target reading support to the 9th graders. Although poor reading skills might not explain all the behavioral issues of this group of students, it did help teachers understand the genuine difficulty students were having in meeting their academic expectations. As a district, we speculated that this "notorious" class must have felt academically inadequate for several years, contributing to their uncooperative behavior, which had been apparent throughout middle school. What was most significant about the focus on data is that it took the school in a completely different direction than it would have taken based on student anecdotes. The teachers originally thought the problem was purely behavioral and simply wanted students removed from the regular class. In fact, the teachers came to believe that the behavior issues were symptoms of a deeper educational problem, weak reading skills, that would not have been remedied had we pursued reactions simply based on student actions. For the long term, it led to a systemwide reexamination and revision of the reading program, beginning in the elementary school, and included a redefinition of reading support that extended through the 8th grade.

A second example of using data analysis to inform practice illustrates the challenges of trying to examine student achievement data. Of the four elementary schools in another district, one had disappointing results on a state reading test, while students in the other schools appeared to be doing just fine. Because I was aware that an analysis of the tests could show how well our students were doing at the mastery level as well as identify those in need of remedial help, I asked all schools to analyze their results to determine how students were performing at all levels of achievement.

Our first experience with data analysis had mixed results. One of the first responses to the task of test analysis was criticism of the test itself: The test was not consistent with classroom practice; the test discriminated against the most needy students by using a procedure in which students fill in blank spaces in reading passages—the test did not truly test reading. Because the district did not have other systematic measures for assessing student achievement, I believed there was merit in reviewing the data for what it did show, despite the limitations of the instrument itself. For the staffs of the schools to begin to examine and learn from the data, the central administration first had to help the principals become comfortable with the data and then support them in spending enough time with teachers for them all to see the link between the test analysis and instructional practices.

As in the first example, this experience uncovered some unanticipated problems and led the district to think differently about the use of data to determine the allocation of resources based on real need. One school responded to its reading scores by mapping the reading resources available in the school, only to discover that they had more than they thought, but that there was little coordination of effort. Based on those findings, the school redistributed its personnel and redefined the role of the reading specialist to enable him to coordinate and follow up on reading initiatives. For example, teachers decided to expand a practice of having all reading support staff work with a particular grade level at the same time during the day, allowing all students to be involved in small-group intensive reading support. This meant that schedules for teaching aides and assistants had to be changed. It also resulted in a decision that there would be more support in the early grades rather than an even distribution across the school, consistent with research about early literacy acquisition. The higher-performing schools were also surprised by the results of data analysis, finding that students in the early grades were not achieving the level of mastery they expected. The schools reexamined their literacy programs and helped teachers expand their teaching strategies for reading. This emphasis on literacy readiness as early as prekindergarten resulted in dramatic increases in the numbers of students achieving mastery by grades 3 and 6 (see Figure 8.2, p. 172).

A third situation that illustrates the benefits of data analysis involves a high school math program and provides another example of how understanding the needs of a particular group of students can influence an entire system. In June 1997, the chairman of the high school math department was concerned about the results of nonaccelerated students on the state test for the first-year high school math course (in New York State, Integrated Math Course I). As a conscientious teacher who cares deeply about student achievement, he was extremely anxious to develop a plan to help all students pass this course. Rather than begin with a series of next steps, a traditional way to solve problems in schools, I asked him to apply the feedback spiral. Instead of generating solutions I asked that the department do an item analysis of the test results in order to develop data-driven interventions.

The analysis raised many systemic issues related to math instruction that the high school teachers alone could not address. For example, their analysis showed some gaps in student learning that had implications for the elementary and middle schools. Given the scope of the required high school curriculum, if these students were going to do better at the high school level, the middle school would have to revise its curriculum to include some of the topics required in 9th grade. The data, then, helped inform the system that in order for all 9th graders to improve their math achievement, math teachers in kindergarten through 8th grade would have to rethink the skills they expected of students in light of the high school requirements. That led to the beginning of a

FIGURE 8.2

Reading Scores in the Mamaroneck School District Before and After Data-Driven Changes in the Literacy Program

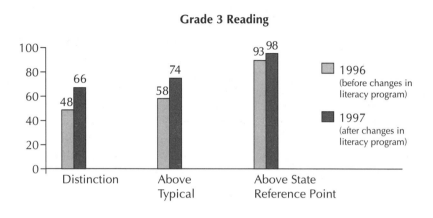

Grade 3 Reading

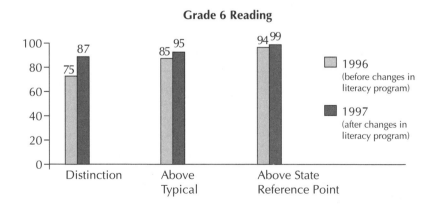

Grade 6 Reading

K–12 math initiative for the district, one that probably would not have been created and implemented without a hard look at actual student achievement data. Perhaps most important, because the conversations with colleagues from other schools were based on actual data, the joint meetings did not have the tone of "blaming" the feeder schools that so often characterizes such discussions.

CURRENT AND FUTURE CHALLENGES FOR DATA-DRIVEN SYSTEMS

Moving from an impressionistic system to a data-driven one is not easy work. Despite the fact that our schools are filled with information about student achievement, we have not been accustomed to using it to inform our decisions. Schools that are interested in becoming "data driven" are doing so in a high-stakes political environment in which scores are printed in local newspapers. These comparisons, which ignore the limitations of the available data, present test scores as the only picture of school achievement.

Furthermore, as teachers pointed out in the item analysis of New York State's 3rd grade test in reading, many tests are not aligned with the curriculum or with instructional strategies that best support learning. There is also some skepticism about the public use of test scores because they have historically been used to sort students, not help them all reach higher standards. Despite the limitations and reservations, school and district-level leaders must be accountable for student growth. We must identify or create assessment systems that provide reliable information about real student performance. Leaders must ensure that data is used to help all students, not to limit them. Among the challenges of the next century will be to develop, refine, find, and use instruments that will provide public accountability and define the areas where we must continue to improve. Parents, students, teachers, and the wider community have a right to know how our students are doing. Figuring out how to involve the entire community in the work of continuous improvement is one of the great leadership challenges of the next century.

LOOKING AT STUDENT WORK

Actual samples of student work are the best evidence of how students are doing, what our standards look like in practice, and how our students are doing in relation to those expectations. Student products—their knowledge work, as Phil Schlechty (1997) calls it—tell us much more than decontextualized columns of test scores printed in the local newspaper. Neither scores alone nor student work by itself is sufficient. Absent a shared set of standards, we have no way to determine what is "good enough." If examining student achievement data is one component of a successful school system for the 21st century, a second essential component of systemic improvement is the development of a shared set of standards. Reading and scoring work together, developing shared standards, and making work public are ways districts can become explicit about their standards. The work of the schools in Mamaroneck, New York, in developing *Milestones in Literacy* is one example of how a district can develop shared standards and create an inclusive model of curriculum development consistent with Costa and Kallick's (1995) model of continuous improvement.

Developing districtwide standards for literacy led the district to support teachers in meeting jointly to read and score student work. This work with the staff was also a catalyst for changing the structure of monthly administrative council meetings. Rather than focusing on managerial issues, the meetings were reconceived to model practices that could support the examination of student work. For example, at a summer retreat, one elementary principal brought a collection of student work. The high school principal brought a copy of a student report card with samples of the student's writing on a state exam. Principals and assistant principals observed that there was a great deal of information in student folders that did not necessarily have an impact on instructional decisions. Some administrators speculated that the amount of material made it difficult to focus. In addition, there were clear discrepancies between local standards and those of the state; people who knew the children well expected a higher quality of writing than the state accepted.

The administrative team decided that examining the overlap among curriculum, instruction, and assessment should be our work for the year. Two administrators (chosen in alphabetical order, not by school or area of expertise) would work with the superintendent to plan each of the monthly meetings. For the entire year, the administrative team engaged in a number of activities that would both raise awareness and model practices that could be replicated in the schools. Examples of these activities include the following:

- The administrators read and scored samples of student work from the prior spring's New Standards English-Language Reference Exam and compared their scores to those of outside evaluators.

- Two administrators gathered samples of student writing from 2nd to 11th grade. In small cross-school groups, administrators looked for patterns of growth and gaps.

- Administrators analyzed districtwide test score data and corresponding patterns of student placement.

- Administrators gathered samples of rubrics from various schools and discussed what the rubrics were asking for, how they were being used, and whether we needed some agreed-upon standards.

In addition to administrative professional development, the group knew that it had to create similar opportunities for teachers.

Elementary schools initiated grade-level meetings at which teachers began to make more systematic the casual sharing that characterized interactions in most schools. Teams of teachers and administrators went to colloquia sponsored by the Coalition of Essential Schools and the Annenberg Institute for School Reform, where they learned techniques for sharing student work. Representatives attended workshops sponsored by New Standards™, and the district hosted a workshop for teachers from across the district at which they could learn about the New Standards™ Reference Exams. The assistant principals received support in becoming "assessment experts" and supporting teachers in piloting new assessments being developed by New York State or New Standards™. Most important, the board of education allowed the schools to engage in these pilots for two years without reporting results to the public, thus avoiding a high-stakes environment and allowing the schools to use the pilots to examine practice. With that background, the administrators gathered sample papers, jointly scored them, and in some cases compared locally derived scores to those of outside evaluators. The district, then, became immersed in analyzing student work through a variety of reading and writing assessments.

Reading and scoring student work was a precursor to developing a set of standards that we could agree upon and make public. New York, like many states, has developed a general framework for literacy, but our involvement with student work convinced us that we had to create a document that would be more specific to our community. We were able to build on the grade-level meetings, at which groups of teachers had begun to develop draft documents of what they thought students should be able to demonstrate as readers.

At a districtwide meeting, teachers looked at and edited the draft documents. Coming out of the isolation of their own classrooms, they expressed a great deal of passion as they tried to agree on a shared set

175

of standards for student performance. That meeting was followed by a summer workshop on reading and subsequent meetings at which teacher representatives from all schools crafted the district document on reading, *Milestones in Literacy.* In the fall, parents received a description of *Milestones in Literacy* as part of back-to-school night—a major step toward public accountability around a shared set of expectations (see Figure 8.3).

FIGURE 8.3
Informing Parents About a Revised Literacy Program

Update on Elementary Literacy
Mamaroneck Public Schools, September 1997
What's been happening in Mamaroneck?
• Reading scores are up.
• Teachers have been looking anew at how they teach reading.
• Several new assessments (tests) were piloted in grades 4 and 8 last year.
• We're studying how students are doing in three ways.
• Teachers across the district created *Milestones in Literacy*—consistent with the guidelines adopted by New York State.

The *Milestones* state for each grade, K–5, what attitudes and behaviors, and skills and strategies are reasonable to expect of a child.

What do the *Milestones* look like? Some examples:
Grade 1
• Identifies and forms the letters of the alphabet.
• Increases awareness of conventions of print.
• Uses some or all of the following strategies: picture clues, 1-1 matching, context clues, phonetic elements, sight words, and memory.

Grade 3
• Demonstrates flexible knowledge of phonics and develops increasing control over word analysis.
• Demonstrates increasing knowledge of language.
• Reads increasingly complex text with fluency and independence.

Grade 5
• Revises and confirms predictions and assumptions.
• Identifies elements of writer's style.
• Compares, contrasts, and analyzes elements of text, genres, and works of authors.

The work of developing a document that codified grade-level expectations for students was a dramatic shift toward districtwide coherence. Although teachers had high internal expectations for students, agreeing to put those expectations in writing was a major step toward breaking the isolation of teaching practice. There were rich and passionate debates about what would happen to students who didn't meet all the expectations—a discussion that still continues. There was concern about reducing the educational process to a checklist—a continuing worry. There was fear that the *Milestones in Literacy* document would sit on the shelf like so many curriculum projects we have all experienced— a challenge we face together.

To keep this model of continuous improvement vital, my monthly meetings with individual principals began to include specific reports on evidence of the *Milestones in Literacy* in practice. We identified teachers who were having difficulty with the document and discussed ways to help them with additional reading strategies. The board of education acknowledged the work of the teachers in developing the *Milestones in Literacy* document through a letter to the staff and asked for a midyear progress report at a public meeting, another way of signaling that this was important work.

In essence, we used Costa and Kallick's (1995) feedback spiral to define our work. Although we did not have the spiral before us as a template, we were attempting to internalize the notion of reflective practice and continuous improvement. The *Milestones in Literacy* document had come out of clarifying our goals for reading and agreeing upon developmentally appropriate indicators of progress. Now we had to take action in order to gather evidence and assess whether the *Milestones in Literacy* would serve as a useful road map in helping us improve student achievement. By insisting that all teachers pilot new assessments and look at student results against the *Milestones in Literacy*, we were ensuring that our teachers and students would be prepared for the new state expectations. Equally important, we would gather information that could tell us whether we had selected the right indicators in reading for our students. As another way to honor this systemic approach, the district agreed to support additional purchases of textbooks if the requests were consistent with the issues our study of literacy had raised. For example, several schools used the additional funds to purchase nonfiction material for the early grades, as well as multiple copies of texts for grade levels that wanted to practice guided reading, a new reading strategy many teachers wanted to include in their classroom repertoire.

The work in literacy had a dramatic impact on the work of the schools. For the first time, the district had developed a shared set of expectations for students. The process of developing those agreements led to a renewed spirit of collegiality and experimentation as evidenced by the proliferation of pilot report card forms that have integrated elements of the *Milestones in Literacy*. As the graphs of student achievement show (see Figure 8.2, p. 172), there were immediate results in terms of improved reading scores that suggest that the focus on literacy is having the benefits we intended. The initiative is now being expanded through the middle school, and reading support is now part of certain high school–level content area courses. As suggested by the math example described earlier, when administrators and teachers are involved in shared learning, the results can be shared systemwide.

This model of developing and assessing curriculum, instruction, and assessment as an integrated whole is both old work and a revolution. Good teachers have always looked at student work against a set of expectations and revised their instruction accordingly. Few districts, however, have succeeded at making this model of good practice the expectation of the system. Agreeing upon standards that cross school and teacher lines is the work of the future. Sharing explicit criteria and exemplars of what is "good enough" with students and their parents, so they know what the target looks like, is the work of the future. Using the data on student achievement to inform our instructional practice and check our progress is the mandate of the next century.

COMMUNICATING WITH THE COMMUNITY

Our ability to maintain public education into the next century is based on support, which requires that the community be knowledgeable about the achievement of our students. Systemic reform in the 21st century will require a rethinking of the role of the community in the work of the schools. Although many schools have models of shared decision making, these bodies have not always been invited into the work of teaching and learning. As a matter of fact, many members of boards of education express frustration that once they are elected to the board they become policymakers quite removed from the issues that moved them to become involved in schools in the first place. Board members, parents, and the community-at-large must be informed about the real challenges of schools if we are going to maintain the support necessary to sustain public education.

Over the past few years, my strategy has been to provide the board of education, parents, and the wider community with learning experiences that parallel those of teachers. For example, in one district, we maintained a monthly column in the local newspaper that included information about school reform locally and in the context of the changes at the state level. Another aspect of communication involves translating educational jargon. Many parents want to know what happened to old-fashioned tests, since "authentic assessment" was not necessarily part of their experience.

In Mamaroneck, we have developed a highly professional relationship with the PTA around systemic reform and continuous improvement. New York, like most states, has a schedule for new assessments. But parents don't know what is replacing what. Therefore, we have jointly hosted meetings at which parents take samples of old tests and new assessments. Not surprisingly, the parents quickly understand that the new expectations are more rigorous and will require more of the schools and their children.

Once we raised awareness, we wanted parents to understand what we were doing to prepare their children for the new exams. One approach we have tried has been to share the same expertise with parents that we do with staff. For example, the same reading expert who has been helping teachers think about their practice met with parents to talk about their role at home in helping their children become readers. We have taken a similar approach in content areas such as science, math, and computer technology. The more the community understands the magnitude of demands on schools and on today's students, the more they are likely to support our efforts to help all students meet higher standards.

This also means a different role for the board of education. Continuing a practice I initiated in a district where I had worked earlier, the board has monthly study sessions at which they can discuss in depth the difficult issues the schools face, many of which don't require specific board action. For example, understanding the implications of the *Milestones in Literacy,* or the recently defined outcomes in technology, or the development of a new, problem-based science curriculum takes time and exploration, especially if we want to develop this work in the context of the feedback loop, ensuring continuous reflection and improvement. To help in this effort, the board has developed a protocol (see Figure 8.4, p. 180) for study sessions that allows board members to ask thoughtful questions that are consistent with the critical feedback necessary to ensuring quality work. By having a system for sharing information, presenters are forced to become clearer about their goals and how they will measure success—exactly what we are asking teachers to do in becoming more explicit about their standards in reading.

FIGURE 8.4
Protocol for School Board Study Sessions

Essential Question:

- Research process.
- Criteria: How will the school define success?
- Public engagement: How have parents been involved? Questions that might need to be answered from the public.
- Teachers: Where do they stand on the proposed changes?
- Evaluation: Timeline.
- Financial implications.
- Next steps: What kind of support can/should the board provide? Public comments/questions/concerns the board might hear. Next steps.

Sharing the richness of this work is not an easy task. Our district, like many others, tries to make its newsletter as much an educational opportunity as a celebration of the schools. In the February 1997 issue of *Know Your Schools*, a district publication that is sent to the entire community, we stated the district's focus as follows:

> All work in the district has one aim: to influence and constantly improve instruction and student achievement. Our focus on continuous improvement is consistent with New York State's call for higher standards for all students. The Mamaroneck Schools are seizing this opportunity to reevaluate programs, teaching methods, and resources. Our focus is on teaching, learning, and the use of assessment. Specifically this year, our work falls into four categories: Structure, Curriculum Mapping, Assessment, and Technology.

To help parents and teachers have more meaningful conversations about teaching and learning, the newsletter went on to explain the changes in assessment, including a glossary of terms that might be unfamiliar to parents (see Figure 8.5, p. 181). The glossary also supported the district's consistent use of terminology.

FIGURE 8.5
Glossary of Terms Included in Community Newsletter

Benchmarks—Performances or tasks at a targeted grade (e.g., grade 4, 8, and 10) designed to determine whether students are on course toward meeting graduation standards.

Expectations—Goals that are the same for all children, based on the belief that all children can succeed. What we can expect *all* students to learn.

Frameworks—Road maps of standards and competencies to guide instruction.

Goals—What have been established as targets. They are defined, attainable, and measurable.

Milestones—Reasonable developmental accomplishments expected of all students by the time they reach the end of a given year.

Outcomes—Concrete results in a classroom. What students demonstrate they know and are able to do at any given level.

Rubrics—Scoring guidelines used to evaluate work.

Standards—The levels students must reach for in order to be well educated. New York State defines "content standards" (what students must know as fundamental to each discipline) and "performance standards" (what students must be able to do: the skills, strategies, and applications of what is known). Some people use the terms "thresholds" or "milestones."

Source: *Know your schools* (1997, February).

EXPLAIN THE MEANING

We know that these publications are important but do not ensure that the community is informed. As superintendent, I have also tried to make public, on a regular basis, the priorities of the school system. In addition to formal remarks at the beginning of the year that set forth our goals and priorities, we have developed a midyear presentation called State of the Schools. For several years this has been a multimedia presentation. Because integrating technology into the instructional program is a priority for the district, by creating a multimedia presentation and presenting it to the staff, blunders and all, I hope to model the kind of risk taking we ask of students—and I hope of staff.

Equally important, a summary of how we are progressing toward meeting our goals keeps us focused. Initiatives such as the *Milestones in Literacy* are a reminder that our current approach to professional development is meant to be dynamic, not to create curriculum projects that will gather dust on shelves. In the State of the Schools presentation to staff and the community, I highlight the way in which our literacy efforts (as well as priority work in other areas) is manifest in our curricular, instructional, and assessment work.

In a further effort to help ensure that the community knows about our work, we have put the presentations on local cable television and are about to include the State of the Schools on the district's Web page. I hope that when the community sees examples of kindergartners' study of snails on our Web page, they will understand that naming the animals in alphabetical order and labeling diagrams is as much a part of literacy acquisition as it is the study of science.

LOOKING AHEAD

A cartoon I have seen shows two people on camels. One says to the other, "Don't ask if we're there yet, we're nomads!" The work of continuous improvement has no end point, but it must have clear focus and direction. Having clear standards and expectations, examining student work against those standards, modifying practice and allocation of resources based on the information gleaned from assessments, and trying again is the work of a lifetime.

The challenge to leadership as we look toward the next century is to create balance out of a series of paradoxes. We must celebrate our students' successes even as we present them with new challenges. Educators must simultaneously slow down and speed up the pace of change. We can no longer have a reform of the year—systemic change takes time. But we cannot afford to wait for everyone to be on board as another generation of students passes through our schools before we change. We must pay close attention to the linkages suggested in *Kids and School Reform* (Wasley, Hampel, & Clark, 1997) such as Routines and Repertoires, Caring and Expectations, Rigor and Innovation, Scale and Discourse.

School leaders must be knowledgeable about assessment and pedagogy, about ways to bring the faculty and community together to discuss standards for our children and the partnership we need to have so that all students meet the same high expectations. Schools and districts must avoid becoming shopping malls of change initiatives, but must keep doors open to new knowledge about teaching and learning. The future requires that we pay attention to feedback loops like the one suggested by Costa and Kallick (1995) if we are going to create responsive organizations filled with reflective practitioners. There must be time to evaluate our efforts before we adopt them for all or abandon them for the next fad. As leaders, we must understand the enormous demands being placed on schools and provide appropriate buffers so that people are able to do their work well.

Teachers are being asked to prepare students for new assessments in every major discipline, learn and integrate technology seamlessly into the curriculum, link career and school, and do so in classes that have a wider range of student ability. If we believe, as I do, that all of these competencies are necessary for students to become responsible citizens of the 21st century, then our job is to break down these tasks into doable, measurable pieces. If the list is too daunting, it will be easy for teachers to close their doors and wait for this period of time to pass. If we ignore the challenges, our students will suffer. Rather, we must focus our efforts, beginning with reading—*the* essential skill—and ensure that our systems are structured around the components of continuous improvement. With this clear agenda, we can gather the evidence that supports the belief on which a democratic society relies—that all children can learn.

REFERENCES

Costa, A. L., & Kallick, B. (1995). *Assessment in the learning organization.* Alexandria, VA: Association for Supervision and Curriculum Development.
Know Your Schools. (1997, February). Mamaroneck, NY.
Schlechty, P. C. (1997). *Inventing better schools.* San Francisco: Jossey-Bass.
Wasley, P. A., Hampel, R. L., & Clark, R. W. (1997). *Kids and school reform.* San Francisco: Jossey-Bass.
Wheatley, M. J. (1994). *Leadership and the new science.* San Francisco: Berrett-Koehler.

9

Life Inside a School: Implications for Reform in the 21st Century

Myranda S. Marsh

Picturing the year 2000 was once an exercise in fantastic vision. Futurists would describe the wonders of talking computers, instantaneous transportation, and tin-foil wrapped automation everywhere one looked. But, with the turn of the millennium at hand, we know what that "future" looks like now. Computers do talk and planes have dramatically reduced travel time, but the daily life of a teacher has not evolved as much as we might hope. It is strange that the idealistic visions of young teachers who want to make a difference in the lives of their students have not come to pass even at the close of the millennium (Sarason, 1996).

We are losing teachers. In losing so many, we are surely losing some of our best. The situation in schools is such that dedicated idealists are hard pressed to maintain their vision in the face of reality. In fact, researchers who discuss teacher burnout cite disturbing statistics about the rates at which these idealists are leaving the profession (Sarason, 1996). A RAND survey of teachers confirms that not more than half of women and only 30 percent of men are still teaching six years after they begin (Farber & Ascher, 1991, p. 112). As we set our sights on a shining future for education, we need to think how the year 2000 could be a turning point for the profession of teaching.

CURRENT REALITIES: A DAY IN THE LIFE OF A TEACHER

The teacher arrives to begin the day in a classroom that was built decades ago. The fortunate teacher works in a classroom that has fresh paint, solid individual desks, and perhaps a TV with a VCR. The teacher is not likely to have a computer on her desktop, and if she does, it is hardly reasonable to expect that it will be accompanied by a modem, a printer, or a CD-ROM drive. It is not unusual to find an overhead projector, but do not look for the converter that would project her computer screen for the class to see.

During the day, the teacher meets with five or six groups of students for just under an hour each. During each class period, the teacher spends most of the time at the front of the class talking. Her 20 to 30 or more students spend most of their time listening, writing down her words, and perhaps posing a question that asks for a bit more explanation or clarification of a point. When students speak to one another, it is not about the academic subject at hand.

During those times when the teacher is not responsible for a class, she devotes time to many clerical tasks. Attendance and other forms of paperwork take a piece of that time. She spends a portion of many days at the communal copy machine; most likely waiting in line occupies half of the time necessary to reproduce materials. She may have to call parents or fill out forms to document the lack of effort or success on the part of some of her students.

The teacher has contact with other adults only for social or disciplinary reasons. For example, she may need to see an administrator to discuss a discipline problem. The teacher also encounters an administrator once a year when that administrator delivers an evaluation of the teacher's performance. The teacher may also briefly interact with other teachers over lunch or a quick cup of coffee. The conversation is likely to be of a light personal nature or to consist of rueful complaints about the foibles endemic to the profession or mournful anecdotes about troubled students. The teacher spends all other time in the work day with adolescents or alone.

Work done on the curriculum is mainly done in isolation. An occasional department meeting sets milestones for the curriculum.

Decisions regarding books that students should read at a particular grade level or specific mathematical equations they should master are likely to be decided in a group or handed down from department or district administrators. However, almost all choices that concern pedagogy and methodology are made by individual instructors acting on their own best judgment without reference to or reflection on input from other professionals or even professional literature. The teacher does her most important work—the development of pedagogical style and curriculum—alone, without validation or insight from peers or superiors.

The structure of the school day does not encourage the teacher to be reflective individually or with other professionals. She is left to interpret her classroom techniques according to the merits of her own impressions and without reference to any new thoughts or studies from the academic world of education or her own subject area. Other teachers are not likely to know about what happens in her classroom and would feel uncomfortable offering ideas or observations if they did somehow come to hear of some lesson or activity that she conducted with her students. The only feedback the teacher receives on her pedagogical approach consists of those bits and pieces that find their way into the annual evaluation made by the administration or that are offered in a random comment by a parent or student.

At the end of the year, the teacher will retreat with a sigh. She is hopeful that she has provided an engaging educational experience and is relieved to be outside of the daily pressure of classroom routine. She may, if conscientious, develop a few new handouts or projects that she hopes will improve the experience of her students the following year. This work may, but more likely will not, reflect insights drawn from the 40 pages of professional articles she found stuffed in her mailbox by an enthusiastic member of the administration. She remembers hearing some other teacher mention something about one of the articles while standing in the parking lot at the end of a long day. Unfortunately, she needs to gear up for summer school because it helps pay the mortgage. Perhaps there will be time to discuss the articles with someone in September. . . .

LEADERSHIP AND TEACHER PRACTICE

There is a massive literature on change in schools, reform, and restructuring—much of it focusing on leadership as the key to meaningful change. Sergiovanni (1992) provides an interesting exploration of what leadership means in a school. He describes the usual type of leadership as "Follow Me" leadership. People follow this kind of leader because the leader has the power to command obedience or can make it worth their while by dangling either intrinsic or extrinsic rewards in front of them. More recently, leaders profess that they should be followed because they have done the research and therefore they know what is best. Sergiovanni cautions that all of these motivations create a submission by teachers that will not generate the kind of emotional commitment needed to sustain significant reform. If a principal establishes a hierarchical form of authority, it communicates the assumption that teachers are subordinates who do not share the goals of the administration and must be watched over or they will not perform adequately. The principal who operates with this pattern of authority is telling teachers that they do not practice an art but rather an applied science and that scientific knowledge is more important than classroom practice (Sergiovanni, 1992).

Thus, teachers often fail to step forward because they work in a structure that tells them they don't know anything. In particular, the structure of inservice activities communicates to teachers that what they know is not valuable. In a five-year study of 16 schools, a research group from UCLA led by Jeannie Oakes used interviews, surveys, and site visits to probe the realities behind reform movements. According to their research, the usual inservice activity consists of a few hours of lecture-style presentation by an outsider who is introduced as an "expert" and is usually not a classroom teacher. The outsider does not have credibility with the faculty, and often there is no follow-up or support (Quartz, 1996). Many articles and books echo the fact that teachers feel that they are not treated like real professionals.

In November 1993, Secretary of Education Richard Riley called a forum of teachers together to discuss the Goals 2000 education reform program. The very title of the report summarizes what those teachers most desire: "Honor What We Know. Listen to What We Say." Teachers voice their strong and consistent belief that "they are not taken seriously. If they were, they would be actively involved in policy making at all levels" (U.S. Department of Education, 1993, p. 20). These sentiments highlight the need for schools to establish a way of working that honors the experience of all participants and lets everyone feel ownership of any ideas or changes intended to improve a school.

Unfortunately this structure does not exist in most modern schools. It is not difficult to find documentation and descriptions of the adversarial relationship between teachers and administrators. Not only is there an "us-them" tone to the relationship, but often all issues are handled in a way that leads to a "winner and loser" outcome. Someone gets something at the expense of someone else. Consensus, collaboration, and cooperation are not normal operating values in most schools (Barth, 1990).

Contemporary schools tend to operate from what Wenger (1998) would describe as a dominance model of influence. To be effective, he asserts, dominance implies a meaning-making structure in which followers are reflexively obedient. This orientation requires constant renewal through demonstrations of dominance. In a school, this happens when the administration makes decisions that profoundly change the working conditions of teachers without consulting them. For example, concerned with the level of stress and unhappiness among students, a school administrator may announce that all teachers are to meet individually with their homeroom students to discuss the students' feelings about their school experience. This is a demonstration of dominance because it requires obedience and does not come from any consensus on the part of the teachers that this action is necessary or will be effective in solving the problem that concerns the administrator.

Sustaining this dominance requires rules pertaining to obedience, duty, and consequences of insurrection. Teachers often find that their only contact with the administration stems from a failure to comply with some administrative dictum. It is rare for a teacher to have an administrator drop a note that says "Well done" instead of "Why weren't you at the last faculty meeting?" This is typical of the modern school, but it sounds more like something from Orwell's *1984* than a futurist's school of the year 2000.

Unfortunately, our schools are not even functional at the dominance level. Cynicism and withdrawal are practically programmed into teachers who stay in the system. Failure to obey and to serve as duty requires often brings consequences, and positive participation and competence rarely garner attention from parents or administrators. But often a new teacher will come to see that obedience can be given its superficial due, and real competence is not evaluated. Failure to create fascinating lessons and maintain idealism results in no criticism, whereas doing so requires extra effort on the part of the teacher.

Teachers who attempt to use new methodology open themselves to the criticism of peers and parents who are most comfortable with school looking the way it did when they were there. As social support for obedience and duty erode and a practice of no consequences (positive or negative) for insurrection evolves, anarchy or stagnation results.

In schools where the children differ significantly in terms of skills and expectations, including diminished expectations of duty and obedience with a paradoxical incentive to insurrection, chaos or indifference takes over. Alternatively, teachers retreat and barricade themselves behind their classroom doors.

The current school organizational structure based on "rules, duty, and consequences" creates barriers to collegiality and sharing. In schools, the people who are in positions of authority in the accountability hierarchy have three dominant themes: (1) Keep Quiet (Kids and Teachers) and Stay in Your Seats, (2) No Lawsuits—No Headlines, and (3) Results Don't Count. School administrators' actions within this dominance model do not create a "common sense" in which the meaning of schooling is learning. Drath and Palus (1994) would suggest that these administrators are not leaders; rather they act to force teacher practices to serve the institutional apparatus. When push comes to shove, the administrators and noted outside experts can offer proof, training, instructions, workshops, schedules of reforms, and mandates for change, but the individual teacher shuts the door and does what he or she thinks is best. The external experts do not have to live the reality of the classroom day in and day out. By invalidating the expertise and experience of teachers in the classroom, those desiring reform have alienated the only members of the educational community who can make a real difference in the lives of students.

Angry at what they feel is resistance to improvement, the administrators may step in and force change. At this juncture, teacher culture and school structure collide with unfortunate results. After reading that group decision making is a good idea, an overzealous administrator may create mandatory discussion groups. On this subject, one researcher notes that collaboration can often become an administrative dictate forcing people of differing philosophies to work together on a goal received from an external source. The teachers react with distrust, and often, because they receive no training on how to run meetings effectively or ameliorate conflict, they end up having defensive confrontations and leave feeling even less trusting of their coworkers and more determined to work in isolation (Hargreaves, 1991).

Teachers can gloss over personal differences in the faculty room, but the real diversity of the faculty comes to light when people must agree on a direction for action and discover that they each want to head toward a different compass point. Lacking trained moderators and accustomed to a norm of not criticizing peers, many teachers choose to keep their feelings to themselves. Supporters don't want to be seen as administrative pawns or "eager beavers," and dissenters are bound by the norm of noncriticism. No one tells the truth, and then the administration is stunned by a lack of implementation (Weiss, Cambone, & Wyeth, 1993).

Research does offer some signs of hope. Teachers trust and converse with their colleagues at much higher levels when they feel that they are participating in decision making and are working with an authentic, or nonmanipulative, principal. Not trusting the administration is directly correlated to not trusting other teachers (Busman, 1992).

HOW TEACHER CULTURE WORKS AGAINST REFORM

Why do teachers continue to do their most important work alone and without collegiality? Surely it is not a profession that primarily appeals to those who are lazy. On the contrary, educational leader Ted Sizer echoes the sentiments of many when he praises teachers for their idealism and commitment. He notes that although there are "malingerers," teaching is not a profession usually chosen by those who don't want to work hard. Sizer points out that most teachers face a baffling juxtaposition. They must pit their commitment against the negative tide of public apathy or criticism or the depression of isolation, and against a reward and recognition system that is entirely internal to the individual (Sizer, 1984). Even critics of failed reform efforts believe that "practitioners passionately, even desperately, want to help young people" (Pogrow, 1996, p. 662).

Is it that teachers prefer to work alone? It is hard to conceive of a profession that is based entirely on communication skills being populated by members who don't really want to share ideas. Research shows that teachers are desperate to have someone take an interest in what they are doing in their classroom. Educational author Roland Barth shares a poignant anecdote that highlights the competing interests for a teacher working in isolation. The teacher reported that he had taught more than 17,000 class sessions in his 30 years of service, and during that period he had had only eight adult visitors, each of whom was a principal conducting a formal evaluation (Barth, 1990, p. 20).

Barth then offers an explanation for the dilemma of teachers wanting to have colleagues interested in their work but not being able to create a culture that enables that to happen. His theory of competition, which I think might better be described as "communism," holds that among teachers, no one can be seen as better or more expert than another. Teacher culture has come to a dangerous crossroads, not unlike that of Mao's peasants, where to become more successful or to profess expertise was to risk ridicule at best, or, more likely, exile.

Barth's insight has a strong ring of truth for practitioners when he notes: "Woe to the teacher who stands up in a faculty meeting and offers: 'I have a great idea about grouping children in mathematics. I want to share it with all of you'" (Barth, 1990, p. 16). This observation accurately documents the unspoken cultural rule in teaching that no teacher should be considered more talented or more capable than any other teacher.

For many teachers, a major source of frustration is the misalignment between society's expectations for educational reform and the realities of school culture. Society, academic institutions, researchers, administrators, and even teachers agree that change comes down to what happens between teachers and students. But teachers look at mandated professional development, administration speeches about how important it is to nurture children, and even popular films that focus on school settings as placing the responsibility on the shoulders of teachers alone. Michael Fullan may be voicing a teacher's greatest fear and frustration when he remarks, "Perhaps deep down many leaders believe that teaching is not all that difficult" (Fullan, 1993, p. 117). That observation certainly rings true among classroom teachers. It is not a surprising fear in a society in which a common cliché is "Those who can't do, teach." Reformers and researchers at every level may see themselves as a resource and not an obstacle to teachers' efforts to get the job done, but they will have to go a long way to persuade teachers that that is the case. If reform of any kind is to succeed, teachers must believe that they will have a meaningful voice in decisions and will not become the lone scapegoats of a failure to reach goals. Life is different in the trenches of the nation's classrooms.

Whatever fascinating discussions are taking place at other levels, decades of reform efforts and debates have not meaningfully changed the life of the average teacher in the United States (Glickman, 1998; Sarason, 1996). Administrators' unwillingness to hear and honor teacher knowledge and experience has created what one author has called a "carousel of reform." On the "carousel," veteran teachers watch cynically as a cycle of new administrators say that they have found "the answer" to a school's problems. The new administrators then create a flurry of superficial rearrangements of the school's structure—which leads to the reform slowly fading away and then reemerging as the carousel comes around again (Deal as cited in Evans, 1993). Various studies and reports repeat this sentiment. Glickman, for example, says,

"Such waves of top-down change appear to the experienced teachers to be periodic and endless. If one waits long enough . . . then the current mandated reform shall pass" (Glickman, 1998, p. 140).

Cynicism and bitterness are added to the carousel ride when experienced teachers work very hard for a new idea and see their efforts wasted. When offered a new idea, these former idealists say, "Let somebody else take a turn. They'll wait and see" (Weiss, Cambone, and Wyeth, 1993, p. 5). Administrators often misinterpret such caution as the grumblings of incompetents who are unwilling to change. Frustrated veterans in one study resented being labeled as resisters because they approached reform ideas with caution. One expressed displeasure with the lack of long-range vision of the young reformers:

> They don't see the commotion they will cause, don't really understand all the work involved and they don't want to hear about it. . . . I know there isn't only one way to do things, but we don't need to change for the sake of change. (Rusch & Perry, 1993, p. 11)

Those who express caution may view the young reformers as agents of the administration and "may resent the self-importance of those who become active participants, particularly if the activists are new, young teachers who haven't been part of the informal leadership structure of the school" (Weiss et al., 1993, p. 6).

The presence of this form of peer pressure makes changing the teacher culture an imperative that takes precedence over all other issues of reform. Encouraging individual teachers to do their utmost ignores the sociological reality that "people behave as they do not only because of who they are and the abilities they possess but also because of where they are and what those around them believe" (Schlechty, 1997, p. 136). Teachers must operate in the structure and peer group that surround them. A negative milieu can erode and distort the energy and initiative of the most idealistic, morally grounded teacher.

The final factor to contemplate is that teachers are overwhelmed by the burden of keeping their own classroom in order and dealing with the mind-numbing demands of day-to-day paperwork. Teacher are front-line victims of what David Lewis, a British psychologist, has described as "information fatigue syndrome" (as cited in Murray, 1998). Parent and community expectations for teachers as fix-it artists are overwhelming; schools have become the proposed miracle pill for modern social ills (Bennis, 1997). As discussed in Allan Odden's chapter on resources (see Chapter 7), teachers do not have the time or the tools to create a new paradigm under current conditions. They have no time and little incentive to plan a revolution of their own. They will need partners in reform efforts who can provide support for their viewpoints and leadership initiatives.

THE TEACHER'S ROLE IN EDUCATIONAL REFORM: SOME KEY ELEMENTS

HONORING TEACHER VOICES

Linda Darling-Hammond makes an effective analogy that compares teachers with physicians immersed in the controversies over managed care. Physicians were accused of being out of touch and elitist when they had primary policy-making power in hospitals. Now that more and more decisions are being taken out of the hands of medical practitioners, consumers of health care are concerned that administrative decision makers are not well-versed in the realities of patient care (Darling-Hammond, 1997). Similar concerns should be voiced about an educational system in which the most profound decisions concerning reform are removed from the hands of the person charged with delivering the product—the teacher.

It does not make sense for each teacher or even each school or district to decide what success will look like. That model provides no way to quantify progress or provide sustaining policies and incentives. Hill and Crévola's call for various types of standards (see Chapter 6) is a necessary discussion of an end point that will help schools measure whether or not they are achieving desired results. In no way should a discussion of process be divorced from quantifiable end points. Responsible educators want to do things that work. Honoring the teacher voice does not exclude buying into national-level goals and discussions of standards. It does mean respecting teacher interpretations and designs for delivering instruction at the local level.

Good teachers are not afraid to put themselves in front of peer reviewers or to agree on what would constitute national standards for subject mastery. Resistance to standards is not rooted in a desire to avoid accountability but rather in a fear of being left out of the discussion of what constitutes success. With a change to a community-of-practice model, the implementation of standards should be easier and more effective. It is important to remember that the discussion of end points is utterly moot without first making a commitment to acquiring the genuine cooperation and understanding of classroom teachers.

"When all is said and done, what matters most for students' learning are the commitments and capacities of their teachers" (Darling-Hammond, 1997, p. 164).

CREATING COMMUNITIES OF PRACTICE

Genuine leadership emerges when one person or group risks stepping forward and proposing a new meaning or approach, and the others say, "I believe that, too." The reform literature has put too much emphasis on leadership by individuals. Effective leadership is essentially creating a "common sense," a shared meaning across the group (Wenger, 1998). The group then can take responsibility for change and subsequently for movement toward agreed-upon standards and outcomes.

This sense of things being understood in common, or across a group, occurs through a process of culture building (Drath & Palus, 1994). The culture solidifies through processes in which a vision is articulated, problems are framed, goals are set, and activities are undertaken. These elements of community become accepted and implemented through arguing, dialogue, theory building and testing, storytelling, and making of contracts and more informal agreements. For those skeptical of this happening in a school setting with a strong "us versus them" polarity among stakeholders, it is encouraging to note that research has shown that the greater the initial disagreement within a group, the more accurate and effective the final decisions are likely to be (Henry in Bennis, 1997).

People in a group are united by more than membership; they are involved in practices that bind them together. If people are a valid part of the policy-making process, they become committed in a way that allows others to make claims on them (Farley in Drath & Palus, 1994). They become a community with practices that reinforce what they share. This concept, which reflects the wisdom of many writers, has recently been crystallized into a conceptual framework called a "community of practice" (Wenger, 1998).

Organizational effectiveness happens only when practice is changed. Leaders become effective when their priorities are seen to be part of the routine practices of an institution. This is the real key to change and improvement in schools because of the unshakable reality of "street-level bureaucracy." Schools, as institutions, provide a context for practice. Institutions define roles, qualifications, and the distribution of authority, but if these roles don't find echoes in practice, they do not

connect with everyday affairs (Wenger, 1998). Practice is where competence and effectiveness are defined. Correspondingly, communities of
practice within the school must integrate the institutional system of accountability in their definition of competence to be effective.

Wenger (1998, p. 248) suggests the following guidelines for a good
community of practice:

- Construe learning as a process of participation.
- Place emphasis on learning rather than teaching.
- Engage "communities" in design of their practice as a place of
learning.
- Give "communities" the resources they need to negotiate their
connections with other practices and their relation with the organization.

Construe learning as a process of participation. In a school, this means
ordinary full-time classroom teachers should be present in any group
debating and deciding on policy. This participation must be honored by
giving the teachers the same amount of power as other members of the
group. Department chairs, although they may teach, will not be viewed
by the faculty-at-large as one of their own. A principal in Philadelphia
reported that successful results in recent reform efforts happened because of his belief that ". . . participant research and practitioner inquiry
would encourage principals, teachers, and support staff members to
become a community in which we would think, learn, and work
together . . ." (Lytle, 1996).

Being a participant means that the leader must interact with the
faculty as a colleague rather than an administrator. If a clearly administrative tone characterizes every interaction between an administrator
and a faculty member, then the "us versus them" sentiments will be reinforced. Administrators must approach faculty members as consult-
ants and as people. If an administrator is only seen flying through the
faculty lounge in the midst of a crisis, the gulf widens and resentment
builds. Retreats at which faculty are the facilitators and administrators
join the ranks of the common educators can go a long way toward promoting a sense of teamwork.

Place emphasis on learning rather than teaching. Teachers are in the
classroom to help students become effective, independent learners, not
to provide large bodies of content that must be memorized for a test.
This notion goes back to some of the classic authors of school reform
ideas. John Dewey in his various works talked about the need for the
applicability of learning. The same philosophy would be useful in regard to all participants in the school. Adopting the principle of lifelong

learning, teachers, administrators, and parents should also identify themselves as learners in the school community. People in traditional positions of hierarchical authority can begin to be seen as learners by going to classroom teachers to ask questions and seek solutions to problems instead of only to evaluate performance or pass on complaints. Leaders in reform will be successful when they make it clear that they believe they have much to learn from other stakeholders. Visiting classrooms in a nonevaluative mode is a great way to start. The administrator can build confidence by acknowledging in public what has been observed "behind the classroom door" and setting it out as an example to emulate. Some of these public forums need to include teachers who can bask in this recognition and pass the word back to their colleagues.

The most effective way to engage teachers is to put them in leadership positions without taking them out of the classroom. For an administrator, this means finding a teacher who is recognized for having leadership qualities or expertise and supporting this teacher in his or her attempts to engage the policymakers in dialogue. Top-level administrators must make clear that teachers will be taken seriously.

This call for engaging teachers in policy discussions may seem to be an obvious measure. However, many schools are still in the habit of importing outside experts who may not even have been classroom teachers to offer their opinions on how things should be done. When one principal used teacher experts from various schools to provide much of the inservice activity for a district, another principal "took umbrage at having to sit through workshops conducted by teachers . . ." (Lytle, 1996, p. 668). Administrators can make it clear that they see themselves as learners by deliberately stepping off the pedestal of authority and by putting another member of the learning community in charge of a seminar or discussion and joining in as a participant who sits with the teachers and other learners.

Engage "communities" in design of their practice as a place of learning. An administrator who sets up the entire structure for new communities of practice or learning on behalf of teachers is creating a recipe for disaster or indifference. Being involved in the design phase is critical to promoting ownership. In a school environment, design-level participation means classroom teachers are included at each policy-making level. The faculty should elect a dean of faculty or create a similar position to act as a liaison between the faculty-at-large and the highest levels of administration. Compensating the selected teacher with a stipend or a reduction in course load makes the position feasible. Issues and concerns raised by this representative should be addressed in public forums.

Another strategy is to be clear about what decisions the principal or district will make and what decisions will be made in concert with all stakeholders. It is better to exclude the faculty from the beginning of a decision-making process than to appear to solicit feedback that is then disregarded. When administrators are taking a survey for informational purposes only, making that clear in the request avoids morale-bruising miscommunication.

Communities of practice, Wenger observes, are about the negotiation of meaning and agreement on enterprises to undertake. They can't be legislated or decreed; only recognized, supported, encouraged, and helped. The institution can design a vision, a curriculum, procedures, and work processes, but it must recognize that practice is a response to a design. The allegiance needed to realign cultural values and required work habits cannot be designed. Highly prescriptive designs, Wenger warns, may result in a response that appears to satisfy but may be at odds with the intent.

Give "communities" the resources they need to negotiate their connections with other practices and their relation with the organization. For most schools, the most precious resource of all is time. Time for involvement in communities of practice should not be time in addition to what is required to fulfill all other obligations, but rather time that is set aside. The administration of every school must decide that this process is important enough to supersede other duties, or ask teachers in what way they could best be compensated for the additional responsibility. Teachers must function in triage during most school days. They will give top priority to tasks that have serious consequences if not carried out. If not turning in attendance records means receiving a reprimand, attendance records will take priority over reflection and planning. True dialogue requires deliberately creating a space and time for reflection.

Reaching consensus will take a great deal of time. Demands for consensus are antithetical to dialogue. Consensus is not a requirement in first meetings. The first demonstrable goal is intelligent debate.

Public reporting of the progress of various debates can promote accountability. Leaders should ask for discussion only on topics that are actually going to take into account the opinions solicited. Setting aside time for lengthy debate and then having administrators take opposite action will make faculty unwilling to participate in future discussions. Consensus is not necessary. If it appears that a large segment of the faculty has been listened to, all faculty members will be more willing to participate.

COMMUNITIES OF PRACTICE IN CONTEXT

Institutional designs and national standards function as a focus for communication and negotiation, something on which the community of practice can take a stand. Communities of practice within a school build from their histories of doing something together to respond to the proposed design.

Educators who adopt Wenger's (1998) model of learning appreciate that schools gain relevance by providing "experiments of identity" that students can engage in. The goal is deep transformative experiences that involve new dimensions of identity and ownership of meaning that are more significant than extensive coverage of a broad, abstractly general curriculum that may be of limited relevance in the coming millennium. Experiments of identity may be equally critical for administrators and teachers who agree to undertake reforms.

Administrators and teachers alike must be patient and realize that reform is a process and that culture changes only with the passage of time. This runs counter to the established American value system that seems to reflect the expression "God grant me patience, RIGHT NOW!"

Teachers and administrators approach problems from very different angles. Administrators tend to view reform efforts as fairly easy to implement and straightforward in nature. They are inclined to focus on the potential benefits and gloss over potential difficulties. Similarly, policymakers behave as though the change is made when the law is signed. Linda Darling-Hammond offers insights on the actual process. She cites one study that showed legislators were given three times more time to write the policy than they gave to teachers who were to implement the reform. Furthermore, explanations of the policy can be translated as in the child's game of "telephone," until the policy bears little resemblance to the original intent (Darling-Hammond, 1990).

It is the teachers who must bridge the gaps between the old methodology and the new. They must create ways for students to move from old learning patterns to new ones. They must synthesize their current classroom with a distant bureaucrat's vision of their new classroom. Administrators tend to intervene promptly when a change doesn't quickly produce visible results. Teachers often see more potential problems. It is instructive to take note of research that shows that in the early stages of implementation, teachers are much more accurate in their predictions of how the reform effort will go than are administrators (Huberman, 1993). As one researcher succinctly suggests, ". . . changing one's teaching is not like changing one's socks" (Cohen & Ball, 1990).

The Ideal: Teaching in the New Millennium

With a nod to pop culture, let's go back to the future and check on our teacher in the new millennium following a real revolution in education. Our teacher arrives at school a few minutes early to log on to her computer and get her e-mail. The latest memos are all there, along with a reminder that her grade-level team will be meeting during the common planning period. She turns on her printer and prints out the quiz she wrote last night and e-mailed to herself at work. She recalls how one of the other teachers helped her use this technology to support a curriculum-sharing meeting. When she saw how her colleague was able to use this computer software she was intrigued enough to ask for a few quick lessons. It was a good thing that she was on the committee that apportioned the facilities funds and could speak about the need for desktop computers for everyone.

Her students file in. They will be hearing a guest speaker who will conduct an interdisciplinary lesson on environmental activism. The science teacher who shares her common planning time mentioned that the science curriculum was covering pollution, and so the two teachers pooled their resources to create a unit around the visit of the activist. Students take notes for the paper that they will write for credit in both classes. The teacher makes a mental note to pick up extra red pens for the next common planning period when she and the science teacher will grade the papers together. The chair of the science department has asked to sit in and observe so she can learn some tips for helping other teams develop similar projects.

At lunch, the teacher sits with various teachers she has gotten to know in a variety of discussions of philosophy and curriculum. A colleague asks if she could come and watch him conduct a Socratic seminar using the guidelines she presented at a recent curriculum sharing meeting. The teacher nods and puts a note in her organizer.

When she returns to her computer, an e-mail survey asks her to rank which discussion topics she feels are most urgent for the next faculty meeting. The teacher chuckles when she remembers how these surveys used to end up in the trash after too many "preemptions" of teacher-chosen topics. The teacher knows that a sacred time has been carved out in the meeting schedule. Priorities have changed. New behaviors are being rewarded! Just last week, her department chair presented her with an application for a teacher leadership grant and offered to help her get a stipend for her work in mentoring new teachers.

The journey of 1,000 miles . . .

Everyone wants schools to get better. Everyone hopes and dreams that the year 2000 will be a catalyst for fundamental change. There are many good teachers sitting in their classrooms feeling isolated, paralyzed, and disenfranchised. Imagine what our schools could be like if they were active and empowered in their schools. A futurist might see the classroom teacher rising to a respected stature in our society as teaching shifts from a job to a profession. All members of a school could take part in choosing how to meet benchmarks for achievement.

The urgency of these issues has not dimmed in the nearly 30 years since Goodlad & Klein (1970) noted that what happens "behind the classroom door" is what counts. Who will be the one to open the doors and convince the teachers that the educational world is eager for their full participation in the improvement of the lives of their students in the next millennium?

REFERENCES

Barth, R. (1990). *Improving schools from within.* San Francisco: Jossey-Bass.

Bennis, W. (1997). *Managing people is like herding cats.* Provo, UT: Executive Excellence.

Busman, D. (1992, April). *The myth of the teacher resister: The influence of authenticity and participation on faculty trust.* Paper presented at the meeting of the American Educational Research Association, San Francisco.

Cohen, D., & Ball, S. (1990). Policy and practice: An overview. *Educational Evaluation and Policy Analysis, 12*(3), 347–353.

Darling-Hammond, L. (1990). Instructional policy into practice: The power of the bottom over the top. *Educational Evaluation and Policy Analysis, 12*(3), 233–241.

Darling-Hammond, L. (1997). *The right to learn: A blueprint for creating schools that work.* San Francisco: Jossey-Bass.

Drath, W., & Palus, C. J. (1994). *Making common sense: Leadership as meaning-making in a community of practice.* Greensboro, NC: Center for Creative Leadership.

Evans, R. (1993). *The human face of reform: Meeting the challenge of change through authentic leadership.* Wellesley, MA: The Human Relations Service.

Farber, B., & Ascher, C. (1991). *Urban school restructuring and teacher burnout* (Report No. EDO-UD-91-5). New York: ERIC Clearinghouse on Education. (ERIC Document Reproduction Service No. ED 340 812)

Fullan, M. (1993). *Change forces: Probing the depths of educational reform.* London: The Falmer Press.

Glickman, C. D. (1998). *Revolutionizing America's schools.* San Francisco: Jossey-Bass.

Goodlad, J., & Klein, M. F. (1970). *Behind the classroom door.* Worthington, OH: Charles A. Jones.

Hargreaves, A. (1991). Contrived collegiality: The micropolitics of teacher collaboration. In J. Blase (Ed.), *The Politics of Life in School* (pp. 46–72). Newbury Park, CA: Sage Publications.

Huberman, A. M. (1993). *The lives of teachers* (J. P. Neufeld, Trans.). New York: Teachers College Press.

Lytle, J. (1996). The inquiring manager: Developing new leadership structures to support reform. *Phi Delta Kappan, 77*(10), 664–670.

Murray, B. (1998, March). Data smog: Newest culprit in brain drain. *APA Monitor, 1,* 42.

Quartz, X. (1996). Becoming better: The struggle to create a new culture of school reform. *Research in Middle Level Education Quarterly, 19*(1), 83–112.

Pogrow, S. (1996). Reforming the wannabe reformers. *Phi Delta Kappan, 77*(10), 656–663.

Rusch, E. A., & Perry, E. A. (1993). *Resistance to change: Fact or stereotype.* Paper presented at the meeting of the American Educational Research Association, Atlanta, GA.

Sarason, S. B. (1996). *Revisiting the culture of the school and the problem.* New York: Teachers College Press.

Schlechty, P. C. (1997). *Inventing better schools: An action plan for educational reform.* San Francisco: Jossey-Bass.

Sergiovanni, T. (1992). *Moral leadership: Getting to the heart of school reform.* San Francisco: Jossey-Bass.

Sizer, T. (1984). *Horace's compromise: The dilemma of the American high school.* Boston: Houghton Mifflin.

United States Department of Education. (1993). *Honor what we know. Listen to what we say: Voices from the Goals 2000 Teacher Forum.* Washington, DC: Author.

Weiss, C., Cambone, J., & Wyeth, A. (1993). Trouble in paradise: Teacher conflicts in shared decision making. *Educational Administration Quarterly, 28*(3), 350–367.

Wenger, E. (1998). *Communities of practice: Learning, meaning, and identity.* London: Cambridge University Press.

Section III.

The Year 2000 in Schools: Celebrating, Synthesizing, and Reflecting

10

Using the Year 2000 in Schools: Celebrating, Synthesizing, and Reflecting

PATRICIA O. PEARSON

Celebration seems to be an integral part of elementary education. In one building, the entire school prepares to honor the memory of its founder. Skits are developed, poems are written, murals are painted, songs are rehearsed. In the process, the students improve their research skills and learn about a significant piece of history, discuss the importance of meter and rhythm in poetry, work on perspective and depth in art, come to appreciate a style of music they have not heard before, and, in the end, use oral presentation skills in the most authentic of assessments: a performance in front of parents and community leaders. There is nothing contrived in the celebration. It is student-driven but clearly guided by professional educators. It demonstrates the genuine respect the children have for the woman who founded the school some 50 years ago. The celebration is built on

205

tradition and pride, it involves many disciplines, and the final product is of high quality.

Although secondary educators might recognize the value of such a celebration, rarely do such learning experiences occur in middle or high schools. We are boxed in by the demands and constraints of our individual curriculums. Our students must pass statewide tests in algebra or county assessments in English and social studies, or finish the course in time for the AP tests. We can't take time out of real instruction for "parties."

But celebrations are important in schools—all schools. The change of pace they offer from the daily schedule, while a welcome break, may be disruptive and certainly shouldn't be overdone. But celebrations present us with opportunities to try innovative methods of teaching and learning. More than that, they give us a jumping-off point for reflection on what we do and why we do it. They give us a new context in which to think about learning. They can enliven our classrooms with energy and enthusiasm, not just for our students, but perhaps more importantly, for ourselves.

The experienced classroom teacher knows how good and how bad celebrations can be. The 9th grader who brings in soggy baklava at 7:30 in the morning for "Greek Civilization Day" has probably not learned a great deal about the ancient Greeks. The teacher who finds herself lying about allergies to honey to avoid eating the aforementioned baklava is likely to veto Greek Day in the future. Who among us hasn't suffered through celebrations of the arts during which one-fourth of the students sunbathed on the lawn near their exhibits while three-fourths of the students left campus and headed for the local hangout? Celebrations or commemorations of important events can be disastrous wastes of time. But when the planning is done with clear-sighted emphasis on *meaningful* learning, celebrations push us to improve both what we teach and how we teach it.

CELEBRATIONS IN U.S. SCHOOLS:
LESSONS FROM TWO RECENT EXAMPLES

Many of us have found meaning, either as teachers or as students, in celebrations of major historical events. At the national level, two examples stand out.

In 1976, schools all over the United States explored ways to mark the nation's Bicentennial. There were, of course, the requisite colonial fairs and solemn readings of the Declaration of Independence. Some were done very well, others were not. But the Bicentennial went deeper. How Americans defined "all men are created equal . . ." was not, in 1976, what it had been in 1776. Nor was it what it had been in 1876. The 200th anniversary of American independence nudged us to learn and relearn our history. Teachers who grew up in the schools of the 1950s were steeped in Paul Revere's ride and George Washington cutting down the cherry tree. They had to reconsider that version of the past. What we teach about the founders today has changed, not because the founders have changed, but because our search for meaning has grown.

Would our teaching and thinking about the American Revolution have grown without the Bicentennial as celebration? Yes. But it would not have grown in the same way. Teachers weren't alone in thinking about 1776. Publishers focused on the Bicentennial with commissioned popular fiction like John Jakes's series, *The Kent Family Chronicles* (1974–1976), a multigenerational saga, as well as scholarly works. Movies, television specials, the renovation of several historic sites, an upsurge of visitors to the places connected with the event—the nation focused on a particular year and educated itself in a variety of ways.

The year 1992 marked the 500th anniversary of Columbus's first voyage to the Americas. Much of the world commemorated in one way or another. Not all were celebratory by any means. Although Columbus is a hero for some, he represents the end of whole cultures for others, something schools overlooked for decades. The anniversary gave people a reason to study the world from a new viewpoint. Today, teachers focus on native cultures that existed before Columbus. The Smithsonian exhibit "Seeds of Change" presented the significance of Columbus's voyage in terms of plant and animal life, something most of us did not learn in school. The children we teach today learn about the Columbian exchange because we, their teachers, learned. Of course, we would have moved in that direction with or without the anniversary, but our knowledge base and access to resources were expanded because society as a whole focused on a particular year as a milestone.

So why the millennium? It does not mark a particular event as an anniversary does. Scholars have revised their estimates of the actual date of the birth of Jesus of Nazareth on which the Gregorian calendar is based. For that matter, those who really understand these things tell us that the new millennium begins in 2001, even though we know that the celebrations will center on 2000. There are other problems to address as well. Not everyone in the world uses the Gregorian calendar, and some will argue that time is, in a sense, imaginary to begin with.

But the very difficulties that celebrations of the millennium present become positives in the curriculum if we use them well. Vague in meaning though it may be, the millennium pushes us to look forward as well as back. It nudges us to acknowledge the remarkable achievements and failings of the last thousand years and to stand in awe at the brevity of our lives. It is one thing to view a century; many of our students will live long enough to do that firsthand. It's quite another to peer a thousand years into the past or future.

THEMES FOR CELEBRATION AND STUDY

Because we are marking the passing of both a century and a millennium, our celebrations can be twofold. We can seize the opportunities each offers. The possibilities for the school or the classroom are enormous. The suggestions below are intended to generate thought and discussion of what could be done, nothing more. If each teacher suggested just one way to make use of the passing millennium as a teaching tool, we could fill a millennial day-planner with ease. The point here is to offer a few ideas as kindling.

CALENDARS

Not everyone in the world is impressed by the millennium. Not everyone follows the Gregorian calendar. Even many people in the United States or elsewhere in the Western world follow more than one calendar. What year is it in the Islamic world? In China? In India? How does a civilization choose a starting point for a calendar? How long after the key event do people recognize its significance? How has Western civilization revised the current calendar over time? Why? Will it change again?

The more central question related to the calendar as a symbol of a society is this: Why do we have calendars? What are they for? We pull in the astronomers at this point, and the historians. Who had the first calendar? Why did they think of it? Granted, our world studies students should be able to shout out the answer to this, but could they look at the calendar in a new way? How were the Egyptians like us in wanting or needing a calendar? Would their panic at not being able to predict the Nile's annual flood be the equivalent of our fear of computer meltdown when the clock runs out in 2000? The ancient Egyptians may not be of our millennium, but the questions about their ideas are much the same as the questions about ours.

Why are we drawn to round numbers? What difference does it make that a hundred years have passed, or a thousand? If there is no real significance, then why are people so enamored of New Year's Eve, the turn of the century, and so on? Are people in other cultures who use different calendars like that? Are there important numbers in their minds? Are the numbers 100 or 1000? Perhaps students could compare the Gregorian calendar with the Aztec calendar and formulate their own questions.

They might also look at the labels we put on centuries or even decades. Society moves constantly. When we examine that movement we tend to see the trends that carry us from one era to the next. Hence, the "Roaring Twenties" or the "Fab Fifties." What do those trends say about a society? What trends are pulling us forward now?

TRENDS

There are several publications by organizations that study societal trends in order to think in terms of the future. *Megatrends* by John Naisbitt (1984), for example, synthesizes trends in American society. These include things like workplace changes (in 1982 Naisbitt suggested that more people would begin to work from home using computers), population shifts, and the move to a global economy. These assertions are not the result of guesswork, and the amount of information that goes into them is enormous.

Students could read sections of such publications and analyze not only the information but the gathering of the information. What should go into the research to produce a book like *Megatrends?* Could students devise a scaled-down version? What do the trends that futurists see mean for the lives of our current students? These are not dire predictions of doom and gloom; nor are they high-tech visions of life at the push of a button. They are simply movements in society, some subtle, some not. What they tell us is that our children's lives will not be exactly like ours. Students might consider what they need to do to prepare for the changes their lives will hold. Their predictions may or may not prove to be accurate, but the acknowledgment that change will occur may, in itself, be of benefit.

PREDICTIONS

Did scholars in the year 1000 make predictions for the future? How accurate were they? Students might see what they can find of these predictions and then trace their accuracy through history. What were the limitations of those who lived a thousand years ago? What kinds of things have happened that would have been virtually impossible to imagine nearly a century before the First Crusade?

This kind of activity might be more accessible in terms of the end of the last century. There are print copies of predictions made in the late 1800s about the 20th century. Students could analyze these predictions. They might discover conflicting opinions about what the future held and suggest reasons for the differences. After looking at the accuracy and failings of the predictions, they could make predictions of their own for the new century. Even a look at the 1939 World's Fair could be a good starting point. Just 60 years ago, futurists thought we would all be riding in hovercrafts by now.

Literature offers a similar mode of thought. Science fiction authors often create entire worlds of the future. How accurate are they? A close look at the worlds that Jules Verne envisioned in 1870 might give students insight into the worlds that contemporary authors create. They might then build their own visions of the future. A watch-making company is now producing a combination wrist watch and cell phone. Dick Tracy used his years ago.

Science fiction isn't the only literary genre that deals with the future. George Orwell's *1984* chilled many readers when it was published in 1949. But the society he described did not come to pass even though it could be argued that the technology to sustain it may have. Why is this? What happened instead? And what was it in the society of 1870 and 1949 that led Verne and Orwell to see what they did? What is it in today's world that allows or perhaps forces our authors and screenwriters to see the future as they do?

POPULATION STUDIES

One ongoing trend that all of us recognize is the continuing growth of the world's population. For many, the future of our population is a cause of concern. Graphs of population growth over the last 1000 years are astonishing and are likely to interest students. But what they make of the data should not be uniform.

The explosion in numbers that took place after World War II can be alarming, but longer views—as far back as two or three hundred thousand years—show a somewhat different picture. In 1798 in England, Thomas Malthus published his views of the future in terms of population growth. He foresaw dire consequences of the rapid population growth taking place at the time because the food supply could not grow nearly as quickly as the number of people. Students might plot Malthus's population predictions and compare them with the real growth that took place. Then they could plot the actual growth in food supply, noticing yield per acre as well as other factors. Science comes into play at this point. What changes in crops, farming techniques, and so on allowed the food supply to grow far more quickly than Malthus could have imagined? What geography and technology factors played a part? And why was there an enormous outmigration of people to other parts of the world? Malthus's predictions did not come to pass. What about our own? What limitations are there on what we can know about the future?

Another visual presentation of population growth is a six-minute film by Zero Population Growth Inc. and Southern Illinois University at Carbondale. Lights appear on a map of the world each time a million people are added to the population of a region. Why do the lights come on so slowly as the clock ticks off the years at the beginning of the film? When do they start coming on faster and why? In the 1300s lights go off in a surprisingly effective reminder of the bubonic plague in Europe, not far distant in time from the plague of smallpox and chicken pox that killed whole tribes of Native Americans. As the clock ticks into modern times, single lights are no longer discernible. They appear in clumps like wildfire. How many more lights will fit on the map?

What are population experts of today predicting for the next century or two or three? They certainly don't all agree on what will happen. When they use the term *overpopulation*, what do they mean? Where will future population growth occur? Why? This is geography and mathematics and biology and botany and chemistry. It is also a cultural issue students will be reading about and perhaps discussing and acting on throughout their lives.

CULTURAL PERSPECTIVES

All of us are guided in our thinking by our own culture's view of the world. The ancient Chinese, for example, thought of China as the middle of the earth. Even those who conquered them took on their ways. During the era of manifest destiny in the United States, Americans generally believed that they were destined to control the continent from sea to sea. The fact that several thousand natives had lived in the new region for centuries didn't dissuade them. Why is it that societies throughout the ages have thought of their own culture as the only one worth acknowledging? And how much of that is there in us?

Most schools in the Western Hemisphere have had a Eurocentric approach to history and culture for quite some time. Has that always been the case? Europe was not the dominant part of the world in the year 1000. According to *The Timetables of History* (Boorstin, 1975) Mayan civilization in the Yucatán was at its height while many Europeans were convinced that the end of the millennium signaled the end of the world. Was there a dominant force at all, or was communication not strong enough to allow any one place to have worldwide influence? What parts of the world are taking center stage now? The Pacific Rim countries have had enormous economic growth in recent years. But events in Japan and Indonesia and Hong Kong threaten that growth. Will the downturn continue? Or will the potential of the region be realized?

What about art? Is there a part of the world where artists flourish right now? Is there a renaissance in literature or music somewhere outside of our small piece of the sphere? How will mass communication affect culture and economics as time goes on? Will there be a world culture, a loss of ethnicity in the new millennium? A McWorld, so to speak?

This theme could run through curriculum all year. The entire notion of cultural diffusion is an avenue for thought. How is art or music or literature or scientific inquiry different from one place to another? Perhaps more importantly, how is it the same? And has that changed through the centuries? Will it change in the future, and if so, why?

If we celebrate our diversity, as many schools do so well, can we also identify the length of our traditions? How long ago did the tea ceremony in Japan develop? When did tulips first bloom in Holland or fireworks come to signal celebration? Will these things go on forever or are traditions lost? What traditions are worth holding onto into the next millennium? Why? Do they tell us something about ourselves that we are unlikely to learn in other ways? And if that's the case, how do we defend ourselves against the onslaught of a universal culture?

Accomplishment

Most societies define themselves in large part by their accomplishments. Europe of the Middle Ages looked to heaven through its cathedrals. Augustus Caesar looked on his reign in Rome in terms of the buildings he erected. What do we choose to feature about ourselves?

The end of the last century was filled with technological showcasing. The Industrial Age was upon us, and it seemed that humans were capable of just about anything. Expositions were fashionable because they provided an opportunity for the industrial world to demonstrate what it could do and for the public to be awestruck at the wonders of the modern world. Paris hosted a world exhibition to celebrate the end of one century and the beginning of another, and the Eiffel Tower was built as its centerpiece.

As the 20th century comes to a close, and with it the millennium, Germany will host Expo 2000. No one building or exhibit will symbolize this celebration. The centerpiece at this exposition will be the technology that allows people all over the world to come to the fair without leaving their homes. Whereas the architecture developed at the end of the last century was inspiring and amazing (the United States' contribution to architecture is the skyscraper), computers are the marvel that we "show off" today. There isn't a school district in the United States that doesn't currently have some policy or plan or funding for technology. What better way to greet a new century and era than by participating in its celebration via satellite and the Internet?

Vantage Points

Who will choose to join in Expo 2000? Europe seems to be more "into" millennial celebration than the United States. There appears to be more focus there on the year 2000. Germany is hosting an exposition; Scarborough, England, has developed an enormous project to commemorate the event; and so on.

Students might do some research into this apparent phenomenon. Is it really the case that the United States is paying less attention than European countries to something of significance? If so, why? This question could present students of United States history or government or literature with a new perspective on the provincialism Americans often tend to have.

Time is difficult to imagine. How old is old? If, in fact, Europeans are taking more interest in the millennium than are Americans, could it be because they have more direct connection with "old" than Americans do? How many American students (or teachers) can walk out their front doors and see a human structure dating to the year 1000? Weren't any people here a thousand years ago? Of course they were. So why aren't their structures still with us? What are the oldest structures in the United States, and how old are they? The answer is probably the pueblos of the Anasazis of the Southwest, and they were built very close to the year 1000. Why nowhere else? How much of the millennium went by before Europeans settled permanently in what is now the United States?

Our image of time is far more than historical. It is mathematical—a mental graph, as it were, of lifetimes. Time is verbal; students should be able to apply descriptors to it. It is spatial and visual in those pictures that should come to mind when we say "a thousand years ago" or "four centuries before the Reformation." The brevity of United States history may put our students and our population as a whole at a disadvantage in evoking those images of time. If that is why Europeans seem to be more in touch with the millennial celebration than we are, we should use that very celebration to correct the disparity. At the same time, we might look at our differences in vantage points when we choose the focal pieces of the last 1000 years.

PEOPLE AND EVENTS

The telephone book of any small town is likely to hold more names than the index of a history textbook claiming to cover hundreds or even a thousand years. Billions of human beings have lived and died in our millennium. Uncountable events, discoveries, inventions, and accomplishments have occurred. When we study this segment of time, however, we have no choice but to focus on only a few people or events. Somehow we have to decide what makes one more important than another.

Life magazine (Fall 1997) chose Thomas Edison as the most significant individual of the last thousand years. The *Washington Post* (Fisher, Page, Hinson, Von Drehle, & Forgey, 1995) gave that honor to Kublai Khan. What criteria did they use to arrive at such different conclusions? Students might use these publications or any of dozens of others to assess the merits of the choices made. They might follow up with

214

well-researched candidates of their own, using their own criteria or that of other authors.

Interestingly, both *Life* and *The Washington Post* rated the printing press as the most significant invention of the millennium. That may present a wonderful starting point for discussion of the importance of language and communication to civilization and the individual. What does the future hold, good or bad, as our ability to communicate increases?

ACTIVITIES FOR CELEBRATION AND STUDY

STUDENT ACTIVITY

Celebration of the millennium provides an opportunity for students to take ownership of their learning and give it meaning in a way a teacher-driven assignment can not. But what to do with that learning? How to share it, both process and product, with the larger community?

Project Enlightenment, an interdisciplinary extracurricular activity, is an example of the depth of learning that takes place when students have a clear investment in what they are doing. Developed by a physics teacher and an English teacher in a public high school, Project Enlightenment is a partnership between a school and a museum or historic site. Students take on a character from history. They do research on that character and then write dialogue with other students' characters. Finally, in costume at the museum or historic site, they perform these conversations for the public.

The level of research these students conduct is astonishing. Because they become their characters in public and must be able to ad lib in character with the audience, they take ownership of the project. They go to libraries, search the Internet, call universities, and interview experts because they want to. No one gives them written instructions. No one tells them they must have at least four sources or that one must be an online source. In fact, the students receive no grade or credit for what they do. They do it because they discover that they love learning. I have been privileged to cosponsor the project, most recently initiating a partnership with Mount Vernon, the home of George Washington and the second most visited historic site in the United States (the White House is first). I never cease to be amazed at what 30 or 40 students can achieve, largely on their own. When, after untold hours of historical research and thinking and writing and rehearsal, they say, "Can't we do it again tomorrow?" and "I don't want this to end," we know they will be lifelong learners. What more could we want for students of the 21st century?

Celebration of the millennium can provide us with a new and challenging focus for curriculum in many areas. It can also give us a connection with what much of the rest of our culture will be doing. By celebrating the millennium with our students, we can give them connections to the bigger world in which they live. We can weave what they do in school and what they see outside of school in such a way that their learning can take on clear meaning. By celebrating the end of this millennium, we may, in fact, help prepare our students to live and learn in the next one.

However they approach the celebration of the year 2000, school communities must imbue that celebration with genuine intellectual meaning. That involves teachers, as well as students, who are eager to expand their thinking.

When ideas for marking the millennium start to flow, they seem to multiply geometrically. Put three or four teachers in a room and throw out a suggestion and the conversation will begin. This exchange of ideas—some of them bold and ambitious, others silly and impractical—is a very healthy exercise. It pulls us away from the papers to grade, forms to fill out, attendance calls to make, and tests to photocopy, and pushes us toward remembering one of the reasons we teach: It's wonderful to watch kids get excited about learning.

Teacher Activity

Millennial celebrations provide us with wonderful opportunities for creating student activities that incorporate the kinds of thinking and performing the new century will require. But there is great benefit for teachers as well in focusing on the year 2000.

As classroom teachers, we too often devote ourselves, immerse ourselves, perhaps bury ourselves in the day-to-day rigors of teaching. We feel guilty if we read a book that is unrelated to our subject area. We count as wasted time any conference or presentation we cannot translate directly into classroom use. We demand recertification courses, even when they are graduate classes, that offer packaged lesson plans. Yet, what better plan could we have as teachers than to show our students the joy and excitement of learning? And how can we show them that if we don't experience it ourselves?

Teachers need an intellectual life outside the classroom. We need it for our own growth and well-being. We need it for balance. We need it to maintain our enthusiasm for learning, something we want for our students but frequently steal from ourselves. The 21st century screams for lifelong learners, and we pay homage to that in our mission statements and objectives. We need an intellectual life outside the classroom to demonstrate to ourselves as well as to our students and the community that we mean what we say. Celebration of the millennium offers a hook for meaningful intellectual endeavor to teachers as well as students.

In northern Virginia, teachers from several school districts have come together over a period of years in a forum called the Intellectual Life of Schools Project. Created by Hugh Sockett, a professor of education at George Mason University, the project has moved in several directions over a number of years. Teachers in some schools have formed book clubs that bring members of several disciplines together to discuss the chosen book of the month. No one has time for such a thing, but in those schools where a principal and a librarian have been supportive, the book discussions have been very successful. Teachers gather to discuss books, not students or attendance policies or discipline. They return to teaching refreshed and renewed.

In other schools, teachers have organized monthly lunch programs. For a brief, shining 23 minutes, someone from the outside or an expert from within makes a presentation on a topic and offers suggestions for further reading. Are the topics related to educational theory or the latest sure-fire delivery system for instruction? Thankfully, no. Are they intellectually stimulating to people from all disciplines? Thankfully, yes.

Every year, the Intellectual Life of Schools Project hosts a spring seminar that brings together the various school groups and all others who might be interested in a Saturday morning of good, intellectual dialogue. In recent years, the spring seminar has been followed by a two-day institute in August.

The focus of the institute in 1997 looked at the fin de siècle, the surge in intellectual activity at the end of the last century. Europe was awash in political and cultural achievement, particularly in Vienna, Austria, but across the continent as well. Music, literature, architecture, and science all flourished in Paris, London, and much of the rest of Europe, and in North America. There was a sense that all things were possible but also, in some quarters, a sense of despair. Although the term *fin de siècle* refers to the late 19th century, the phenomenon of cultural achievement at the end of a century is not unique to that period. Certainly, the 18th century ended with remarkable intellectualism as well. The last quarter of the 18th century brought us the work of Mozart, Lavoisier, Franklin, Adam Smith, and Jefferson, just to scratch the surface. As we approach the end of our own century, it seems appropriate to wonder if such a thing is occurring now. The Intellectual Life of Schools planning committee chose to use the fin de siècle theme for the three years leading to the new millennium because it offers so many questions for historically based study, and also because it parallels our current societal interest in the passing of this century.

The ends of centuries tend to be times of great action in many fields. We find ourselves now at the end of another century, this one perhaps more notable because it is also the end of a millennium. Have we seen heightened intellectual activity and achievement? That may be hard to measure in the moment. But certainly significant aspects of how we live and think are changing more rapidly than at any other time in history. Those changes, if not a particular year or day or hour or minute, warrant our attention. As teachers, we should be leading the way in asking questions and giving serious thought to the answers. After all, we touch the future every day.

As teachers, we should also be planning the celebrations of an event we know to be contrived. The actual change of a date may be meaningless. But the enthusiasm it can generate is far too good to ignore. If by celebrating the passage of time we renew our enthusiasm for trying new ways of learning or refresh our desire to know more than we did last week or last year, we have accomplished a great deal. If we remember how energizing it is to learn and stretch our minds, we have accomplished even more as human beings and, therefore, as teachers.

REFERENCES

Boorstin, D. (1975). *The timetables of history.* (3rd ed.). New York: Simon and Schuster.

Expo 2000. www.expo2000.de

Fisher, M., Page, T., Hinson, H., Von Drehle, D., & Forgey, B. (1995, December 31). . . . And a few other maddeningly subjective millennial milestones. *The Washington Post,* pp. F1.

Jakes, J. (1974–1976). *The Kent Family Chronicles: Vol. 1–8.* New York: Jove Books.

Naisbitt, J. (1984). *Megatrends.* New York: Warner Books.

100 people who made the millennium. (1997, Fall). *Life, 20*(10A), 136.

Zero Population Growth Inc. and Southern Illinois University at Carbondale. (1990). *World population* [Videotape]. Washington, DC: Author.

About the Editor

David D. Marsh is the Robert A. Naslund Professor of Curriculum and Instruction and Director of the Center for School Leadership at the School of Education, University of Southern California. He is coauthor with Judy Codding of *The New American High School: Educating for the 21st Century* (Corwin Press, 1998). The book grew out of his work as a critical friend at several high schools, as regional director of the Coalition of Essential Schools, and as director of several research studies of high school reform. He was coauthor of the California high school task force report *Second to None,* and has recently completed studies of middle school reform, the role of state curriculum frameworks in school improvement, and the enhancement of principals as instructional leaders. He has also been codirector of an International Principal's Institute, a two-week institute held at USC. The institute gathers school principals from England, Australia, and the United States in an intensive exploration of how to dramatically improve performance for all students. He served on the ASCD Publications Committee from 1995 to 1997. Address: 702 Waite Phillips Hall, University of Southern California, Los Angeles, CA 90089-0031. Phone: (213) 740-3290. Fax: (213) 740-2198. E-mail: dmarsh@mizar.usc.edu

About the Authors

Brian J. Caldwell is a professor with an endowed chair and Dean, Faculty of the College of Education at the University of Melbourne. He is coauthor or coeditor of 10 books, including *The Future of Schools: Lessons from the Reform of Public Education* (Falmer Press, 1998) with Don Hayward. Two previous books, *The Self-Managing School* and its sequel, *Leading the Self-Managing School,* have helped shape decentralized school management in a number of countries. A book coauthored with Jim Spinks, *Beyond the Self-Managing School* (Falmer Press, 1998), expands ideas found in Chapter 3 of this book. Address: G.457, Alice Hoy Building, University of Melbourne, Parkville, Victoria, Australia 3052.

Phone: 61-39-380-8308. Fax: 61-39-347-8315. E-mail: b.caldwell@ edfac.unimelb.edu.au

Todd Clark is the Executive Director of the Constitutional Rights Foundation in Los Angeles, California, a community-based organization dedicated to educating youth for citizenship. He is a former president of the National Council for the Social Studies and the California Council for the Social Studies. He currently chairs the California Commission on Improving Life Through Service, which is responsible for the management and distribution of the AmeriCorps program in the state. Address: Constitutional Rights Foundation, 601 S. Kingsley Drive, Los Angeles, CA 90005. Phone: (213) 316-2103. Fax: (213) 386-0459. E-mail: todd@crf-usa.org

Judy B. Codding is Vice President of the National Center on Education and the Economy in Washington, DC. She was principal at one of the United States' most successful suburban high schools—Bronxville High School in Bronxville, New York—and at a very challenging inner-city high school—Pasadena High School in Pasadena, California. She recently coauthored *Standards for Our Schools: How to Set Them, Measure Them and Reach Them* (Jossey-Bass, 1998) with Marc Tucker, and *The New American High School: Educating for the 21st Century* (Corwin Press, 1998) with David Marsh. Address: National Center on Education and the Economy, Suite 750, 700 11th Street NW, Washington, DC 20001. Phone: (202) 783-3668. Fax: (202) 783-3672. E-mail: jcodding@ncee.org

Carmel A. Crévola is a lecturer in the Department of Learning, Assessment, and Special Education within the Faculty of Education at the University of Melbourne. She is Codirector with Peter Hill of the Early Literacy Research Project, which has led her to do extensive research and consulting work across Australia, New Zealand, and North America. She is also Program Coordinator for the Reading Recovery Tutor Training Program at the University of Melbourne. Address: Centre for Applied Educational Research, Level 5 Science Building, University of Melbourne, Parkville, Victoria, Australia 3052. Phone: 61-3-344-8201. Fax: 61-3-347-0945. E-mail: crevola@edfac.unimelb.edu.au

Delaine Eastin is Superintendent of Public Instruction in the California Department of Education. As State Superintendent, Eastin is an elected constitutional officer and the highest-ranking official in the California K–12 system. She is a Regent of the University of California and a Trustee for the California State University System. She is past president of the New Standards Project. Prior to her election, she served four terms in the State Assembly, where she chaired the Education Committee. Address: California Department of Education, 721 Capitol Mall, Box 944272, Sacramento, CA 94244-2720. Phone: (916) 657-5485. Fax: (916) 657-4975. E-mail: deastin@cde.ca.gov

Peter Hill is a Foundation Chair of Education and Director of the Centre for Applied Educational Research at the University of Melbourne. In 1986 he was appointed Chairperson of the Victorian Curriculum and Assessment Board and assumed a leading role in the development and implementation of assessment and certification reforms for students in the final years of schooling. In 1989 he became Chief General Manager of the Department of School Education in Victoria, with overall responsibility for more than 2,000 schools, 52,000 teachers and other staff, and an annual budget of some $2.8 billion. Currently, he is also chair of the Board of Directors of the Australian Principals' Center. He and Carmel Crévola lead the Early Literacy Research Project, which is being adopted statewide in Victoria because of its proven effectiveness. Address: Centre for Applied Educational Research, Level 5 Science Building, University of Melbourne, Parkville, Victoria, Australia 3052. Phone: 61-3-344-8201. Fax: 61-3-347-0945. E-mail: p.hill@edfac.unimelb.edu.au

Sherry P. King is Superintendent of the Mamaroneck Union Free School District in Mamaroneck, New York. From 1992 to 1996 she was Superintendent of the Croton-Harmon Schools, Croton, New York. She has been a high school principal, assistant principal, and teacher of English, beginning in 1973 at Scarsdale High School. Dr. King received her Ed.D. in education administration from Columbia University in 1984. She is involved with a number of educational movements, including the Coalition of Essential Schools, and works closely with the National Center for Education and the Economy. She is an Annenberg Fellow at the Annenberg Institute for School Reform, a Trustee on the Board of Directors for Jobs for the Future, and a Senior Researcher for a Study of Chicago Small Schools, funded by the Joyce Foundation. Address: Mamaroneck Union Free School District, 1000 W. Boston Post Road, Mamaroneck, NY 10543. Phone: (914) 698-9133. Fax: (914) 698-9659. E-mail: kings@mamkschools.org

Myranda S. Marsh is a Social Science Teacher at Marlborough School for Girls, an independent school in Los Angeles. She has also taught at an award-winning inner-city high school, Pasadena High School. While a teacher at Pasadena High, she served as cochair of the restructuring committee that guided the school's use of a comprehensive state grant to improve education. In 1994 Ms. Marsh was one of 35 educators recognized for teaching excellence by KTTV-Fox Television in Los Angeles. Address: Marlborough School for Girls, 250 S. Rossmore Avenue, Los Angeles, CA 90004. Phone: (213) 935-1147. Fax: (213) 933-0542. E-mail: Myrandas@earthlink.com

Allan R. Odden is Professor of Educational Administration at the University of Wisconsin–Madison. He also is a codirector of the Consortium for Policy Research in Education (CPRE), which is a policy research collaborative that includes UW–Madison, the University of Pennsylvania, Harvard University, the University of Michigan, and Stanford University. His most recent books include *Financing Schools for High Performance: Strategies for Improving the Use of Educational Resources* (Jossey-Bass, 1998) with Carolyn Busch; *Paying Teachers for What They Know and Do* (Corwin Press, 1997) with Carolyn Kelley; and *Educational Leadership for America's Schools* (McGraw-Hill, 1995). Address: CPRE, Wisconsin Center for Educational Research, University of Wisconsin, 1025 West Johnson Street, Suite 653A, Madison, WI 53706. Phone: (608) 263-4260. Fax: (608) 263-6448. E-mail: odden@macc.wisc.edu

Patricia O. Pearson is a classroom teacher at McLean High School in Fairfax County, Virginia. She has taught world history and geography at the 9th and 10th grade levels and currently teaches United States history at the 11th grade level. She is cosponsor of Project Enlightenment, an interdisciplinary, extracurricular partnership between a public high school and historic sites and museums in which students take on characters of the past and write conversations that are performed for the public. Project Enlightenment has performed at the Corcoran Gallery in Washington, D.C., at Decatur House in Washington, D.C., and, most recently, at George Washington's estate at Mount Vernon. She also serves on the planning committee for the Intellectual Life of Schools Project in conjunction with George Mason University. Address: McLean High School, 1633 Davidson Road, McLean, VA 22101. Phone: (703) 714-5700. Fax: (703) 714-5797. E-mail: ppearson@fc3.fcp3.k12.va.us

Marc S. Tucker is President of the National Center on Education and the Economy in Washington, D.C. He also serves as codirector of New Standards and chairs the policy committee of the National Skill Standards Board. Mr. Tucker is the author of *Thinking for a Living: Education and the Wealth of Nations* (Basic Books, 1992) with Ray Marshall, and *Standards for Our Schools: How to Set Them, Measure Them and Reach Them* (Jossey-Bass, 1998) with Judy B. Codding. Address: National Center on

Education and the Economy, Suite 750, 700 11th Street NW, Washington, DC 20001. Phone: (202) 783-3668. Fax: (202) 783-3672. E-mail: mtucker@ncee.org

Belinda Williams is a Senior Research and Development Specialist at the Northeast and Islands Regional Educational Laboratory at Brown University. As director of the Urban Education Project at Research for Better Schools, Belinda guided the development of the Urban Learner Framework (ULF), a synthesis of research to help educators make decisions about enhancing learning in the urban context. She is on ASCD's National Program Advisory Committee and recently was editor of the monograph *Closing the Achievement Gap: A Vision for Changing Beliefs and Practices*. Address: Northeast and Islands Regional Educational Laboratory, 222 Richmond Street, Suite 300, Providence, RI 02903. Phone: (401) 274-9548 x236. Fax: (401) 421-7650. E-mail: Belinda_Williams@Brown.edu

ABOUT THE 1999 YEARBOOK COMMITTEE

David Marsh, University of Southern California, Los Angeles
Brian Caldwell, University of Melbourne, Melbourne, Australia
Judy Codding, National Center for Education and the Economy, Washington, DC
Patricia Harvey, Chicago Public Schools, Chicago, IL
Sherry King, Mamaroneck Public Schools, Mamaroneck, NY
Allan Odden, University of Wisconsin-Madison, Madison, WI
Marc Tucker, National Center for Education and the Economy, Washington, DC
Belinda Williams, Northeast and Islands Regional Educational Laboratory, Providence, RI
John O'Neil, ASCD Liaison

ASCD 1998–99
Board of Directors

Elected Members as of November 1, 1998

Executive Council

President: Thomas Budnik, School Improvement Planning Coordinator, Heartland Area Education Agency, Johnston, Iowa

President-Elect: Joanna Choi Kalbus, Lecturer in Education, University of California at Riverside, Redlands, California

Immediate Past President: Edward Hall, Dean, Division of Social and Professional Studies, Talladega College, Alabama

Bonnie Benesh, Change Consultant, Newton, Iowa

Bettye Bobroff, Executive Director, New Mexico ASCD, Albuquerque, New Mexico

John W. Cooper, Assistant Superintendent for Instruction, Canandaigua City School District, Canandaigua, New York

Michael Dzwiniel, Teacher, Edmonton Public Schools, Alberta, Canada

LeRoy Hay, Assistant Superintendent for Instruction, Wallingford Public Schools, Wallingford, Connecticut

Sharon A. Lease, Deputy State Superintendent for Public Instruction, Oklahoma State Department of Education, Oklahoma City, Oklahoma

Leon Levesque, Superintendent, Lewiston School District, Lewiston, Maine

Francine Mayfield, Principal, Clark County School District, Las Vegas, Nevada

Raymond McNulty, Superintendent of Schools, Windham Southeast Supervisory Union, Brattleboro, Vermont

Robert L. Watson, High School Principal, Spearfish 40-2, Spearfish, South Dakota

Peyton Williams, Jr., Deputy State Superintendent, Georgia State Department of Education, Atlanta, Georgia

Donald B. Young, Professor, University of Hawaii, Curriculum Research & Development Group, Honolulu, Hawaii

Members at Large

Patricia Ashcraft, Chimneyrock Elementary School, Cordova, Tennessee

Judith Dorsch Backes, Carol County Public School, Westminster, Maryland

Beverly Bjork, Colorado Springs District #11, Colorado

Gerald L. Brown, Education Equity Center Region VIII, Denver
Cathy Bryce, Weatherford, Texas
Evelyn Chatmon, Baltimore County Public Schools Southeast Area Office,
    Maryland
Cheryl Clark, Conway Public Schools, Arizona
Ronald Costello, Noblesville Schools, Indiana
Nancy Tondre DeFord, Park City School District, Utah
Diann Gathright, Rich Mountain Community College, Mena, Arizona
Kolene Granger, Washington County Schools, St. George, Utah
Lou Howell, Urbandale Community School District, Iowa
Lisbeth Johnson, Walnut Valley Unified Schools, Walnut, California
Donald Kachur, Illinois State University, Normal
Carol Mackey, Evergreen School District, Vancouver, Washington
Patricia H. Marshall, Jefferson County Board of Education, Louisville, Kentucky
Saundra McCray, District of Columbia Public Schools, Washington, DC
Marie Meyer, Thornton Fractional Area Educational Coop., Calumet City,
    Illinois
Michaelene Meyer, Elkhorn Public School, Nebraska
Ronald R. Musoleno, Parkland School District, Allentown, Pennsylvania
Joann Mychals, Puget Sound Educational Service District, Burien, Washington
Carol Renner, Kearney Public Schools, Nebraska
Mary Ann Reynolds, Fort Bend Independent School District, Sugar Land, Texas
Sarah Booth Riss, Riverview Gardens School District, St. Louis, Missouri
Wayne Starnes, Dayton Independent Schools, Kentucky
Barbara Warner-Tracy, Susan B. Anthony School, Sacramento, California
Edward Weber, Lakeway Learning Center, Gillette, Wyoming
Jill D. Wilson, Riverland Elementary School, Fort Lauderdale, Florida

Affiliate Presidents

Alabama: Betty A. Edwards, Shelby County School District, Columbiana
Alaska: Ernest B. Manzie, Fairbanks
Alberta: Dixie Roberts, Edmonton
Arizona: Mary Lou Gammon, G2 Educational Services Inc., Flagstaff
Arkansas: Joyce Littleton, Hot Springs School District 6
British Columbia: Bruce Mills, Terry Fox Elementary School, Abbotsford
California: Mary Beall, San Diego County Office of Education
Colorado: Chris K. Palmer, Academy School District 20, USAF Academy
Connecticut: Alida D. Begina, Hamden Public Schools
Curacao: Suze M. L. Giskus, Fundashon Material Pa Skol
Delaware: Terry B. Joyner, Colonial School District, New Castle
District of Columbia: Paula K. Boone
Florida: Allan Dornseif, Punta Gorda
Georgia: John A. Jackson, Athens

Germany: Joyce Christian
Hawaii: Carmielita A. Minami, Hawaii School Leadership Academy, Honolulu
Hong Kong: Daniel Yuen Oi-Ming, Wanchai
Idaho: Bonnie A. Farmin, Kellogg
Illinois: Debra A. Hill, Joseph E. Hill Administration Center, Evanston
Indiana: Roger Fisher, Paoli Community School Corp.
Iowa: Bill Wright, Denison Community School District
Israel: Tali Friedman, Levinsky College, Moshav Bnei Zion
Japan: Stephen Middlebrook, Osaka
Kansas: Judy Scudamore, Pittsburg Unified School District 250
Kentucky: Carmen Rader-Bowles, Fayette County School District, Lexington
Louisiana: Cynthia Caliste, New Orleans
Maine: Gregg Dowty, Good Will/Hinckley Homes for Boys and Girls, Hinckley
Manitoba: Linda Thorlakson, Winnipeg
Maryland: Marcella Emberger, Maryland Department of Education, Baltimore
Massachusetts: David S. Troughton, North Reading Public Schools
Michigan: Marie Neil, Kent Independent School District, Grand Rapids
Minnesota: Ann Goldstein, Edina Public Schools 273, Minneapolis
Mississippi: Leslie Johnson, Hinds County Public Schools, Raymond
Missouri: Gary Reed, Carthage Reorganized School District 9
Montana: Mike Birrer, Poplar School District 9 & 9B
Nebraska: Katie Mathews, Park Elementary School, Kearney
Nevada: Danielle Miller, Las Vegas
New Hampshire: Leo P. Corriveau, Fall Mountain Rural School District,
    Charlestown
New Jersey: Kathleen S. Moreland, Evesham Township Board of Education,
    Marlton
New Mexico: G. C. Ross, Clovis Municipal Schools
New York: Sandra J. Voigt, Holley Elementary School
North Carolina: Donald T. Lassiter, Elkin City Schools
North Dakota: Jay Diede, Watford City Junior and Senior High School
Northwest Territories: Gordon Miller, Harry Camsell School, Hay River
Ohio: Louise Baehr, Gahanna-Jefferson Public Schools, Gahanna
Oklahoma: Bill Beierschmitt, Bartlesville Public Schools
Ontario: Jim Tayler, Trillium Elementary School, Orleans
Oregon: Kathryn Holboke, Clackamas
Pennsylvania: Linda Bigos, Derry Township School District
Puerto Rico: Luis A. Burgos, Upsala A-1, San Juan
Rhode Island: William R. Fasano, Riverside
Singapore: Kwang Yap Tan, Ministry of Education
South Carolina: Mildred S. Huey, York School District 1
South Dakota: Grace Christianson, Lennox School District
Spain: Irene Conway, The American School of Valencia
St. Maarten: Roberto Arrindell

Tennessee: Sue Carmichael, Bon De Croft Elementary School, Sparta
Texas: Vernon Newsom, Mansfield Independent School District
United Kingdom: Sue Raven, Cambridgeshire
Utah: Kevin D. Hague, Granite School District, Salt Lake City
Vermont: Judith M. Ouellette, Westford School District
Virginia: Gail Pope, Virginia Beach City Schools
Washington: Arthur O. Jarvis, Enumclaw School District 216
Wisconsin: James Sorensen, Delavan
Wyoming: Cathy Hemker, Washington Elementary School, Green River

ASCD Review Council

Chair: Corrine Hill, Salt Lake City, Utah
Quincy Harrigan, Insular Department of Education, St. Maarten
Nancy Oelklaus, Texas ASCD, Austin
Arthur Steller, Kingston City School District, New York
Sandra Wegner, Southwest Missouri State University, Springfield

ASCD Headquarters Staff

Gene R. Carter, *Executive Director*
Diane Berreth, *Deputy Executive Director*
Frank Betts, *Deputy Executive Director, Operations*
Melody Ridgeway, *Assistant Executive Director, Information Systems and Services*
Douglas Soffer, *Assistant Executive Director, Constituent Relations*
Michelle Terry, *Associate Executive Director, Program Development*

Holly Abrams
Diana Allen
Barry Amis
Joanne Arnold
Holly Baker
Monica Barnette
Eva Barsin
Kimberly Bell
Jennifer Beun
Steve Blaufeld
Gary Bloom
Cecilia Boamah
Meltonya Booze
Alexandre Bouche
Maritza Bourque
Dana Bowser
Joan Brandt
Dorothy Brown
Beverly Buckner
Colette Burgess
Simon Cable
Angela Caesar
Christine Calorusso
Roger Campbell
Kathryn Carswell
Sally Chapman
John Checkley
Katherine Checkley
Raiza Chernault
Sandra Claxton
Judi Connelly
Andrea Corsillo
Agnes Crawford
Marcia D'Arcangelo
Michael Davis
Jay DeFranco
Keith Demmons
Becky DeRigge
Clare Driscoll
Stephanie Dunn
Shiela Ellison
Don Ernst
Olivia Evans
Honor Fede
Gillian Fitzpatrick
Harriett Forster
John Franklin
Christine Fuscellaro
Julie Garity
LaKiesha Gayden
Barbara Gleason
Troy Gooden

Nora Gyuk
Dorothy Haines
Joan Montgomery Halford
Charles Halverson
Vicki Hancock
Nancy Harrell
John Henderson
Helené Hodges
Davene Holland
Julie Houtz
Angela Howard
Debbie Howerton
Todd Johnson
Jo Ann Jones
Mary Jones
Teola Jones
Pamela Karwasinski
Betsy Kelaher
Laura Kelly
P. Diane Kelly
Leslie Kiernan
Crystal Knight–Lee
Tamara Larson
Shannon Lomax
Gabriel Lynch
Angelika Machi
John Mackie
Indu Madan
Larry Mann
Helen Marquez
J'Anna McCaleb
Jan McCool
Michelle McKinley
Clara Meredith
Ron Miletta
Frances Mindel
Nancy Modrak
Kenny Moir
Karen Monaco
Jacqueline Morrison
Margaret Murphy
Dina Murray
Charwin Nah
Julie Nardella
Mary Beth Nielsen
KayLani Noble
Tom O'Grady
John O'Neil
Margaret Oosterman
Jayne Osgood
Millie Outten
Diane Parker

Rose Parmantier
Kelvin Parnell
Mark Cantor Paster
Margini Patel
Elisa Perodin
Terrence Petty
Maryann Pheulpin
Carolyn Pool
Ruby Powell
Tina Prack
Pam Price
Gena Randall
Karen Rasmussen
Hope Redwine-Ford
Judy Rixey
Erik Robelen
Rita Roberts
Gayle Rockwell
Carly Rothman
Jeff Rupp
Jamie Sawatzky
Marge Scherer
Jan Schmidt
Beth Schweinefuss
Timothy Scott
Bob Shannon
Lisa Shannon
Katherine Sibert
Darcie Simpson
Tracey Smith
Valerie Sprague
Karen Steirer
Brian Sullivan
Michelle Tarr
Beth Taylor
Carol Tell
Jocelyn Thomas
May Kay Thompson
Janis Tomlinson
Lindsey Verble
Mia Wallace
Judy Walter
Tisha Ware
Ingrid West
Vivian West
Kay Whittington
Linda Wilkey
Helena Williams
Scott Willis
Carolyn Wojcik